T0086414

BACHELORS ABOUNDING

BACHELORS ABOUNDING

THEIR MUTINOUS MARCH ON MATRIMONY

TERRY REED

Algora Publishing
New York

Library of Congress Cataloging-in-Publication Data —

Names: Reed, Terry, 1937- author.
Title: Bachelors abounding: their mutinous march on matrimony / Terry Reed.
Description: New York: Algora Publishing, [2016] | Includes bibliographical
    references and index.
Identifiers: LCCN 2016001803 (print) | LCCN 2016004601 (ebook) | ISBN
    9781628941746 (soft cover: alk. paper) | ISBN 9781628941753 (hard cover:
    alk. paper) | ISBN 9781628941760 (pdf)
Subjects: LCSH: Bachelors—History. | Bachelors in literature.
Classification: LCC HQ800.3 .R44 2016 (print) | LCC HQ800.3 (ebook) | DDC
    306.81/52—dc23
LC record available at http://lccn.loc.gov/2016001803

Printed in the United States

For bachelors everywhere: Dum vivimus vivamus!

("As long as we're living, let's live!")

Table of Contents

Chapter I. "Where the devil are my slippers, Eliza?"

Our enviable task in these pages is to explore, explain and defend the unsteady reputation of wondrous bachelordom against its traditionally soiled reputation, its questionable eccentricities, its ill-comprehended motivations and its ostensibly nefarious ends. If that sounds like a mouthful, it is, and it requires a bit of doing. Bachelors, as a rule, are not especially well received. Befuddled married men are jealous of them; petulant unmarried women are more than a little frustrated by their understated but still firm resistance to matrimony. The origins of this perpetual dilemma lead us inexorably back to the mythic Pygmalion, the young and incomprehensibly talented sculptor, cited by Ovid in Book X of his Latin *Metamorphosis*. The bacheloresque Pygmalion does not entertain a particularly favorable view of women because of what he somewhat prudishly views as their shameless behavior. Ovid also tells us (in Rolfe Humphries' translation) that Pygmalion was so "shocked at the vices / Nature has given to the female disposition / Only too often, [he] chose to live alone, / to have no women in his bed." What to do? He sculpted a woman of his own; that's what.

In the real world this is patently impossible; in the world of mythology, anything goes. Thanks to his extraordinary creativity (as Ovid tells us), Pygmalion "made with marvelous art, an ivory statue, / As white as snow, and gave it great[er] beauty / Than any girl could have, and fell in love / With his own workmanship." The virgin he has created appears "almost living and seemed to move," since (as we are reminded) "the best art, they say, / Is that which conceals art," that is, it hides behind its own artfulness. Hence, Pygmalion falls in love with his magnificent handiwork, has touched it, and is inclined to believe that his ivory has miraculously become flesh. He speaks to her, fears that he might bruise her tenderness, then "pays his compliments and brings her presents." Later, "he decks her limbs with dresses and places rings on her fingers." He notices that "she seems / Even more lovely naked," finally "takes her to bed," and "calls her darling," then "my darling love." When the love goddess Venus enters the picture, Pygmalion prays for a tailor-made wife "like my ivory girl," and Venus hears the prayer. Pygmalion kisses his maiden, later identified as *Galatea*, while her ivory miraculously appears to soften and her body becomes human. He praises Venus lavishly while she blesses the marriage.

With a little help from above, our bachelor boy has managed to fashion a woman to his own erotic specifications, although Ovid's account leaves us with the impression that Galatea is as much the creation of his romantic imagination as it is his artistic hands. Nevertheless he succeeds in getting what he was after, to wit: the perfect woman. Today we recognize this circumstance as the *Pygmalion Effect*, sometimes called the *Rosenthal Effect*, meaning that the greater the expectation one places on people, the greater they perform. The *Galatea Effect* assumes that the more people are encouraged by what they're doing, the greater will be the result. Misogynistic though he once was, Pygmalion appears to be a bachelor no more. In time, however, the ivory lips he's been kissing don't kiss back. He is eventually made to realize that his ideal woman is no more than a fleeting artistic image so ingeniously sculpted that, as we were told, art has concealed art. His romantic expectations have been dashed.

Classical myths are such that they turn up endlessly in subsequent places. George Bernard Shaw's 1913 stage comedy *Pygmalion* eventually gave rise to a 1955 play and 1964 film called *My Fair Lady*, which has to do with the Galatea Effect's transformation of an apparently simple Cockney flower girl named Eliza Doolittle into an apparently authentic English lady, by emending her mutilation of the King's English. The author also, to be sure, makes implications about the fragility and fatuousness of the British class system, by illustrating that a guttersnipe can be transmogrified into something that appears to be so elegant as not to be believed possible.

Much has been made of Professor Henry Higgins' priggish bachelorism. Shaw commented that "his manner varies from genial bullying when he is in sound humor to stormy petulance when anything goes wrong; but he is so entirely frank and void of malice that he remains likable even in his least reasonable moments." Higgins' message to Eliza is that, by way of some fairly simple adjustments to her voice and demeanor, she can presume to be, or at least pretend to be, someone who transcends the limitations of her class, culture and social station. One is not, given Shaw's commitment to socialism, surprised to find that nearly anyone can be transformed into just about anything. The same applies, of course, to the possibility of transforming some ordinary chap into the appearance of a bachelor and possibly a gentleman.

Like Pygmalion, Higgins detests women, although in the end the tables are turned. He falls for Eliza; and in the Alan Jay Lerner–Frederick Lowe musical, she assumes the upper hand, chastising him by saying that she will one day have the king's ear, and that his majesty will proclaim the 20th of March as *Eliza Doolittle Day*, when she will demand Higgins' severed head. The king will of course agree to all her demands, even her wish to see Higgins stand before a firing squad.

"And the king will tell me: 'Liza, sound the call.'
And as they lift their rifles, higher, I'll shout, 'Ready! Aim! Fire!'
Oh ho 'enry 'iggins, Just you wait!"

Such is her response to Higgins' bachelorish arrogance, his insufferable pretension, preposterous posturing and absurd misogyny—features that Ovid assigned to Pygmalion prior to his fashioning an elusive dream girl. Higgins becomes a little less attached to his mother and a bit more attached to the woman he's refashioned.

We must, before any more's said, reach an understanding upon what *bachelor* means and has meant, and how it's spelled and has been spelled. Its *etymology*, by which we mean its *linguistic history*, is confused enough to be contestable. A bachelor was once taken to mean a male (occasionally female) in the employ of a *calonuus*, meaning a manor. The term *calonis* has as its Latin designation a menial servant, a drudge. It's also understood to have meant an apprentice knight who has yet to prove himself by showing the world out of what he's made. The word *knight* itself has had various implications, among them one who sews (combines), a man of military rank, one who is honored, is possibly in the service of a lady, a gentleman of rank and reputation. But he has yet to acquire *vassals* (via Middle French, from Medieval Latin *vassallus*), meaning servants who, for one reason or another, pledge their fealty (fidelity), which is to say their devotion, support. But he's currently a knight, symbolically or literally, displaying an identifying banner of his own or of another's. A knight of this description has also been identified as a novice in arms, or a *bas chevalier*, a lesser (base) knight, hence a knight-bachelor, a knight of the lowest order, possibly a gentleman who has been knighted without belonging to any of the so-called *orders*, meaning a community of those affiliated with some fraternal group (military or Christian, for example).

Bachelor has also been taken to mean a *yeoman* (attendant, retainer, petty officer, one who is sturdy, loyal, brave, or possibly a small farmer who cultivates his own land). We should not fail to mention that a bachelor is tellingly one of the young, inexperienced and inept of the fur seal species that the adult bull seals prevent from entering the mating grounds for a try at some of the older female seals. Lest we forget, a bachelor is also a lowly fresh water fish (*pomyys annularis*) of the lowly bass family, common in southern American waters. Today it's taken to mean one (be it man or woman) who has taken the first, which is to say lowest, university honor, (the bachelor's degree) and wears a bachelor's hood, signifying the possession of an AB (*artium baccalaureus* in Latin) or in English a BA (bachelor of arts). The Latinized *baccatarius*, by the way, was on occasion rendered as the pun *buccalaurs*, as if to suggest *baccalauri*, a laurel berry.

Bachelor, as we usually spell it, has evolved through a range of other orthographic mutations of letters or other symbols, among them: *bachilere, bachelere, baccalere, bachiller, bachelar, bacheler, bachiler, batcher, batcheter, batcler,* et cetera. There are bachelor-related expressions, old and recent. Today the word generally refers to unmarried men of marriageable age, but it still contains the dreaded root *bas* (base, inferior, vile sordid, decadent, subdued) that may account for the word's having, shall we say, pejorative (deprecatory, belittling, altogether negative) connotations. As we intimated earlier, being a bachelor is not, in some circles, necessarily admired and applauded. Hence we have among other commonplace expressions bachelor's wife, an obvious oxymoron, a self-contradictory utterance. No bachelor has a wife, but still and all the expression is taken to mean an unimaginably ideal woman, so universally endowed and splendidly situated that even Pygmalion would jump at the chance to marry her. A true bachelor, one might presume, is so confirmed in his bachelorhood that nothing in all womanhood could possibly tempt him into matrimony, although he may be tempted to invite her into his chambers. There is also something called a bachelor lady, signifying a maid (in the old sense of the word) meaning an unmarried, self-sustaining woman who may have her own resources and lives independently. A bachelorette is a bachelor of the opposite gender, which is ostensibly impossible. A bachelor apartment, otherwise called a bachelor pad or bachelor room, is usually quarters occupied by a bachelor and, by invitation, others. The term bachelordom, used often here, refers to the estate (rank, station) of bachelors collectively.

Bachelors can be, and usually are, deucedly difficult to catch, since they are disinclined to snap at common forms of bait, such as the erotic, the monetary, the promissory, the religious or other such enticements into which they may be lured. We refer to things such as supposed companionship, similarity of interests, not to mention the social, the romantic, the travel, the holidays—all of them dampened by the prospect of the wedding, the parenthood, the marriage counselor, the child support, the lawyers, the remorse and the psychological and other damage that marriages leave in its wake. Some married men and women secretly long for their spouses to die, although if death should occur they appear to be depressed, lonely and needy. It's often seen as an affront to one's former spouse to attract another partner and begin the hideous marital process anew. For men, the problem begins if and when they forsake their bachelorhood and walk, (not without some misgivings) into marriage that, as is often said, is an *unnatural* way to live. Men find it difficult to remain true to a woman for more than a weekend, let alone a half century. It's a nearly unanimous problem among men who understand that marriage is dreadful, that they'd made a huge mistake and that they'd rather not admit that it's been a parade of frustration, boredom and emotional captivity. When they admit anything, it's to concede (on the sly) that marriage has been tolerable at best.

"It's a woman's business to get married as soon as possible," Shaw wrote, "and a man's to keep unmarried as long as he can," which treats matrimony as one of life's inescapable penalties to be compared with heart disease, cancer, mental impairment and hair loss. Marriage is all about women; in fact, its Latin *matrimonium* means something like "the condition of motherhood." Apparently there are responsible people who regard marriage as socially respectable, supposedly for mental, psychological and reproductive purposes. Even so, by 2012 the average age for marriage among men was 28.6, men, 26.6 women, as compared with 30 years earlier when it was 25.2 for men, 22.5 for women, which seems to imply that some prudent hesitation has gone into this bewildering lifelong commitment to which most intelligent bachelors take a cautiously dim view. Toward what else would young men agree to a lifetime binding contract? Were *polygyny*—the complicated act of wedding, say, six women on the same day—to remedy any bachelorship dilemmas, is at best absurd, and out rightly problematic as well as horridly expensive. It is better, all considered, to maintain four women at a time without marrying any of them.

If there is anything men love about women, it's more women. The same evidently does not apply to the absurd notion of polyandry, a woman's marriage to more than one man, since women seem conditioned to concentrating open taming one bloke at a time. Simultaneous marriages, commonly regarded a bigamous (literally two marriages) begs questions of other multiple civil (read uncivil) unions, all of which are patently preposterous. Some years ago the Mormon Church supported that impossible marital proposition, but eventually thought better of it. Average people seem to agree, paradoxically, that marriage is a good idea, especially if it consists of bonding social equals, otherwise known as endogamy, endo meaning within, although the probability of a bachelor's marrying what we'll call a female bachelor, seems to have small chance of lasting more than half an hour following the marriage ceremony, after which the newlyweds' next big event will unravel in a divorce court. Bachelors are by nature independent fellows to whom even the merest suggestion of marriage is abhorrent, celebrating, as they do, the occasional indiscretions of personal liberty. A man who marries has presumably lived through at least two decades of glorious freedom and ought to know better than committing matrimony.

There is a phrase derived from the Sport of Kings called playing the field, which means betting on two horses for the price of one. The animals upon which the bets are placed are called field horses, which suggests that their probability of winning, placing or showing is perilously improbable. Bachelors with whimsical dispositions hugely prefer to play the fields of cooperatively-inclined women, graciously moving more or less effortlessly as a butterfly wafts through a splendid field of Buttercups, before any dark clouded battles of the sexes (to be discussed later) begin to descend. He devotes himself not to some woman, but to a life governed by Liberty and his brother Freedom. As Bob McNamara used to say, coercion "merely captures man; freedom captivates him." To wish matrimony on a bachelor is recommending that he subject himself to as much captivity as a caged condor under the supervision of a jailer. If he succumbs to marriage, he will by stages be driven into a state of *celibacy* which means being married while not being married. The word derives from the Latin *caelibatus*, which signifies the unmarried state, sometimes interpreted to mean taking a vow to *abstain*, a medieval idea for promoting Platonic purity, urging people into abbeys, monasteries and other drearily grey quarters that in every respect conflict with routine mainstream bachelorism.

The popes are presumed to be celibate all, but we wouldn't bet a bountiful collection plate on it. Martin Luther, if what we hear be true, was every bit (so it seems) the bachelor, but who married, of all improbable women, a fertile but not yet fertilized nun who commenced to deliver six children into the world, each holier than the last. Henry VIII shelved his Catholic upbringing and cranked up his own church so that he could marry as often as he wanted, rather than (who knows why) opting for bachelorhood. Married men are presumed to be celibates, sort of, which is to say that they allegedly keep sex, if any, inside the family and in accordance with a marriage vow that has condemned many a married man into a sexless postmenopausal pother. Buddhism seemed for a time to have viewed sex an impurity, and then loosened that policy. We've been told that Judaism prescribes seasons of abstinence that often raise the unbachelarian subject of chastity, something not necessarily endorsed by the rank and file of generously equipped bachelors. Being *chaste* means giving up chasing women while giving the impression (anyway) of being unusually devoted to the high purposes behind modesty, purity, moral cleanliness and rectitude. Such things describe certain bachelors who entertain a penchant for undoing women without so much as a trace of regret and without fear of chastisement or other expression of disapproval.

The Catholic Church, in a directive called "Is Chastity Possible" (1994) viewed chastity as "in conformity with God's eternal law," a reining-in of reprehensible behavior not limited to lust, but extending to other vices such as promiscuity. Such delicate matters are soundly addressed in the holy pages of its "Declaration of Sexual Ethics" (1975), where it argues furthermore that "any voluntary sexual arousal or act outside of normal (uncontracepted) marital union of husband and wife is seriously sinful." The word chastity comes down to us (as some say) from the 12th and 13th centuries by way of the middle English *chastite*, and possibly the old French *chastete*, high-jacked from the Latin *castitat* or *castitasatis*, more or less synonymous with the highest purity. Aristotle mentions it in his *Seven Moral Virtues*, arguing also (more or less) that it is to be considered as a heavenly virtue rather than as an unbridled lust, unless it occurs in some sort of loving arrangement when it becomes (to the contrary) somehow quite pure, promoting good health and even wholesome education, all the while discouraging intoxication. Aquinas, in the privacy of his monastic cell (we'll greet him again in Chapter V), knew his Aristotle well, and enthusiastically endorsed the old fellow, saying that sexual appetite must be subject to *reason*, the same word Aristotle used. Yes, he said, there should be a time when even lusty folks must rise above it as a way of elevating their sublime thoughts closer to Platonic levels, because too much non-chastity leads us, yes again, to imprudence.

Consider, for instance, a military fellow named *Holofernes* who actually lost his head over a woman with whom he was lost in lust. So too, Aquinas allegedly had such less than likely *experience* of his own, if the truth be known. He'd been locked so long in his cell that, after spying a tantalizing woman, he felt a certain *bacheloristic urge seizing* possession of His Holiness, if that's to be imagined. Surmising her seductive ends, he grabbed hold of his firebrand and chased her the hell out, but not without inscribing a sign of the cross on his cell door with that same firebrand, after which (according to other sources) he tossed it in the fire (whether literally or figuratively) and thereafter took his place upon what's been called the seat of sedentary scholarship, a chair of philosophy, that elevated throne of contemplation from which he never rose (literally or figuratively) again. Hence we find a splendid instance of what may be mind over matter, when the head allegorically prevails over the heart. Chastity wins out; Reason assumes command.

For those ill-suited to monastic life, quite the opposite approach may seem more entertaining and more fulfilling, not withstanding, so to engage in one of life's casual, if covert, pleasures. Bacheloristic chastity (another of our oxymorons) may be encouraged by taking up with women, if one must, who safeguard their chastity with a device that comes to us from the endlessly creative Middle Ages. It renders intimacy virtually impossible, thereby serving at least two other purposes, one of which was a primitive form of birth control, the other an ingenious, if hideously uncomfortable, means of preserving their favors for whomever padlocked the belt, which may have been constructed from leather and metal. There still are chastity belts out there, some of them fitted out with mild electrical currents that can apparently transmit covert messages of some sort and can track women's whereabouts electonically. They can also thwart criminal attack and deny entrance to anyone not possessing the appropriate key. We also have, so to speak, a male chastity device that comes with a training video. There are, so we are told, male chastity belts that serve other ends, certain attendant problems, as one might surmise. One of them is to interfere with hygienic necessities; the other is being held in permanent bondage for want of a key.

This is outrageously confining, something that most normal people, most certainly bachelors, find abhorrent. Freedom, as we have suggested, is one of the mainstays of the bacheloristic life that thrives upon such things best described as salacious, a wonderful word, rich in implications that involve, but are not limited to, lasciviousness, lecherousness, lewdness with an occasional dollop of the bawdy, not to cite other forms of indecency with deliciously limitless implications. Salaciousness comes to us like so many other extraordinary things, from the Latin, where it turns up as *salax*, or maybe *salac*, denoting the *lustful* maybe even the provocative. Bacheloric salaciousness is ordinarily associated with lasciviousness which yes, falls to us through the Latin of our forerunners who spelled it lascivious that in turn means wanton, but not the sort of wonton that, with its pockets of dough one discovers covertly concealed in his consommé. This wantonness comes to us through the Middle English wantoun, meaning unrestrained and ill-educated, and in later years came to be read as undisciplined, lustful, bawdy and even tending toward the mercilessly inhumane, not to say excessively sensual. Its later generally accepted meaning trended toward being a pampered, self-indulgent, often flirtatious person with an aggressively frolicsome disposition.

By *bawdiness*, we all agree that it more or less connotes a woman *of easy virtue*, one who may maintain and promote a *house of pleasure* where unbridled lewdness prevails. The term *bawdry* suggests unchastely, coarseness, boisterousness and other forms if ill-mannered behavior that, in the minds of some, tend toward an amusing indecency. *Bawd* comes to us apparently from the German *baird*, meaning (in the old sense of the word) gay, and may well (for all we know) have sifted through the Old French *baud* (merry, licentious). Some are of the persuasion that it evolves from the Old High German *baldbold*, with a low bow toward the Old French *boudetrot*, which is to say a bawd who trots, i.e., runs errands, if you know what we mean.

As to the familiar term lecherous, we may as well concede that it applies in certain unanticipated circumstances in the lives of otherwise well-intentioned bachelors as well as other men of other tantalizingly descriptive designations. In early English it seems to have suggested things like craving and longing, probably for something more pleasingly erotic. The awful truth is that the word's etymological origins may be, shall we say, open to question, and may never be known, unless perchance the word derives from letch, which is a muddy quagmire. We have also cited the word indecency, since it is a regrettably necessary term, useful toward our exploration of the bacheloristic life as it has persisted over lecherous generations. The word obviously directs our attention to matters that are less than decent. This in turn directs our attention to what, on the other hand, we judge to be fit and appropriate, not to say seemly as it may occasionally be applied to the bacheloric life, since it need not be lived any other way. The best of bachelordom is evidenced by its gentlemanliness, its sense of appropriateness and its recognition of our mother language when it's cunningly well-articulated. Bachelors are more than usually attuned to how well they may be received, particularly by women who appreciate, even demand, assuredness, attractiveness, propriety, decorousness and (to a point) fashion. The ideal bachelor is ably equipped to present himself by demonstrating good taste, decency and decorousness, leavened with a dash of common etiquette, civility, formality, modesty, rectitude, comeliness, correctness in discourse, patience, generosity, understated strength, more than ordinary modesty and understated strength reminiscent of the so-called Renaissance Gentleman.

To possess very many of these engaging features is to become what we might be tempted in a compromised moment to call a *bachelor extraordinaire*— with all the advantages that accrue to such gentlemanly presentment. Features such as these *appear* (at least) to have belonged hereditarily to a fellow of noble, possibly gentle, ennobling, chivalrous, honorably distinguished and blessed with elevated social station (conceivably belonging to the landed gentry), with a refined sense of propriety, (inherited) wealth appropriate to a family of position, well bred, endowed with a certain *je ne sais quoi*, an exceedingly good and elevated sense of decency, an ingratiating wit, along with a keen sense of generosity and courtesy, not to say ordinary politeness. By *civility*, we have in mind a man graced with a generously liberal (in the traditional sense) education, admirably well connected, endowed with a certain understated polish and refinement, a humane chap, unfailingly courteous, well-spoken and articulate in more than one language (preferably one *ancient*, more than one *modern*), with a commitment to promoting the enduring ideals of *civility* at its most polished, probably conservative in the sense of his maintaining traditional values. Such a fellow is more than likely to be advantageously tailored, constitutionally subtle, and more than able to speak in tones barely above a Poe-like whisper. We cannot say with any authority that gentleman prefer blondes, but we have no hesitation in saying that they are prepared to receive women in most of their multifarious manifestations, all of whose hands they eagerly kiss. A gentleman refrains from displaying emotion, and is disinclined to treat anyone rudely, having learned his behavior inside the finest drawing rooms and gentleman's clubs that have shown him, among other facetious things, how *to tip his hat*. We have been repeatedly told that "a gentleman will do anything in his power to pursue and court the woman of his dreams," all the more so given his constitutionally romantic, not to say *idealistic* approach to receiving women.

The Renaissance Gentlemen may have originated in 14th century Italy with its revival of classical art and learning, discussed at excessive length and detail in John Ruskin's *The Stones of Venice* (1851–1853) where are celebrated the ideals of universal genius best represented by Leonardo da Vinci. Out of this evolved the idealized *courtier* (originally meaning one who attends the court of a sovereign) and ideal gentleman, commented upon at some length by a chap bearing the unlikely name *of Baldasare Castiglione* (1478–1529) who pretty well wrote the handbook on renaissance gentlemen, known to most of us through Sir Thomas Hoby's English translation as his *Book of the Courtier* (1528) that had a great deal to say about impeccable etiquette and the gracefully aristocratic life. Baldy called it in his Italian, *Il Cortegiano*, something that literary historians classify as a *courtesy book*, which purports to address the education of a young courtly gentleman, which is to say an elegant fellow endowed with diplomatic capabilities befitting a royal court, possibly little more than an elegant princely flatterer. Courtesy books were still in vogue in the 18th century, having turned up in such places as Henry Peacham's *Compleat Gentleman* (1622), Richard Braithwait's *The English Gentleman* (1630) and Francis Osborn's *Advice to a Son* (1658). Such crucially influential books as these purveyed gentlemanly behavior that informs Edmund Spenser's *The Fairy Queen* (1590–1596) and Ben Franklin's extraordinary but never completed autobiography, begun in 1771.

Castiglione, who was entirely capable of writing comedy, recommended that the courtier (read *gentleman/bachelor*) presumes numerous and precise social skills, among them a sense of grace, pleasing countenance, a certain discretion in discourse, a flair for entertainment, a competence at rhetoric, an ability to handle arms properly, a gallant personality, a more than nimbleness of body and wit. He also recommends that the young fellow be resolute, industrious, valiant, profound and invincibly bold, life-embracing with amusingly pleasant characteristics. His apparel (like himself) must be more than ordinarily understated and handsome, refined and clean (so to avoid contempt) but not so gorgeous as to provoke "envy or suspicion of pride, vanity and self-love" or other imperfections. Finally, he must project a "pattern of worthy, fine and lovely virtue." Presuming that he marries, that marriage is strongly encouraged to be Platonic, since ideal love is the bonding of mind and spirit, not merely the joining of two bodies. Hence true marriage surpasses the physical and ascends to an airy abstraction, a divine union of minds that evolve from ignorance into sublime understanding. In other words, it transcends sexuality and moves ever toward the spiritual and the ideal. The big idea is to develop what Castiglione calls "the qualities of the ideal courtier," the object being to stand as an example of *courtly love*, the proper thing for a courtier to embrace as part of his upbringing and presentment, since "it will stand well with him to be a lover" of the right sort, such that "boys [might] not [chide] him for his ineptitude, nor women make him a jesting-stock." He is to become the kind of lover "that brings him praise," such that "in his riper years" he may disavow "all filthiness of common love, and so enter the holy way of love with the guide of reason." All such earnest matter strikes us as too bloody much of a good thing, but even so.

Historians peg the Renaissance from the 14th century to its greater fruition in the middle 17th. The development of the Renaissance Man represents the convergence of several vaguely expressed features, among them a refined sense of self-expression, heightened individual consciousness and immense understanding of such things as the arts, international culture and religion—all of them lofty ideals inherited from the Middle Ages. Out of this emerged humanism that, true to its name, advocated the human over the divine, with its emphasis upon the secular (which is to say the worldly, the temporal) instead of the religious, the clerical and the ecclesiastical. Out of such a cultural hodgepodge emerged a new kind of gentleman, an ideal sort of bachelor, influenced in part by his understanding of courteous conduct not necessarily shared by men of lesser station and sophistication. He gave the impression, at least, of high mindedness, natural elegance, a refined drawing room presence, polite to a fault, with an understanding how to present himself as a gentleman in attire that is conservative, understated and correct. He was powerful in his influence, confident but inoffensive. He was concerned about the welfare of others; he was self-effacing and kind, tolerant and forgiving, accomplished but evermore modest.

The Romance of the Rose (The Roumaunt of the Rose), a dream allegory composed by two authors (Guillaume de Lorris and Jean de Meun) 39 years apart in the 13th century, introduces us to a romantically-inclined young man who nods off, discovers a passage through a high wall with a Freudian opening into a magnificent garden, comes upon a rosebud, submits to the god of love, secures permission to kiss the rosebud, and over time receives earnest advice on how to be the lover to which he aspires. In other words, it is, among other didactic things, another sequence of practical instructions pursuant to becoming a courtly lover, something that entails a considerable amount of coaching since, as in Castiglione, it occasions a discussion of carnality as it differs from Platonic love. It's all treated in a rather self-consciously artistic manner. *The Romance of the Rose* proffers a curious piece of advice for women, as well, namely that since all men are faithless, it is therefore incumbent upon them all to retaliate by fleecing them of every last nickel and dime, in addition to which they too may be every inch as unfaithful as they are wont, since (and we'll mention this later) marriage is by its very nature unnatural. This introduces us to *the battle of the sexes*, about which we will also have further comment. The narrative continues by saying that the world is heartless, and the state of mankind has nothing to recommend it. A bit later the subject of chastity reasserts itself, along with the question of whether or not an act of fornication is an offense to God, and whether, since it is a natural occurrence, it is to be considered sinful. Aquinas, of all people, enters the narrative for having held in his *Summa Contra Gentis* (c. 1270–1273) that men should be given a pass on chastity, because if they were entirely pure, the human race would vanish. Still and all, since chastity leads to heavenly salvation then it must apply to both genders. We are not suggesting that bachelors are necessarily gentlemen, nor are they by any romantic stretch of the imagination courtly lovers, albeit those historical influences are, and will always be, part of the prevailing culture of courtship. We prefer to believe that a gentleman is warmly received anywhere that civility prevails, including in casual encounters with women. Meanwhile, the extreme romanticism of courtly love still lingers in our culture. Courtship, or what passes for it, is still part of the psychology of seduction.

There will always be erotic alternatives for men (including a large part of the bachelor population) who feel that seduction is a sporting pursuit and may on occasion direct their amorous attention to sporting houses, a decorous name for brothels, something that demands some inquiry inasmuch as it regrettably pertains to bacheloric culture. The current meaning of brothel, so *The Oxford English Dictionary* explains, derives from the Middle English word with a similar spelling that means ruined and degenerate. Brothel once referred to a lewd person, a worthless fellow, a scapegrace, a good-for-nothing. It later referred to an abandoned woman, later still a prostitute, later still to a brothel's house, a brothel house, a bawdy house and so elegantly forth. Even gentlemen have been seen and heard in such lewd places, although Shakespeare in his King Lear prudently advises us to "keep thy foote out of brothels." From these etymological origins come such charming variations as bagnios (bathhouses). Brothels have been called cat houses, a term of uncertain origin dating only from about 1931. Call them what we will; there have always been houses of remarkably ill repute, with their reprehensible reputations.

Suffice it to say that such things are, on the surface of it, no places for gentlemen, although such men have been known to call there for less than elegant purposes. Other names for these entertainments still turn up, such as *call house, stew, crib*, and even a *seraglio* which is a *harem*, a lodging place, an enclosure and (more to the point) a veritable heaven (we jest) for gentlemen who know how to comport themselves socially in such circumstances. One must, of course, present himself to best advantage at all occasions and places, even when it means relying upon pretense and posturing. None other than the less than discriminating Huckleberry Finn, by Jove, knew a gentleman when he saw one, and remarked with profound amazement that a certain Colonel Grangerford, a kind of riverboat dandy, was indeed every inch a study in chivalry. "He was a gentleman all over," Huck tells us. "His hands was long and thin, and every day of his life he put on a clean shirt and a full suit from head to foot made out of linen so white it hurt your eyes to look at it; and on Sunday he wore a blue tail-coat and brass buttons on it...there weren't no frivolish about him, not a bit, and he weren't never loud."

Bachelors, be they gentlemen (the real ones), are remarkably adaptable to an array of life's occasions, not all of them elegant, where they can blend and participate with exemplary ease and aplomb in situations involving common exchanges and encounters such as funerals, weddings (as long as they're not their own), holidays, birthdays, sporting events (not the ones in sporting houses), concerts (real ones), picnics and pig roasts. They intermingle smoothly and engage others in their chivalric persuasions. Such abilities are in part the influence of having spent their youths in some of the better universities where they have at least been given far more than a perfunctory exposure to the arts and sciences. Socially they've been exposed to a broad range of examples and experiences intended to provide them with fundamental decencies without which they could not hope to address other civilized personalities, what few remain.

Others have matriculated through colleges of commerce and business where they have attempted to appreciate the manifold differences between wholesale and retail pursuant to creating the appropriate appearance and glib discourse appropriately and generously laced with recent clichés directed at the correct people, so to foster the impression that they are leading while they are indeed following. To acquire such social tools as these entails an almost obligatory involvement with social fraternities that destroy and then rebuild their eager applicants, so to fit the fraternal mold. This is accomplished by belittling them and insisting that they enthusiastically participate in humiliating rituals that, upon fulfillment, permit them to join the brotherhood after a disgraceful initiatory ritual. What motivates these insults is the rabid desire to be accepted, to *fit in*, which is so intense that they will consent to any degradation to add their names to some secret society, pursuant to which they submit to beatings, insults, threats, and a variety of other time-tested outrages. Young men with bachelor's degrees in business devote much of their college years pointlessly singing fraternity songs and eventually marrying sack-dancing sorority girls who squandered their undergraduate careers learning how to teach silly things to school children.

Chances are that bachelors, especially the confirmed ones we will examine in later pages, are disinclined to push any signal of conformity quite that far. Odds are also that they will flirt in some way or another with any presentable woman. To bachelors, women are a bit of a *lottery*. Some men do their best to conceal their decidedly counter romantic attitudes, including their disguised misogamy that, plain and simple, is an old word with an old meaning (in Greek) *misein* (to hate) and the English word *gamy*, meaning marriage, union, ergo *hatred of marriage*. Misogamy is not to be mistaken for *misogyny*, once spelled *misogine*, meaning the hatred of women and girls, used in contexts such as spitefully calling someone a *misogynous old bachelor*. There is not necessarily any pretext for detesting females, since women themselves have been the most virulent of misogynists. We might also add that the word *philogyny* means quite the opposite, namely, the love and admiration of women and girls.

While it is obviously misleading to presume that all women are alike, they are nonetheless more alike than they are different. One is led to assume that the genders are wired differently, which is true, although the implications of that are also mysterious and therefore troublesome to explain. They are as different as an apple and an orange or more likely a dog and a cat. This has not inhibited those who purport to explain gender differences aside from physiological ones. Most marital discord has been passed off as being a result not of misogamy and misogyny, but the near impossibility of even the most elementary of communication. Writer James Kent, with or without psychological credentials, assumes that "all men have direct forms of communication," and that "men do not play games and tend to say exactly what they mean," the implication being that women possess an evasively indirect form of communication, play games, and tend to say something other than what they mean, whatever that may be construed to communicate.

Meanwhile, Amber Hensley, writing on behalf of something called *Masters of Healthcare*, concedes "that there are actually differences in the way women's and men's brains are structured" that helps us understand why "they react to events and stimuli" the way they do, noting, as others have, that women communicate best when their ideas are group-oriented and when they rely upon non-verbal cues such as "tone, emotion and empathy." Men, to the contrary, tend toward the "task-oriented, less talkative and more isolated." She then raises the delicate subject of right and left brain hemispheres that we use to differentiate the rational (left) from the intuitive (right), wherein the left distinguishes itself as structured, controlled, mathematical, logical, versus the right which is more toward the emotional, aesthetic, intuitive and personal. Whereas one might identify men with the former and women with the latter, clinical evidence identifies men with the left hemisphere, but women with both. Nonetheless, this begins to explain why men are more task oriented while women, as Hensley says, "typically solve problems more creatively and are more aware of feeling while communicating, [whereas] men generally prevail in solving mathematical problems." She also observes that whereas men react to stress with a fight or flight (confront or flee) policy, women react with a tend and befriend reaction, borrowing that expression from psychologist Shelley E. Taylor, who associated it with hormonal causes, noting that when under stress, women look after themselves and their children. Emotionally, she notes, "women possess a larger deep limbic system than men," *limbic* denoting that region of the brain associated with motivation and emotion.

The pronouns *we* and *us* belong to the female gender that tends to excel more in language because, as Hensley explains, two regions of the female brain are verbally-related, whereas men "process language in their dominant hemisphere." Men have larger brains simply because they are themselves larger, although the sexes feel pain differently. Women demand more assistance with pain control than do men, and appear to feel pain more intensely, and articulate it. Men are more inclined toward physical problems unrelated to gender, among them *dyslexia*, and are less likely to suffer from anxiety, autism and depression. Other researchers have observed other gender differences, clinical and medical. Michael G. Connor has noted some of the more obvious things, among them that, on balance, men have more upper body strength, develop muscle more readily than women, bruise less, and (in contrast with Hensley's observation about pain) "have a lower threshold of awareness of injuries to their extremities." Obviously too, men are better armed for "physical confrontation and the use of force." Men are more thick-headed, as women have long perceived.

Connor has concluded that women have four times as many neurons (brain cells) that coordinate their left and right hemispheres, which may be why young girls find young boys' conversations *boring*. Boys would damned well rather be on a playing field than listening to girls' confusing conversations that appear to address three subjects simultaneously. All of this supports the view that relations between the sexes can be difficult and at times impossible. Connor concedes that psychological differences "can be difficult to describe," something we're not inclined to challenge. And what about understanding the opposite sex? That too can sometimes be somewhere between *difficult* and *impossible*. He does say, and we've heard this before, that "women are usually more concerned about how problems are solved than merely solving the problems themselves. Men, on the considerable other hand, proceed to the problem, assess it, then presume to resolve it. So too, when trapped in a maze, a hall of mirrors, "girls tend to work their way...as a group that appears not to have a designated leader," then attempt to solve matters with a committee. Boys, however, have structured links and a chain of command with a designated leader.

All in all, Connor observes that women are, as one might presume, intuitive. Tuition derives from the Latin, meaning to guard, protect and watch over. Intuition means to peer into something, contemplate it, understand it in the way that Hamlet contemplatively raises Yorick's skull and deduces some astutely metaphysical observation from it. It was De Quincey who remarked that "God must see; he must intuit, so to speak; and all truth must reach him simultaneously." Some women claim to possess a generous gift for ontologism, an uncanny awareness of certain metaphysical abstractions, if what we hear be so. Opinion is still divided over whether their ontological capability is real or imagined. Ronald Riggio, writing for *Psychology Today* (July 14, 2011) infers that "women are more likely to pick up upon the subtle emotional messages being sent by others," whereas men "are better at controlling felt emotions." He also suggests that women, who have been historically lower in social power... become more attuned to non-verbal clues," partly too because "evolutionary elements" have better ability to decode."

Colleen Oakley of *WebMD Magazine* calls it the "sixth sense," and refers us to Judith Orloff, MD, Assistant Professor of psychiatry at UCLA who writes that "there are neuron transmitters in the gut that can respond to environmental stimuli in the now." Moreover, she notes that "American women...are encouraged to be receptive to their inner thoughts, so it appears that they have more intuition than men," adding that "girls are praised for being sensitive while boys are urged to be more *linear* in their thinking rather than listening to their feelings," which strikes us as not altogether rational. Connor believes that "women are prone to become overwhelmed with complexities," whereas men "tend to focus on one problem at a time." He also suggests that women have an exceptional ability to recall particularly emotional memories, suggesting too that "women possess an enhanced physical response to danger or threat." Addressing the endlessly discussed relationship question, from which bachelors characteristically disengage themselves, Connor argues that men feel closer and more validated through shared activities, while women would prefer instead do far better with their celebrated skill at communication in the form of dialog, thereby sharing experiences.

An article entitled "Men Vs Women" published at *differencebetween.net* chastens us that "though men and women signify opposite forces in Nature, the complementary nature makes them inseparable," continuing that "women seem less able to solve problems, [but are] better at intuitive tasks," whatever those may be. They are also presumed to be more sensitive and emotional, which is patently obvious. One probably views gender identity as inside-out, which is to say that one is born into one gender or the other and, coming to terms with that identity, makes do with it. An illuminating piece called "Femininity/Masculinity" by Jan E. Stets and Peter J. Burke in the department of sociology at Washington State University, stresses the role of society in recognizing and certifying gender identity by determining "what it means to be a man or a woman in society," then clarifying whether one is "dominant or passive, brave or emotional," the result being that obviously "males will generally respond by defining themselves as masculine while females will generally define themselves as feminine." This much determined, the authors hold that "gender roles...are shared expectations of behavior, given one's gender." They go on to say, somewhat surprisingly, that "it is not the behaviors themselves that are important, but the meanings implied by those behaviors." One of the outcomes of these rather stereotypical observations is that "men are aggressive, competitive and instrumentally important while women are passive, cooperative and expressive," assuming "that their role division was predicated upon innate characteristics identified with one gender or the other which began when somebody in an obstetrical delivery room identified them as either boys or girls. After that, they identified themselves accordingly. We are told that, by the age of four, children classify other children in this manner.

Stet and Burke explain that gender identity is part public perception in the sense that "usually [boys and girls] are identified by certain key terms such as soft, hard, weak strong, emotional, not emotional." Another inroad to that identity arrives through the subjects themselves by way of self-descriptions, such as when they begin a statement with "as a [boy or girl] I usually am..." et cetera, that directly bear upon gender identity and gender roles. Gender beliefs are subject to change and contradiction, such as when an Indiana high school football team designated a girl as place kicker, simply because she could kick more ably than any of the boys on the team. This raises the question of what Stets and Burke call *gender-appropriate* and gender *inappropriate* behaviors that may provoke occasional disapproval. Children exhibiting cross-gender behavior "were more likely to have low self-esteem." They conclude by saying that "to modify the social system may mean first modifying individual beliefs about masculinity and femininity."

Gender recognition understandably plays a role in ritualistic bachelor parties, the ostensible purpose of which is for men to dispatch one of their number into vacuous matrimonial bondage, as if to pack a comrade off to war or other perilously secret mission from which he is unlikely to return alive. It's what might be called a watershed event, a water-parting, a parting of the ways, a profound turning point. It is also to be interpreted as an initiatory introduction to the miseries of married life, from which the poor fellow may never be quite the same. An intellectually-inclined woman named Clover Nolan Williams tells of having, as a result of *miscommunication* been a guest at her brother's bachelor party, where she was the only woman present except for an *ecdysiast* whom she befriended and with whom she arrived at certain pointed conclusions about bachelors and their gender identity, later collected painstakingly in a rather overstated but still informative essay called "The Bachelor's Transgression: Identity and Difference in the Bachelor Party," published in the Winter 1994 issue of *The American Journal of Folklore*. It interprets Williams' brother's being obliged to don women's clothing and then, like the ecdysiast, disrobe. Ms. Williams describes the spectacle as "the bachelor's feminization and humiliation," similar to fraternity hazing, expelling the groom "from the group by making him into *another*, which is to say transforming the groom-to-be as an ersatz *woman* that Williams chooses to equate with *degradation*. That much accomplished, the poor fellow has been supposedly humiliated as a way of demonstrating his friends' heartfelt *affection* for him, a contestable conclusion, to say the least. To say the most, she may (however subconsciously) be suggesting that, by submitting to marriage, he's become feminized, another contestable conclusion inferring that he's about to be castrated, in one sense or another, as part of being welcomed into husbandhood. Fear of castration is one of bachelordom's alleged obsessions, at least subliminally, and was something that Freud took seriously enough to assert that to be castrated is to identify with one's castrator. He even advanced the absurd notion that girls are under the impression that they've been castrated.

Certain bachelor party traditions appear to have been long instituted, although a man can presume to marry (something not in his best interests) without being exposed to this supposed celebration which has as its implied message that matrimony is not only a mistake; it's a cardinal blunder. Such occasions also unmistakably promote the opinion that the groom, like some criminal awaiting the noose, lives out the final hours of his freedom in a state of profound dread. Some bachelor parties, so we are informed, have forgone their rowdiness their strippers, their final opportunity for a man to be with a woman not his wife, to whom he will, anon, become bonded (theoretically, anyway) until death parts them. The mere thought of it is outrageous, unnatural, unwarranted, unreasonable, unthinkable and unsound. It's no time for comedy, but in the minds of some, it leads to hilarity, especially among bachelor party revelers, some of whom have somehow evaded matrimony while others have stumbled into it and are looking for their misery to have a little company. Sabah Karim has written an article appropriately and helpfully titled "How to Throw Bachelor Parties" for a source called Culture and Society, where he explains that a wedding's Best Man is allegedly the person in control of the groom's fateful, and in some sense final party, at least of that kind. Karim appropriately calls it "one final depraved fling that the groom-to-be won't soon forget (no matter how much he tries)." One can always resort to the easy and obvious, which is to gather up a merry band of degenerates, engage the de rigueur stripper, and keep the affair quiet and pleasantly erotic. The worst is yet to come.

One of the unspoken, inarticulate messages here is never to marry a woman. One can successfully marry a hydrant or a dead tree, but not a woman. Meanwhile the bachelor party is a last hurrah, a seeming surrender to one of life's ineluctable penalties, every bit that grim. Since the prospect of being driven into marriage is not a certainty, it begs the question of why any bachelor bothers to fret about it. Proceed, if one must, but if the bachelor party becomes (as they say) out of hand, Karim warns that it may offend some party-goers and dip the groom (so to speak) in baptismally bubbling hot water, so that the marriage may well be over before it begins, which will be a blessing not necessarily in disguise. Judy Dutton, writing for a site called *Marie Clair*, cites an account of 37-year-old bachelor who passed his final evening at, where else, a strip club which was conveniently close to a brothel. This gradually came to light when his party guests disappeared, each with a woman, to a hotel across the street. It then crossed the groom's mind that he might just as well join the fun, since this was presumably "his last chance to touch a woman ever again," unless perhaps he took up the eroticism of gynecology. He did the predictable thing by selecting "a statuesque blonde with fake breasts" and crossed the street, in more senses than one, to the same hotel where, according to accounts, he received his money's worth, after which, and for the nonce, he forgot all about his lovely fiancée while his guests "burst into cheers" as if he had earned a Nobel Prize for unpremeditated sex. Before the evening ended, he and those guests devoted some time and attention to the problem of how the groom was to conceal his supposed indiscretion. On the day following, women deeply involved somehow with the wedding (as women invariably are) attempted to explain what had transpired the evening before, but to no avail, since guests (who know about such things) viewed their antics as merely one more *rite of passage*, something that one guest passed off as a "strange ritual, but no more than the wedding itself." One male wedding guest warned the groom that "you're pledging your entire life to one person in a church with statues of bleeding people, and you're spending a fortune." Ms. Dutton, however, concludes her article on a pleasantly, if misleadingly, optimistic note, averring, after all is done and said, that "for some men bachelor party sex is anticlimactic, even depressing," insisting nonetheless that "marriage and fidelity seem appealingly wholesome." As to the compromised groom, she adds, "the wedding was the best day of his life."

We'll see. The groom in question may have formed a contrary take on the contrast between the party and the implied promise of a marital bower of bliss. Karim reminds us that at bachelor parties, "there is an unwritten code of silence among the attendees who apparently hadn't a great deal of confidence in its sinister marital implications, or they wouldn't be assembling in a marginally antagonistic gesture in opposition to it. Appearances aside, their presence was in support of the poor fellow who was about to compromise his future, since friends don't wish the worst on friends. At least they can do what's possible to forestall the inevitable by appearing to deny it by changing the subject.

There is a firm in Montreal that claims to have organized bachelor parties by the thousand and is prepared cheerfully to fulfill any requests, be they strip clubs, hotels, private shows, and *bottle service* with a staff of fun-loving folks who eagerly scout the city in quest of unimaginatively titillating thrills and spills. A similar stateside service stresses the overwhelming importance of carousing in Las Vegas for the poor bachelor's *last stand*, saying that "if there were one place in the world for the perfect bachelor party, it hands down has to be Vegas. They don't call this jewel of the desert Sin City for no reason," the implication being that eroticism begins and ends here. Grab it while you can. It is the nearly prototypical bachelor, or shall we say *failed bachelor* come-on. In a sense, it's entirely unnecessary, since bachelors will continue being bachelors and will continue to unleash their occasionally less than printable good times. It's an erotically attractive option that seems to go unnoticed. Death is inevitability; marriage isn't. Every astute bachelor understands this.

So-called *bachelorette parties* are a different beast, the object being (according to one source) to "treat the bride-to-be like a queen" greeting the big day by "getting pampered at a local spa while hanging out with the girls and sipping mimosas," then launching headlong into "manicures, pedicures, facials and massages," before passing the night viewing "a live drag show," finally concluding the occasion at a "local bar." Other options? "Try planning a kayak, snorkeling or parasailing adventure." We're beginning to get the idea. Consider visiting a "comedy club," depending, of course, on "the mood the group" happens to have tumbled. Consider too "dancing with fog machines and lights," an experience the bride will cherish for a lifetime. There is even a bachelorette superstore prepared to assemble a *lingerie shower* that one wedding-wise woman knowingly remarked is one of the more memorable parts of any wedding and is always a *fun pre-wedding festivity*. Another, somewhat racier idea is to have the bride's dress be appropriate for a "sassy playmate bunny," while the "bridesmaids dress in cute pastel dresses or as fairies." Sounds good to us, provided that the bride "has a great sense of humor and does not embarrass easily." Don't forget, however, to "decorate the room with great bachelorette decorations." We wouldn't dream of it. What about the menu? Try "sweet salads, celery, cucumber sandwiches and pastel M&Ms."

For women, a wedding is their Big Day. Failing that, it's something less than Big. *The London Telegraph* informs us (March 13, 2014) that two thirds of girls begin to contemplate matrimony when they are children of 13, some as early as six, and that "millions of women have already planned their weddings before they have found a groom," which is anything but surprising, since the objective is matrimony itself. Selection of the groom is merely one of numerous busybody details that need to be resolved before the Big Day arrives. We also learn that half of women polled had selected their bridesmaids by the age of 18. About a third of the hopefuls have considered which blooms they'll be watering, and what sort of wedding dress they'll don only once. One woman commented that "If you've attended the weddings of close friends and family, it's hard not to imagine how you would like your own big day." We understand perfectly. About one in 20 have perused wedding magazines, and about 17 percent have seriously investigated a *wedding fair*, but 68 percent say that they advisedly never discuss wedding contemplations with a new boyfriend, confirming that marriage begins as an undercover objective, one quite incomprehensible to most men. Anna Breslaw, writing for *Jezebel*, cites a UK website that queried about 2,000 single women and discovered that nearly 60 percent had begun planning for the Big Day and ten percent had a dress in mind, while 55 percent contemplated the kind of hair style and makeup they preferred, along with precisely who their bridesmaids were to be and the sort of engagement and wedding rings they had in mind. Only about a third notified their *intendeds* that all this chicanery was afoot, lest they beat a sudden and rapid retreat.

It's safe to say that women are *wedding obsessed*, since it is estimated that "one in three single women already own a wedding dress." One woman disclosed that since high school she and her mother attentively viewed Friday night wedding television, sipped champagne and perused wedding magazines. Another woman recalls that "one night in grade 11 or so a girlfriend and I planned out our weddings (bridesmaids, how many family members are coming, where it might be, types of flowers...the style of hair and makeup and rings)." Still another woman recalls that "a former colleague of mine bought her dream wedding dress at 16 years of age, and had spent the entire intervening period—eleven years—maintaining an insanely strict diet in order to ensure it still fitted. Somehow, it always came up in conversation during the first date that she already possessed 'the dress,' and she couldn't work out how come they'd never quite progress to the second date..."

It's surprising that a bachelor would naively consent to being dominated by wedding vows for the balance of his life, but it happens. Married men will invariably reply, when queried, that married life is no more than *all right*, but that they'd *never do it again* (a remark that may not be statistically supported). One woman said that "nothing compares to the heart-warming feeling of a bride['s] listening to the wedding vow of her husband-to-be in front of family and friends close to her." The exchange of wedding vows is the academy award, the shining moment "of the wedding ceremony, and nothing is ever more delightful than a groom['s] delivering a message of love and commitment to his bride." There is something more than a little vindictive in all this, suggesting among other vatic things that the hapless sap is being taken for the joy ride of his life, in a direction he doesn't want to go, on a not so merry merry-go-round.

Weddings are all about women and the prospect of their reproducing, even if they're unable to conceive. One bachelor quipped recently that "marriage is grand. Divorce is several grand." Another man was so impossibly domesticated that not to wear his wedding ring made him feel *naked*. Other men wear such rings, ironically, to pick up *more* women on the fragile assumption that those women want to be thought of as *unavailable*, if that makes sense. Other men view it as similar to tying a string around their finger as a reminder that, for the rest of their lives, they are supposed to return home to the same person and share a bed and half of everything else that isn't entirely their own. For some men the ring is a badge of submission, although men, real ones, don't find submission manly. Some 50 percent of marriages end in divorce, and they long to be in that 50 percent. One married man declares that he will advise his son never to marry, mostly because, "you will have given up your freedom so that you are a slave to another person."

Bachelorhood beckons men to be freed, to breathe deeply, to answer no one, to reclaim their lives, to launch out alone, and to sleep alone—for a while. Statistics tell us that in 1960, 85 percent of households consisted of families. By the year 2000 it had fallen to 68 percent. Make of them what we will; there are presumably fewer marriages and more adults living outside of marriage for any number of sensible reasons. It's the prevenient (we almost said *prurient*) thing to do, by which me mean *anticipatory*, *preventative* because it derails a bewildering number of insidious problems such as marital confinement, everlasting obligation, subjection, legal threat, financial compromise and so perpetually forth. In the wake of all this, bachelorism has even been referred to as an *epidemic*, sometimes *silent epidemic*, a social disease in immediate need of diagnosis, control and treatment, if not annihilation, since it clearly interferes with all of those girlish matrimonial fantasies, wedding banns, receptions, rehearsals, tailor made ceremonies and such like. Commentator Tim Nudd reports that women have been alerted to beware of men "whose dogs bear women's names, who have burns on their shirts and who eat cereal for breakfast, lunch and dinner." We have also been duly warned by something called *match.com*, which stout-heartedly calls itself "the world's number one dating and relationship company," that "bachelorism runs rampant in men across the country." As is said, forewarned is forearmed.

Henceforth, match.com has committed itself to "taking a stand against bachelorism...nationwide" lending its questionable reputation to "terminating this devastating syndrome" by presuming to condemn every man worth the name to interminable marriage, presumably for the national good. No less than Thomas Jefferson, wishing to utter something upstanding and faintly oratorical, declared that the happiest moments of his life had been the few (notice) which he had passed in the bosom of his family. Make what you will of it. One person said that he had taken early retirement *to spend less time with his family*. That said, it is the ill-considered opinion of some dunderheads, most of them employed by our corrupt government, that marriage (at least half of the time) is the foundation of civilization, the rock and mortar of stability, security and solidity of all things invincibly and institutionally upright Like Grant's tomb. Match.com evidently endorses that view and does everything in its dubious influence to uncover a lasting antidote for bachelorism, even as others have suggested to the extent of soliciting anyone who knows a bachelor, or who is suffering from that vile disease, to report it to the *authorities.*

In the years to come, we imagine with profound approval the establishment of a governmental Department of Antibachelorism bent upon registering bachelors, tracking their movements, requiring them to report regularly to counselors, notifying law enforcement *authorities* of their nefarious presence and suspicious activities. In the meantime, match.com is doing all it conceivably can to unlock "the way by which people "meet and fall in love," and is assuming substantial credit for the more than 15 million former lonely hearts around the world who currently participate in this international community that provides them "a rich tapestry" of ethnic "possibilities for love and marriage," proudly serving, as it does, "satisfied clients not only in the 50 states, but also Europe as well as 32 countries in 18 languages, spanning six continents."

Suffice it to say that the war on bachelorism is now menacingly global. An unsigned October 2001 message entitled "an Epidemic of Bachelorism" assures us that nobody much cares for bachelors, which may be a bit of an overreaction. Married men and other prisoners would like more than anything to be liberated, even for one erotic weekend. Meanwhile, bachelors continue to evade their duty to keep the world populated, but instead "spend their lives drinking Martinis and having an unfailingly good time," illustrating once again that living well is the best revenge. "The Happy Bachelor Forum" provides no fewer than 101 reasons why bachelorism is nothing less than bountiful and beneficial, entirely self-aggrandizing. But when one has only himself to manage, it is necessary to be egocentric, not to say narcissistic, examples of which are nearly endless. We begin by observing that everything (not everyone) in his residence is his own, except of course in instances of good will or maybe expediency, when he takes a girlfriend or other woman (any port in a storm) who may be, say, broke and homeless. Still and all, he remains a bachelor.

Our list continues. One need not conceal things if one is a bachelor, even presuming that 1) he possesses things that are best hidden and that 2) he possesses anything that might be hidden. If he were married, he would also presume to conceal nothing from his bride, as it would be at the very least impractical, unwise and unnecessary. Marriage advocates invariably place a huge premium upon *complete candor, honesty and openness*—it's what halfwits are now expected to call full disclosure, which in situations like marriage would last about one hour, if that. We learn too that to be a bachelor one need not share, because it might be too bloody expensive—another point reasonably well taken. Bachelors living alone may consider continuing doing so for fear of someone's stealing their underwear or high-jacking their toothbrushes. There are, like it or not, certain women (we won't name names) who are pronouncedly possessive, quite possibly even territorial. We haven't a problem with that, and remind our readers that one's possessions are crucial to one's identity.

Our list again continues. Another anti-marriage complaint is that one's wife may somehow be entitled to demand, suggest, infer, allude, intimate how her husband is to dress which, as most of us understand, is traditionally a personal matter. We see no fault with taking umbrage at the way he, or anyone else, chooses to present himself, sartorially speaking. Style, we need hardly say, evolves over time, during which one has the option of keeping pace with current inane fashions or dressing in a manner that others may view as less or possibly more than fitting, be it for the seasons, or for the sake of submitting to other people's current whims and less than astute preferences.

It is more than conceivable, nay probable, that a bachelor may prefer to be alone and entirely unfettered. After all, he is by nature and inclination a solitary fellow, and advisedly so. Otherwise, he'd be married, or earnestly inclined to seek some other affiliative company. But no; his evenings are entirely his own. He is jealous of his hours, not wanting to squander them by tolerating the annoyance of ordinary rabble. This is exactly why he evaded and avoided the displeasure of collegiate fraternity distraction during his reclusive university years. The bachelor is, to put it quite bluntly, far and away happiest in his own company where he can impose order his own life and arrive at decisions without first consulting with anyone else. When motoring blissfully down a road he can, for colorful example, execute a sudden and unanticipated u-turn without securing permission from a chorus of nitwits and without having to explain his dubious rationale, even to the constabulary.

Life is easier and far more efficient when one is in command of his own hours. Similarly, his quarters are ordered, or possibly disordered, to suit himself without having to beg clearance before proceeding. Nights are for spending alone, without having to exact consent from some Ophelian woman or reach an understanding about what he's to opine, how to deport himself, what to devour, what to think, how to react, how strongly and for how long. He rather enjoys his own explicable idiosyncrasies and is free to develop engagingly new ones. Bachelors need not remember holidays, birthdays, holy days, or anniversaries, nor do they need to suffer fools and other jackdaws whom they find annoyingly irrelevant, irritating, inane and insipid. In short, they create their own personal microcosm inside of which they play out their days as they would have them be played out. They adjust their own temperatures and draw their own baths. They balance their checkbooks, pay their own bills, launder their own clothing, unclog their own sinks, walk their own dogs, swab their own decks, stir their own pots and pop their own pills.

The Happy Bachelors Forum concludes by alerting all who have ears that being and remaining independent is not quite so self-indulgent and blatantly selfish as it might first appear, since attending to one's intellectual nourishment is of the utmost priority. To this end some bachelors are uniquely prepared to pursue what was once called *the life of the mind*, through which they may explore their own eccentric ends and not always predictable purposes. This entails a reliance upon in the divine light of metaphysical speculation, contemplation, painstaking investigation of ideas ancient and modern, scientific and humanistic, religious and philosophic. He accomplishes this by examining critically the world's most intellectually baffling theories, by reading selectively and discerningly, evaluating astutely, availing his intellect to things and ideas hitherto overlooked but accessible in pages not yet turned. It is essential to the development of their bachelorhood to reinforce their intellects and tastes on their own terms, unaffected by fads and frenzies. Bachelorhood is anything but eccentric pose and pretense; it is a life commitment to impose structure into one's days, unaffected by the commonplace and the clichéd.

It strikes us as odd, somewhat bizarre and a little peculiar that bachelorhood can find expression in monasticism, characterized by an intensely personal inclination toward holy orders and a devotion to life (such as it may be) inside a monastery, a word derived from the Greek that means dwelling alone, living in isolation. This in some respects informs and expands our understanding of bacheloristic independence, inasmuch as it may demand living a determinably solitary life, as is prescribed by monastic culture, and applicable to persons electing to insulate themselves from incivility, to the end that they more than ably nurture the inner life. Bachelors, most of them, aren't always quite so apparently isolated, but neither are certain monks and friars who ostensibly flourish, lost in divine meditation while camped in an ambiance hardly characteristic of flirtatious bachelors.

Evangeline Holland has written that even in Edwardian England (c. 1901–1914), for "the unmarried gentlemen of high society, the world was his oyster," and that at "no other time in history was bachelorism such a widespread and pleasurable, pursuit," which begs the question of why especially eligible men declined to marry, the answer being that there was obviously nothing in it for them, since they "were inclined to dash from cricket match to house party to hunting grounds with nary a thought to acquiring a spouse."

Precisely. Any further questions? Times were changing, as times ordinarily do. Women were ever more striking out on their own, independent of men and invading professions that men traditionally controlled. While that was happening, as Ms. Holland aptly reminds us, bachelors clustered around the theaters and struck it up with women who were, shall we say, freer with themselves. In America, bachelors flourished as never before. There was then even a popular magazine aptly called The Bachelor Book that was both descriptive and prescriptive in its characterization of bacheloristic life, proclaiming that "bachelorhood is surely one of the fine arts," averring too that "no man becomes a bachelor other than by selection," noting that a man may elect that sort of life, or have it selected for him by others, which is somewhat more than doubtful. It further declares that the bacheloristic life is little more than "a mere failure to connect on the matrimonial time-table," i.e., at the reproductive convenience of women.

Whether man (in the universal sense) should customarily live his/her life with a mate of the opposite sex remains a moot question, a matter capable of being questioned, contested, disputed and challenged. The generally held view is that, besides being an element of social stability, marriage is religiously and legally sanctioned on the tacit assumption that it will sustain itself until death mercifully intervenes. For men and women to live naturally in complete harmony again raises questions of gender equality, even though those genders are anything but equal, except under the law and in the eyes of God, as some people insist. Adam and Eve understood this, or at least learned it when it was too bloody late. The Catholic Church teaches that men and women represent two polar opposites analogous to God and man, and to intelligence and reason—but don't tell that to anyone except a Catholic, who already knows it but may not believe it. One is best advised to ascertain which party represents the intelligence, and which the reason, then keep it under his (or her) hat.

Gender relations are a hopelessly entangled, bungled up mess, far better left unexplored, since marital and gender politics can, if one makes the effort, be altogether dismissed, even ignored, by remaining single. There is immense satisfaction in managing one's own time, apportioning blocks of it toward carefully contemplated purposes for amply defined, somewhat exotic ends. One has the rare privilege of setting his own hours, be they day or night, weekends and holidays (without considering someone else's holidays, birthdays, dog days, wash days, et cetera) absorbed in inscrutably transformational interludes of mystical contemplation. This can be accomplished without the problem of being censured, having one's views and opinions subject to someone else's endorsement.

One can always experiment with the appearance (at least) of uxoriousness. By *uxorious* we mean the unconditional, wholeheartedly unequivocal devotion to a wife, probably one's own. This uncommon devotion exacts an uncommon submissiveness and extraordinary declaration of devotion, not to say extreme expression of affection (heartfelt or not) until death do you derail, or at the earliest possible moment that you can escape. Until then, it's a cunning way of maintaining temporary peace and order, not ordinarily commonplace features of matrimony. It's decidedly better, for the nonce, than placing one's neck in a yoke, maybe a noose. Uxoriousness, or the *pretense* of it by an apparently devoted husband who, having little or no perceptible identity of his own, can temporarily come to terms with his termagant (but all the same) indescribably lovely wife who by this time has become his task mistress, his amply decorated commanding officer, his jailor and censor who supervises his thoughts and assigns orders to this submissively wilted husband whose mind, by this time, has turned to mush. This dismal union, enthusiastically endorsed by church and state, leaves the poor husband searching for innovative ways to survive it. In the meantime he's comparable to a war prisoner. He's a pawn in the dreadful conflict between the sexes (to be discussed in greater depth in Chapter III) found guilty but not yet shot.

Speaking of shots, Bill McCleery of the Associated Press reported that on October 6, 2014, a physician in Terre Haute, Indiana, shot and unfortunately killed his bride and himself about 12 hours after their inexpressibly joyous wedding, making it one of the briefer marriages ever recorded in that state. Guests reported that the couple had begun to quarrel "toward the end of the reception," over something no one else quite seemed to comprehend. Obviously the poor fellow ought never have been married in the first place, but he knew no better, and nobody, not even a friend or a counselor, advised him against being captured in a matrimonial net so confining that it might require an act of guerrilla warfare to rescue him. Until then he might arrange a real or imagined business trip, and never bother to return. The objective is to slip *out from under*, especially if there are no children to consider. In other circumstances, one can invent nearly any pretext, any alibi, and any ruse to elude his captor. The idea is to put as much daylight as possible between him and his wife and then summarily vanish. The object is to rely upon the joys of temporary invisibility. Such acts of desperation become necessary, especially considering that some escaped husbands are still too young to comprehend into what vile trap they unwittingly stumbled. Having finally realized it, they've discovered themselves stranded in a psychological and sociological maze from which it is exceedingly difficult to exit gracefully.

A certain unidentified woman essayist we happened upon contributed a piece she called "Signs That a Man is Marriage Material" as a way of offering women *pro bono* counsel on courtship and marriage. It's a bit of down home advice for women hankering to get themselves married. "Many women," she advises, "waste their time dating a man who will never commit to marriage," as one might be committed to a psychiatric ward. Such men, however, may have no financial prospects because they clunk from one paycheck to the next, and therefore aren't the best bets for marital prosperity. Women ransacking dumpsters in search of husbands may conceivably turn up with some miraculously unmarried bloke. If so, the fellow may properly be properly evaluated in two other illuminating ways: 1) as matrimonial candidate, and/or 2) on the chance that there may be (stranger things have happened) something psychically the matter with him that may suggest, nay demand, consultation with a *mental health professional*, as blockheads call them. Even so, the marital candidate may require professional scrutiny, during which his head may require psychiatric candling (in the manner that chicken hatcheries used a candle to scrutinize eggs) and his personality resourcefully investigated for any aberrant matrimonial *issues*, as *cliché artists* refer to them. If, as we were more than implying, the fellow has devoted a disproportion of his waking hours to the metaphysical contemplation of erotic literature, we have on our hands what some *perfectly sane people* would earnestly interpret and hoist as a *red flag*. We are all familiar with red flags, and they aren't the best of portents.

There are women who are inclined to imagine the miraculous appearance of a suitor, a mythical knight on a mythical white horse. However, anyone who has been married for longer than a mythical weekend knows how mythically monotonous it becomes. This begins to account for why well over 50 percent of marriages implode, occasioning a potentially injurious violent inward compression. Given a little encouragement, an unhealthy percent of them will terminate in portentous billows of smoke and cinder. Such marriages are self-devouring; they consume their participants and, worse still, make it exceedingly difficult to escape. Somebody (we forgot who) inclined to similarities, cunningly observed that "boredom in marriage is like a hairline crack in a wall, until time and inaction transform it into an irreparable fault zone." Be it one or the other, it's likely too late to redress it. There have been numerous remedies advanced by psychologists, marriage counselors, and such like well-intentioned (we presume) interventionists, but it's a hopeless cause, stale as last week's leftovers.

This more or possibly less explains why apparently rational people rightly call marriage *unnatural* and worse, even though some married couples are ostensibly contented and even doggedly resigned preserve it; but even a little monotony is too much. It is unnatural to assume that even two more or less attractive and accomplished individuals can be happily marooned in a mineshaft. We've known marriages to remain duct taped more than a half century while the husband, at least, has been wistfully sizing up all the women that he's forsworn by his wedding vows to leave reluctantly alone. It's a hideous way to exist, especially since it's been the acting out, quite unnaturally, of women's notion of eternal love, devotion and unremitting adventure, when it's been quite the opposite. Any mature and relatively sane person need not be told that, when people in their early middle to late twenties create a production number out of wedding ceremony enacted before as many invited people as they or somebody else can afford, their nuptials have a shaky future. By that time children figure in the equation. Eventually, some 90 percent of marrieds report that their presumed *relationship* has long since begun to slump and crumble, even clump and scrumble. Once it begins to slump, it doesn't unslump, but the marriage grinds inexorably on. The only natural thing about marriage is its initial appeal to romantically-inclined individuals who believe that they can overcome the odds through the application of *gusto* and *aplomb*, but can't. All goes middlingly well until the cracks begin to surface and become one of the early diagnostic signs that the ambitious marital experiment is heading ominously south, buried beneath a mountain of kudzu.

It's at this time that the groom begins (if he hadn't long before) to view bachelors with something more than envy: it's now morphed into jealousy. It's also small wonder, because it makes married men long to be the free chaps they thought they once were. Even divorced men seem a bit foolish for having tumbled headlong into their matrimonial morass. That long, lively, lovely romantic life together didn't exactly *pan out*, and in the meantime it exacted an awful emotional price. Bachelors could have seen the whole hideous cycle approaching. It didn't require much insight and imagination, and more than suspected it was infinitely better to remain on their own, free and (mostly) easy, not wanting to pass the rest of their less than precious days trapped in a mason jar with the other masons. One doesn't often encounter a rational-appearing gentleman circumspectly window shopping for a wife. Although more unlikely things have happened, we can't summon any to mind. Possibly, such a person isn't thinking clearly, or possibly he's looking for a live-in cook, a high-dusting housekeeper or dishwashing diva.

We've heard, mind you heard, that more than one eligible man has claimed that the single life ruined him, possibly because he's had extraordinarily too much of a damned good time, and is damned well prepared to settle down like nearly everyone else. He'd devoted serious thought to bidding his bachelorism a less than wistful goodbye. Now he's plotting at all costs (and there will be some) to flee single life by marrying what appears at first glance to be the closest thing he can find to a nice girl, at least until the wedding ceremony concludes. We candidly suspect that there are men (of some kind) who have volunteered for marriage as one might volunteer for service as an ambulance driver in an accommodatively bright, brief and glamorous foreign war, on the assumption that things will in one sense or another, *work out for the better*. Now and then married men say that they actually enjoy being married, but it's in all probability a way of camouflaging their manifold discontents. We've also heard of men who require someone to manage their lives, since they seem unable to do so. There is evidently no shortage of women out there who will eagerly apply for the job, especially when it means treating husbands like footmen.

Bachelors obviously want no part of it because it advertises that they're no longer bachelors. Matrimony is out of the question. What's needed in husbanding is a man (we'll tentatively call him) to accept orders gracefully and in the best of spirit. He's also a fellow committed to what he believes are life's inevitabilities, namely that he's expected to marry, kick back, and make the utmost of it, which, as we have amply seen, is no easy assignment, especially when he considers that it's to continue, unabated, until one of the partners in has the immensely good fortune to survive the other. Women, some of them at least, apparently don't much prefer timid men for marital purposes, although such men are far more easily ordered around by someone in presumed authority, such as their hideous wives. Some women have been partial to what they sensitively call sensitive men, which is a code word for a man exhibiting what might charitably be called feminine emotional responses.

Another literate but unidentified person recently captured the rhetorical implications of wimpishness, identifying it with "a timid man [who is ideally] cautious, nervous [we're all for being nervous], hesitant [we like that, too; one can't be too uncertain these days], and [awaits] permission [or at least a good reaction, probably from his commanding officer] before continuing on with what he's been doing." Perfecto! By Jove, he's the kind of fellow about whom every woman dreams, except that fellows like him are regrettably in limited inventory, having been vacuumed up like fleas by other domineering women. Our informant also observes that a "timid man doesn't take risks, and doesn't do anything to put him on the spot." The fellow was a born an ineffectual bloke and is likely to remain so. He knows his place, and by Jove, stays in it. We wish him and his apron well. In the meantime, one nagging problem may arise, that being how to march this twerp to an altar without first sedating him. Onward, chaps! An army of unwed, possibly unweddable women await your surrender.

It has also been reported in certain suitably avant-garde publications that, to the contrary, there are a few women, (only a few), who appear to prefer confident men. Confident! Yes! By all means. Self-confidence (in moderation, of course) is an excellent asset when a fellow is attempting to make himself appear acceptable for consideration (no more than that: consideration) as a marriage prospect. The problem, as we see it, is simply this: a confident man may be significantly more difficult to control, ordered about, and less accepting of stern, uncompromising direction, much less comprehending that he's about to have his temperament adjusted. We refer to ever-evolving parameters of ordinary marriageability, by which we mean the correct sensibilities, for the right sort of social and domestic personality to be considered suitable even remotely for the compromised art of matrimony. Sometimes when a husband-hunting woman encounters an insecure man, she knows she's caught a manageable chap on her matrimonial hook. He's the sort of fellow who jealously holds his self-reliance in check, fearing to be excessively masculine. We don't quarrel with that. A less than secure gentleman needs to be assisted gradually into matrimony. He cannot appear to be even compromisingly self-confident. All the same, he must learn, within reason of course, to appear minimally secure.

Should the poor fellow presume to speak, he must be entirely aware of what women far and away prefer to hear, conveniently couched in language women prefer. This is anything but easy to surmise, since current virulent habits of speech, especially currently fashionable clichés, are more than apt to disengage the poor fellow's train of thought and discourse. He must also moderate the tone and pace of his rhetoric, although his chatter (if it reaches that agitated extreme) may tend to accelerate, suggesting that he's anything but confident of himself—always a good signal for any husband-hunting harridan. He must do what he can to solicit (we're hesitant about deploying this sensitive word) a woman's fickle sense of approval of his attempting (only that: attempting) to articulate it in such a way as to remain diffident and lubricious, all the while avoiding any telltale suggestion of having a mind of his own. Such are the fundamental requirements for any milquetoast's volunteering for marriage. If a man (we'll call him that out of courtesy) exhibits the slightest stitch of confidence, there's danger afloat on the marital sea. He must also refrain from smiling without prior approval, simply because he's permitted to find only certain circumstances amusing. He's got to bloody well mind his steps.

We can't begin to suggest that all but a minority of men are anything close to timid. They more likely may be self-conscious, but they're not what we presume to be deficient in confidence. Normal, average ordinary men are a considerable distance from ordinary timidity and are quite able to defend themselves in nearly any ridiculous eventuality. This does not exclude the ongoing threat of matrimonial catastrophe, especially when, having been amply forewarned, they've wandered naively into one of those dreadfully deceptive-appearing matrimonial ravines. Observe again that the operative word here is matrimony, a word echoing with mother and motherhood. The word isn't patrimony, having to do with men. No. Hence the whole idea and concept of matrimony is expressly feminine. The role of men in all this is rather an afterthought, just as weddings are entirely the property of women who cluster around a bride, adjusting her hair, fussing with her dress, pampering and pestering. Bridesmaids wear dresses that infer that they're the inconceivably lovely brides of tomorrow's weddings. The groom and his best man (whatever that is) have almost no part of this spectacle of fertility and random reproduction. Men are little more than a bother and a nuisance.

Grooms tag along for the trip, and it isn't going to be any hayride. Had they as boys begun to fanaticize about their weddings? Hardly. Had they stashed their bachelor closets with wedding day finery? Never. Do they pass many hours selecting a best man? We don't think so. If anything, they are dragged with some reservations (but not for a honeymoon) into something they understandably don't begin to comprehend at the time. If they have the misfortune to be vacuumed up into marriage, do they enlist a coterie of other men who assist them in dressing? How many people does it require to get dressed? Compromised though he is, he is quite able to dress himself most of the time. Will he, early in life, begin contemplating the world's all-time greatest wedding? Preposterous. Would he fritter away a small ransom of somebody else's money to pull this spectacle off? Don't be silly. Will he have his hair done? Will he recruit some flower boys? Let's hope not. Why on this one-of-kind grand march wedding day does the bride wear white and the groom black? The wedding parade is totally out of hand and out of control. Do men become wired-up about weddings, even their own? We're not certain. It's more probable that the nearer the occasion looms, the more the groom becomes predictably confused and wary, and for a good many sensible reasons. He's beginning to see things he hadn't seen—or thought of—before, and it's an ample cause for alarm. It's called cold feet, and small wonder. The groom could have called the whole matter off, but didn't. After all, there were all those bridesmaids' dresses, the catering, the flowers and the rest.

An endless number of people believe they have at least married the wrong person, as if to suggest that a right person is out there lurking in the weeds.

Bachelors have themselves to blame, especially because it was they who proposed this monstrosity and volunteered for it. It's going to cost them, financially and psychologically. Some men have been known to try to take an *active role* in all nearly all conceivable aspects of the wedding, but they're likely to discover that the wedding is *none of their business*, since it's completely conceived (if we may again deploy that word) advanced and designed (if at all) by women. The bride believes this to be the great climactic, cinematic moment of her otherwise mundane and unimaginably ho-hum existence. It might just was well be said that once the ceremony is over, *so is everything else.* It's all, as we say, *downhill* from there. A bachelor finds that it's far easier to rise in the world, if he can, when he's unattached and nimbly so. Having a wife makes it far more problematic, since he has to juggle his future on one hand with his spouse on the other, seeking her consent and endorsement before he can do much of anything. Had there been no wedding, this never need have happened. It isn't necessary for men to submit to the interference of a wife. Certain men, possibly destined for bachelorhood, may also have had the prescience to see a few miles and a few years ahead.

Chapter II. "There's nothing better than a single life." —Horace

There are other pressing gender differences, for example men's suggestive tendency to avoid eye-contact, whereas women not only rely upon it, but consider it an essential key to mutual comprehension. One might be inclined to see men's disinclination to search other people's eyes as a signal that they're deliberately discommunicating, and are therefore at communicative cross purposes. There are nitwits out there with whom we don't wish to speak; hence there are good and sufficient reasons not to communicate or to communicate as little as possible. It's fairly safe to surmise that men entertain suspicion about, and lack of confidence in, communicating with women, since discourse with them can all too easily run the risk of being misconstrued, misunderstood, and misinformed. There is, after all, an obvious lack of trust and confidence between the sexes, arising out of differences in perception and malinterpretation, especially difficulty with both verbal and nonverbal signals. Marriage counselors have steadfastly stressed the importance of lucid communication, but that may arguably be quite the contrary, since couples would be far better off if they don't say what they're thinking, or think what they're saying. It's all ultimately too impossibly opaque to untangle and sort out.

Topics of communication are apt to be gender-related, as well. It's a masculine tendency to emphasize his authority, his faultless judgment, his universal knowledge his broad comprehension, his unfailing ability to assume control of any situation that confronts him. Men are likely to avoid troublesome discourse, whereas women may deploy that same troublesome discourse to support their views. Women also tend to be more conscious of establishing (when possible) a sense of *shared interests* and standards, a sameness of objectives and points of view along with a breezy accord in prevailing attitudes and (best of all) an intimate *sense of feeling,* by which they mean an empathy to ideas spoken and unspoken, an intimacy of consciousness, openness to atmosphere, emotion, affection (if any) and whatever other subtleties of communication that may happen cross their ontological minds.

It has been posited (suggested, proposed, assumed, affirmed, and postulated) that men are more communicative in public, women in private. If true, one can presume that men do better discoursing with others who are less intimate and therefore more unremittingly open. Women identify more with close and fairly personal communication between one mind and another, far less between one mind and several minds. Men, it may also be posited, are immensely more macro (large) than micro (small), an abstraction that probably applies. It has also been suggested, interestingly enough, that men have a tendency to arrive at a decision and, having accomplished that much, consider it a fait accompli, a done deal, settled, accomplished, fulfilled, carried out, said and done. In still other words, it's assumed to be so, and therefore need no further discussion, although a good deal of discussion may follow, regardless. Men are often of the view that something is self-evident, altogether obvious, or, as Latins used to say, in Latin, *experto credite* ("trust me"), a fatuous suggestion made by people who don't know what the hell they're talking about. To the contrary, it is believed (if you will forgive the passive voice) that women present ideas in quite the opposite direction. They begin with *exploratory discourse* (let's call it) and from there work their way through a maze of mental gymnastics and circumlocutions, arriving gradually at a conclusion in the manner that a bumble bee executes several reconnaissance laps around a begonia before descending upon it. In other words, men are ineluctably *deductive,* meaning they draw a conclusion from evidence. Women, on the other side, are supposedly more inclined to address contentious exchanges by unraveling them, and resolving them piece by part, attempting thereby to settle matters through analysis, compromise, resolution, neutralization of acrimony and application of accord.

Statistics gathered from North America, Europe and Africa indicate that, that there about 100 women to about 120 men. The 2000 census gathered from about 281.4 million people counted in America reveals a different result, namely that 143.4 were women and 138.1 men, which works out to about 51 percent women and 49 percent men. Before we investigate the prevalence of bachelors, it is appropriate to consider some broader (pun intended) numbers. Women are apparently somewhat more sophisticated than men, and on average exercise a somewhat more refined sense of *humor.* Men, if what we're told be true, laugh at something before considering what's funny about it. Women accord that same object of alleged humor some evaluation before committing any laughter to it.

Speculation is that by the 2156 Olympics, women will out-run men in the 100 meter event, since the elapsed time between the sexes has been narrowing. Evidence indicates that 90 percent of women prudently wash their hands after using a public latrine, as compared with 75 percent of men who, since they were boys, have lived a bit more dangerously, as suggested by their being disciplined 80 percent of the time in high schools, compared to the 20 percent of girls. Census figures estimate that, between the ages of 25 and 34, 14 percent of men still live with their parents, as compared to eight percent of women who, by the way, devote two years of their lives narcissistically admiring themselves in mirrors, compared to six months for men, the difference being that women require more routine facial maintenance. They are also far chattier than men, uttering about 7,000 words a day versus men's 2,000. This suggests that the former are far more *voluble* than the latter, or because they demonstrate a more richly fertile vocabulary, or possibly they're inclined to be more empathetic and gush the English language effusively. Men seem not to listen as well as women, possibly because they *filter* what they hear and find most chatter unworthy of much attentiveness.

Research shows that whereas fat men seem to be happier than thinner ones, it's quite the opposite with women, although chances are that thinner people are in general more pleased with themselves. On the domestic front, women are more inclined to take charge of hearth and home. Men candidly report that their domestic relations are better when they cede this and other inconsequential matters to their wives.

More to the point, there are reportedly 86 single men for every 100 single women, which would suggest that men theoretically have more leverage in finding women, but not necessarily with the intention of marrying them. An estimated 40 percent of the adult single population relies upon dating services to provide what they cannot provide themselves, that being a generous inventory of other single candidates. Other estimates estimate that 44 percent of adult Americans are single, which is to say about 100 million folks. New York, with its 50 percent unmarried adults, makes it (from one perspective) the most advantageous environment for singles, including of course bachelors, to carry on their complicated affairs, nefarious and otherwise, exceeded only by the District of Corruption with its startling 70 percent unmarried population. According to other earnest sources, the best way to attract someone is to present a photo. If you are a woman, it is estimated that you have 15 minutes to impress a man. If you are a man attempting to impress a woman, it takes every bit an hour, illustrating once again that men leap to conclusions while women take their methodical time. The main bone of contention between the sexes is money. Men tend to earn it; women tend to spend it. Some 88 percent of women judge money to be important. Nothing more. Just important. A mere two percent of men meet women in bars; about nine percent of women find men there, which are of course, places of unbridled conviviality. It appears that about 63 percent of married couples met through mutual friends. Single women searching for single men report that the best hunting grounds are in Chattahoochee City, Georgia, Union County in Florida, and Jones County in Texas, Decal City, Missouri, and Crowley City, Colorado. Men hunting for women report that they fare better in Bristol and Franklin counties in Virginia, Pulaski and Randolph counties in Georgia, and Monroe City in West Virginia. Why? We don't know.

In other timely signs of the times, 25 percent claim that touching is as good a way to flirt as any. After a first date, current standards of engagement customarily allot a man one week to telephone. There is only a 17 percent probability that someone will approve of a date arranged by a friend. Some 52 percent of singles believe that they're too busy to encounter other singles. Women will date men at least five years older than they are 77 percent of the time, and 53 percent will take up with a smoker.

Presuming that these numbers are statistically valid, we begin to piece together people who wish to partner, and who forge ahead, undaunted by dreadful divorce statistics and other matrimonial catastrophes, intimating among other things that there is something terribly wrong with marriage as an institution, by which we mean an established social structure, even though about ten percent of all existing marriages have separated and reconciled. There are an estimated 59 million American marriages out there. By gender and race, white men amount to about 44 percent, white women 51 percent, black men 32 percent, and black women 43 percent, Hispanic men 43 percent, Hispanic women 45 percent. People who marry without a high school diploma or with a GED constitute 28 percent.

Those with *some college*, meaning that they devoted ten minutes of their lives to sprawling resentfully in the back row of a community college classroom, account for 21 percent of marriages, whereas those with a bachelor's degree comprise only 11 percent. The percentage of married women who claim that religion is important to them is slightly above 61 percent, as compared with their more secular husbands who weigh in at about 51 percent. Married women who regard religion as unimportant represent 36.3 percent, and married men who feel the same way are at 35.4. Married couples are now a minority and those couples amount to one household in every five. Of particular note is the rise of single households from 16.2 in 1970 to 27.5 today. *Bloomberg Businessweek* reports that men comprise most of those living alone.

Prospects for first marriage survival are discouraging, in that its chances of lasting ten years are only one in 15. If there were no children born by that time, the prospect of holding the union together reduces to about one in 27. If a child is born before the marriage, the marriage probability is back to one in 15. If a child is born within seven months after the marriage, its survival is one in 13. If that child is born eight or more months after the marriage, the chances are one in 12. There are even greater discouragements awaiting those who cohabit, assuming their intention is to marry. If they do so within a year, the chances are one in 47. Moreover, there is an alarmingly low rate of success for second and third marriages. Mark Banshick, M.D., writing for *Psychology Today* (February 6, 2012) raises an obvious question with an obvious answer, namely that those who do not learn from history are doomed to repeat it, which is why second marriages are of about the same duration as first marriages. His stats tell him, and us, that 50 percent of first marriages (as we've repeatedly noted) disintegrate, that 67 percent of second marriages fall apart and 73 percent of third marriages flush down a latrine. He interprets this as the tendency of recent divorcees to marry, as they say, *on the rebound*. These same people are less likely to exercise better judgment, having not allowed sufficient time to clear their minds or examine themselves and their marriage prospects disinterestedly. If they had, they'd know that their prospects were somewhere between fair and awful.

Dr. Banshick observes too that such people may view divorces as more manageable than they really are, having experienced them before, and are prepared to recognize their *warning signs*. He also identifies what he calls "the growing independence between the genders" that account for "one of the reasons for the significant increase of divorce in first marriages during recent decades" owing to, among other things, women's emerging financial independence, and men's determination to protect themselves in the face of social change. He also advances the idea that subsequent marriages are bonded by what he calls *less glue*, partly attributed to children who may or may not serve "as a stabilizing factor" and without whom subsequent marriages are all the weaker and less secure. Most of those children were born during first marriages when their "parents [were] up to about thirty-five years old," meaning that second marriages are less likely to have children between them, making it less difficult to part ways. Furthermore, having to adjust to their spouse's previous children can lead to additional marital malfunction. Dr. Banshick concludes by saying that "it gets harder and harder to keep the show on the road as you move onto the next marriage."

One of the numerous bachelarian delights is the avoidance of all such manifold miseries arising out of the near impossibility of making marriages last, in any sense of the word. This isn't quite what those three millions of girls and women had in mind when they shopped for wedding gowns, drew up lists of bridesmaids and floral orders and, oh yes, persuaded some gullible sucker to marry them and then (hand and foot) to wait on them for the next half century, all the while keeping his eyes and hands off of other women, fathering children, supporting them through their university years, retiring as soon as possible, dying discretely and finally floating serenely off to what Scott Fitzgerald called a *select Episcopal heaven.*

It's a mostly carefree way to trot through life, except that it may not shake out in quite the way couples had intended, given the government statistics we've just perused. Evidence indicates that the male population is apparently growing faster than the female. It's not what we'd call a pronounced demographic change, but all the same, between 1990 and 2000 the number of American men increased by an estimated 13.9 percent as compared with an also estimated 12.5 percent of American women. The number of men times 100, divided by the number of women reveals an increase from 95.1 to 96.3 in 2000. Statisticians account for this by citing the period between 1980 and 1990 when male death rates declined faster than female. In 2000, at age 85, there were nearly twice as many women than men.

The 2010 census, if it is to be taken seriously in light of corrupt government declarations of dubious accuracy and credibility, tells us that there were about 82.8 million mothers of all ages. The average number of children born to women aged 40 to 44 was 1.9, down from 3.1 in 1976, which obviously has something to do with birth control effectiveness. Women were earning 23 cents on the dollar less than men, although there were some 29.9 million women aged 25 and older who had earned bachelor's degrees, barely higher than the corresponding number of men (28.7). Women, the census advises us, have earned more high school diplomas, associates, bachelors and masters degrees, whereas men have prevailed in doctoral and other professional diplomas. In 2009, 30 percent of university degrees belonged to women, and 55 percent of college students in the fall of 2008 were women. As a rule, women college students post higher grades than men, partly because a disproportional number of them enroll in teachers colleges that have appreciably lower academic standards.

Women students are somewhat more inclined to perform as expected in their academic studies. *USA Today* (10/19/05) disclosed that, for the first time, the Minnesota Office of Higher Education said that in the previous academic year "women earned more than half the degrees granted statewide in every category." Impressive though it sounds, a group devoted to preparing low income kids for college also said that only 30 percent were boys, although the number subsequently rose to 34 percent, thanks to "a little affirmative action," whatever that may have been. Since that time, we are told that "more boys seem to be falling by the wayside," noting too that a certain Iowa post-secondary newsletter drew attention to the "dwindling presence of men in colleges" that it chose to interpret as a "sign of women's progress" in the wake of boys dropping out of high schools and colleges. One high school counselor noted that, on the sly, "girls are way more likely to pay attention" to academic advice. Meanwhile, authorities in Maine disclosed that there were "154 women for every 100 men at that state's colleges and universities in 2000," and that admissions officers were guardedly alarmed at the gender imbalance of their new acceptances, while others suggested that academic courses were geared more toward women.

Such circumstances play into the cultural fabric of America and relate to such things as marriage, self-determination, financial matters, politics and economics, not to mention that military and sports participation ultimately have some influence upon bachelorhood, a factor that alters lives and limitations. On the athletic front, 3.1 million girls participated in high school programs in the 2008–9 school year, during which 182,503 women participated in an NCAA sport. Figures tell us that 73 percent of women said they were registered to vote, and 66 percent of women citizens above the age of 18 did indeed vote in the 2008 presidential election, compared to 62 percent of their male counterparts. Aside from women who owned businesses, there were supposedly 59 percent of women 16 and older in the work force, or about 72 million women, according to the *American Community Survey*. There were 39 percent of women 16 and older who claimed to have some sort of managerial jobs and claimed also to have some professional occupation as compared to 33 percent of men. Government figures report that there were as many as 111,000 women police officers in 2009, roughly 9,700 fire fighters, not to mention 338.000 lawyers, and 294.000 physicians. There were also 38,000 airplane pilots, and about 197,900 women in active military duty in the fall of 2008 as reported in the *Statistical Abstract of the United States* in 2011, which constitutes about 14 percent of the armed forces, not to mention 1.5 million women military veterans.

By 2010 there were believed to be 65.1 million married women 18 and over, including those who, predictably, were by this time removed from their husbands, speaking of which, 20 percent of them were believed to be earning $5,000 above those husbands who were presumably also out there trying to earn a living, according to figures released from a source called Families and Living Arrangements. If they were not out there earning a living, about 154,000 of them were stay-at-home fathers.

Other figures, some of them discouraging, have come gradually to light, such as a document called "Men, Women and Murder: Gender-Specific difference in Rates of Fatal Violence and Victimization," authored by A.L. Kellerman and J.A. Mercy and published in *PubMed* in July of 1992. Their findings indicated that among 215,273 homicides, 77 percent involved male victims, and 23 percent female, concluding the obvious: that women were substantially at lower risk than men, while being substantially at higher risk for "being killed by a spouse or intimate acquaintance." Unlike men, however, women were far less at risk of being murdered by a stranger, whereas "more than twice as many women were shot and killed by their husband [*sic*] or intimate acquaintance than were murdered by strangers using guns, knives of any other means," whereas women made up "more than half of the U.S. population, they committed only [!] 14.7 of the homicides included in this study." Men killed non-intimate acquaintances, strangers or victims, some of them of undetermined relationship in 80 percent of cases. Women killed their spouses, intimate acquaintances and even family in 60 percent.

One may infer from such numbers that, predictably, women were more discriminating in whom they selected to murder, while protecting themselves from being murdered. Men, by contrast, appear to be less choosey, which results in more dead men than dead women. The same observation applies to male and female driving statistics published by the *Institute for Highway Safety*. Violation numbers tell us that the ratio of male to female citations for reckless operation are 3.41 to 1, driving under the influence 3.09 to 1, seatbelt violations 3.8 to one, speeding 1.75 to 1, failure to yield 1.54 to 1, stop sign violations 1.53 to 1. The ratios (as expressed by age) for fatal automobile accidents per 100 million miles traveled works out to 9.2 (men) and 5.3 (women) ages 16 to 19, 4 to 2 for ages 20–29, 1.8 to 1.3 for ages 30-59 and 4.1 to 4 for ages 70 and above. The composite average is about 2.5 for fatal accidents attributed to men, versus 1.7 attributed to women, who are evidently more careful, more attentive, less compulsive and perhaps a bit more passive.

Now that we've been apprised of ontologically-inclined women, airplane pilots, cops, surgeons, car drivers, discriminating murderers and so forth, it is more than appropriate at this juncture to investigate generally held views among women, regarding what constitutes femininity and feminine behavior. Bachelors then and now find such subjects endlessly absorbing and informative, to the end that they apply such information toward attracting women by attempting (no more than that) to comprehend them and (to be quite frank) deploying these scraps and shavings of speculative information to the high purpose of seduction, but with little to no avail. They merely want to seduce but not necessarily abandon. A comprehensive understanding of women, while patently impossible, is a necessary tool to have up one's sleeve, were it possible. The more learning, the better, especially when it is directed at parsing women's feelings and other sensitive points of incursion aimed at seizing their minds and, more significantly, their bodies. Platonic love be hanged, the objective here is to uncover heretofore unnoticed pathways to their famously elusive vulnerabilities. Such things can be apprehended, learned, committed to memory and applied. This is anything but a simple matter, inasmuch as women themselves seem not to comprehend other women any more than they understand themselves. In the end, there are enormously more questions than answers.

What, then, do women think? Opinion ranges all over the road. Says one, "I see a lot of statements claiming that feminism has taught women not to be feminine or that women have forgotten how to be feminine." Says another, "They [women] are not lacking it, but some people do not like it that 'feminine' behavior is not displayed 100% of the time." Says still another, "Femininity principally refers to secondary sex characteristics and these behaviors [are] better suited to women, [such as] gentleness, patience, vanity [and] kindness...feminine women 'like' men [and] do not have issues with being female; embrace their sexuality; feel the desire to care for [their]mate[s]... put love above money. Feminist women are too often discussed [?] by men in general; dislike the gender they were born in..." Another comments that femininity is "what is attractive to men...the paradox is that women [are] the people who have the biggest problems with femininity."

There is an unsigned treatise out there called "The Art of Being a Feminine Woman," that purveys earnest advice to women wishing to be as feminine as may be feasible. It begins with the fundamental observation that, even at a time when it's fashionable to assume characteristics of the opposite sex, women remain "softer and more emotional than men," an observation with which most people would not quarrel. It also argues that the urge to "liberate" women allegedly began with the observation "that some men were domineering and cruel," but nonetheless are better suited "for stronger, brawnier [sic] tasks," among them protecting women. At least they're good for something. The term female refers basically to the gender that bears offspring. Feminine obviously denotes characteristics proper to women and girls, hence feminine comes to mean woman-like, womanly, and characteristically proper to the female gender. In some contexts it suggests weakness, as in the weaker sex, which in some respects is appropriate, in other respects not. Today it's applied facetiously, but all the same has its history. The Weaker Sex surfaced as a 1948 British film depicting life on the home front in World War II when women were pressed into service performing work traditionally assigned to men in factories that produced materiel crucial for winning wars. The film was therefore ironic, since it was in large part women assigned to assemble aircraft and tanks. Rosie the Riveter was not the most feminine of spectacles, but lent credence to women's being the more deadly of the species, as expressed in some lines composed by Rudyard Kipling that proclaimed "the female of the species is more deadly than the male," a remark that calls out for interpretation. There was an op-ed piece by Marianne J. Legato (evidently but not specifically identified as an ob/gyn) in *The New York Times* on June 17, 2006, also called "The Weaker Sex," that raises the matter of gender-specific medicine. Some of Dr. Legato's women patients had been known to ask, "Do you take care of men too?"

She responds, "I—along with many of my colleagues—have tried to atone for the fact that for so long the majority of diseases that affected both genders were studied exclusively in men" whereas at present "we doctors and researchers may have focused too much on women" while men are "the weaker gender." For example, "while there are more male embryos than female, there are also more male miscarriages. such that industrial nations are reporting a lessening of males-to-females for reasons never quite understood, except perhaps the chances of a male embryo decline as parents (especially the father's) age, Once the babies are born they face up to four times more possibility of disorders such as autism and dyslexia." She also points out that "teenaged boys have a greater probability of suicide. Girls on average learn language sooner and mature sooner and live longer "since some men die sooner from causes like coronary artery disease twice as often as women, who seem to have stronger immune systems. Of the ten most common infections, men are more likely to face seven. Women appear to have twice the probability of depression as men," possibly, as Dr. Legato suspects, "because women are more likely to seek treatment." She concludes, "considering the relative fragility of men, it's clearly counter intuitive for us to urge them, from boyhood on, to cope bravely with adversity, to ignore discomfort, to persevere in spite of pain and to accept without question the most dangerous jobs and tasks we have to offer."

"Crisis Management," a publication of the Catholic Church, ran an article called "Men Are the Weaker Sex" in its July 17, 2012, number. It cites a government publication (therefore not necessarily to be trusted) claiming that 53 percent of high school students abstain from sex, the point being that there is a prevailing *weakness* in men that allows them to accede to every sexual opportunity. This properly identifies them as *weak willed* since they have no intention of abstaining from much of anything and are, we regret to say, poor candidates for the bachelors of tomorrow when they may make it a habit and a policy rarely to resist the temptation of a woman who is, or may be, as we've said, the more dangerous of the genders. We are reminded of the Biblical Judith who, with her sexual wiles, so entranced the leader of an army that one fine day she unhesitatingly killed him.

Speaking of things Biblical, we recall too the example of David, who, because of his sexual adventuring and his having overlooked his relations with God so flagrantly and so long, was (so to speak) *put to sleep* at the behest of his dear wife. The point, obviously enough, is that men are woefully deficient on principles and proper moral perspectives. Women, on the other hand, tend to be virtuous by nature. We are all put in mind of Aristophanes, the Athenian comedian (c. 448–c. 380 B.C.) whose *Lysistrata* depicts women who possess the good and proper sense to embark on a sex strike to end a war. The chorus in that play consists of old women armed with buckets of water they deploy to dampen the conflict, after which a peace conference ensues, a banquet takes place and each woman is reunited with her bellicose husband. It all shakes down to the conflict between smart women and dumb men. Crisis Management counsels us to exercise prudent control over battles and unbridled lust, reminding us that men, to put it as chastely as possible, , if they possibly can, must shoulder the responsibility for promoting chastity, something that we don't see happening in the near future.

As one unidentified rake has wryly written, "Attention passengers! We are now leaving Nun Central and are beginning our journey to Hell and beyond. The captain has turned off the 'no smoking' sign and you may now move about the cabin freely." The recommendation from the folks at "Crisis Management" is to turn off the no smoking sign because it's for the good of us all. It promotes dignity and prudent control of every kind. Some men who are considered marriageable may discover that they never slept alone until they embarked on their honeymoons. To be quite candid about it, it's no circumstance for any bachelor to find himself in, because it's entirely too Platonic and too spiritual, and it's no place for the kind of chap who enjoys forbidden delights for every bit as long as it's feasible and conceivable.

Let no bacheloristic opportunity go uninvestigated for its promises and possibilities. *Carpe diem!* It's an expression believed to have originated with Horace, the Latin poet and aphorist in about 23 B.C. It means something like *pluck the day.* Time is short. There may not be many more days to seize. There may or may not be rewards and consequences that await following death, or whether, having made the most of life, one can look forward to more golden days and happy occasions, or whether it's best to celebrate life in the present because it may be the only one to be celebrated.

Notwithstanding, there are those who pine their time away wishing to marry some as yet unspecified person who will rescue them from the wells of loneliness that reportedly beset unmarried people. In 2010 CNN, if it's to be taken seriously, reported that it knows there to be some 96 million *lonely hearts* (we'll call them for the moment) who are not married, or to say the same thing another way, those 96 million who represent (also reportedly) 43 percent, all of whom have 1) never been married or 2) are divorced, otherwise unmated. There are 31 million (21 percent of all households) who say that they're living alone, as compared with 17 percent ten years before. The numbers become somewhat confusing, even contradictory. The census concludes that 46 percent of households belong to single persons, or to say it another way, about 52 million are among the lovelorn (we're mostly joking) population.

Statistics are merely statistics, nothing more. One anonymous person writes resignedly, "after a certain point in life most people decide that they no longer are going to put up with anyone's crap," in which case divorce or other estrangement becomes another kind of *blessed event*, setting another (possibly married) person free as if being released from a penitentiary. Another anonymous person says "it does take two unselfish people to make a happy marriage, and unfortunately there are not just that many...in the world," ergo, there are concessions, not all of them feasible that apply to people who think they want to marry and take their chances. We're told that marriage promotes happy, stable, morally upright and mentally healthy lives, but it isn't true. Another person writes, "More and more people are deciding that they don't want to be miserable for the rest of their lives," so they bail out of marriage. Another replies, "everyone needs to realize it [certain matrimonial realities] before marriage. It's unfortunate [that] they don't." Then another person chimes in, saying "marriage is supposed to be an equal partnership between two individuals that love each other. Rarely does it work that way," adding that "almost always one gives more or tries harder then [sic] the other. I've been married twice. Both failed miserably. I was just as much to blame as my exes. I would never marry again. I don't think marriage is for most people. That is why the statistics for divorce are something like 50%."

Then there are financial considerations, among them that the federal laws supposedly give preferential treatment to married couples. On January 14, 2013 *The Atlantic* carried a Lisa Arnold—Christina Campbell article called "The High Price of Being Single in America" that in a prefatory statement makes the case that "Over a lifetime, unmarried women can pay as much as a million dollars more than their married counterparts for health care, taxes and more, and later that far more single people, who happen to represent half the population, are made to suffer from what they call "institutionalized singlism" whereby they are "penalized for not marrying." They cite a 2010 case where a single woman earning $40,000 paid $6,181, while a married woman with the same income paid $5,162, about $1,000 less. In a projected 40 year span, the same single woman, still earning $40,000 annually, pays

$645,000, versus the same married woman who shells out $80,000,. The problem spills into such wonderful things as Social Security and IRAs where married people can accommodate themselves and their spouses, but a single person cannot. The same applies to health insurance for the same women. Over 60 years the single pays $189,000 while the married pays $331,200, a $48,000 difference. The long and the short of it is that singles pay hugely more for health care, due, the authors tells us, to the "discriminatory policies of companies and the U.S. government." Imbalances in housing costs come partly, they say, "because of the logistical costs of living alone, are such that "our single woman would pay more to rent a mountaintop mansion in Hawaii than our married woman would pay (as part of a dual-income married couple), but other factors also come into play." None the less, the proportion of singles continues to rise.

In a related matter, Marissa Weiss, in a September 16 issue of *The Experts* with evident alarm reports that "for the first time, most people over 16 in the U.S. are single: eating alone, sleeping alone, watching TV alone and supporting themselves alone," citing a study that claims "being single is as dangerous as smoking or obesity," the corollary of which is that "sharing your life makes you live longer and better," an observation that does not square with marriage statistics. Nonetheless, Dr. Weiss claims also that marriage "has a greater survival benefit than chemotherapy relative to the five most common cancers in women and men, although the benefit is bigger for men." She also advises singles to be aggressively social by "exercising in a class (not on the treadmill in your basement), going out to dinner with friends, walking with friends, joining a club centered on an activity you enjoy (bridge, tennis, cooking, books)...and of course "putting yourself out there' with new methods of dating." One reader commented, "As the majority of men who have ever been married in today's society will advise...Don't do it. You will be sorry."

Meanwhile, *The Daily Real Estate News* reported on September 11, 2014 that "one out of every five homes" had been "purchased by a single woman," that "about 124.6 million Americans" above the age of 16 reported they were single, and that the percentage of them had been trending up in the previous 12 months. The Bureau of Labor Statistics estimated that they constituted 37.4 percent of the population. Indeed, the penalties for being single may be worth the money, considering the other kinds of penalties that await the married. Any devoted bachelor will find it, as they say, cheap at the price. Better to live a better life at a higher cost; and besides, it's cheaper than dealing with the 50 percent probability of costing far more dollars and grief. Be all that as it may, bachelors (if need be) have ways to lessen the outrageous costs of living mostly by oneself. Yes; it's egocentric, but that's one of the delicious rewards of bachelordom, inasmuch as bachelors tend to be more than a little bit narcissistically self-centered and self-absorbed. Why not? Criticize if you will, but many a married lifer (by which we mean a man sentenced to be wedded all of his adult days) would pay through the nose to have enjoyed any of those batcheloresque privileges and perks, most of which come down to having his own way and not having to negotiate his treacherous trail through life with a nagging wife over which films to view, how and when to clean house, what to opt for dinner, how and for what purpose to spend money and so miserably forth.

It is also, shall we say, a character-building form of living, since one assumes full responsibility for his every act and decision. Having someone else on the premises means, among several other things, passing one's days and nights in perpetual negotiation. It is, as we just said, character enhancing, assuming that one has any character left to build. It's altogether possible that a bachelor's character was more than adequately built quite some time ago, and requires no further scrutiny and emendation. What we mean by character in this context is one's distinguishing parts, his fundamental nature, his essence, his characteristic traits, his particularly, not to say invincibly, strong qualities. The best of bachelors have enviably distinguished features, particularly as they relate to their station in life, their rank, their authority and so bloody forth. Best of all, bachelorizing lends itself to heightened existential self-knowledge. By existential we don't mean whether someone exists or not; we mean instead the discovery of one's role in life, the essence of his being. There are people out there, not bloody many, who are intelligent enough to investigate their own existence, their role and objectives for living, and to what purpose.

Bachelors are by natural inclination and by temperament fundamentally loners who, from time to time, may admit certain women into their tents and sensibilities. All the same, loners rather like their own company, and rely upon themselves for guidance and counsel on a variety of crucial fronts, prominent among them the handling their monetary affairs with a mind to being financially well situated through managing wealth, investing, economizing here and there, even under the financial penalties of the single, bacheloristic way of life. A bachelor would not be one to share the costs of a mortgage with a woman, partly because to do so would thereafter undermine the essence of his privacy and financial security. Even so, he has to manages the costs of his utilities, taxes, mortgages, rents, groceries, insurances and of course, his nights on the town. Through it all, he manages, as they say, to live better for less by eliminating the unnecessary, such as cell phones, which is why everyone else proudly brandishes and totes them everywhere. Meanwhile, he may also opt for high deductible insurance policies. He selects his clothing with attention to its quality, and wears it for years, maybe decades. He keeps his thermostats advantageously calibrated; he has no carry forward credit card charges and so like. It's about living within one's means, preparing for one's future in a state of free and unencumbered liberty without wives, in-laws, dogs, tree frogs and children, but always with the ability to carry him to any of life's plethora of destinations, real and metaphoric. It's a life methodically prepared and executed in ways that have not the slightest interest in sociological currents that steer conventional people in conventional directions for conventional purposes. Bachelors don't set about organizing bachelor clubs so to huddle with others of presumed like-mindedness, although such things exist, and have always existed.

Hence, one finds bachelors soliciting only professional advice. Other than that, they may be soliciting, but not counsel. Nonetheless one UK source calling itself "Eternal Bachelor" counsels those who don't wish to be counseled, advising them, (obviously) to refrain from marrying, cohabiting, (not so obviously), begetting children, maintaining joint bank accounts, publishing addresses, taking up with single mothers, buying service men drinks, standing by while feminism implodes, minding no one's business except one's own, playing the system, being anything other than self-employed, enriching anyone but one's self. There is also a load of advice out there, aimed at women, advising them never to take up with bachelors, by which we mean *real bachelors*, not ordinary unmarried blokes. Another anonymous source offers some choice pieces of counsel to other women who may be seeking the company of bachelors, and how they might begin that perilous journey, if that it be. By way of preface, they're encouraged to *give it a try*, since it can be both fun and exciting, but all the same frustrating, simply because bachelors "are used to living life at their own pace," something that doesn't bode particularly well, since there are those who think it would be far better if they lived their lives at someone else's pace. Another problem facing bachelor-seeking women is that bachelors "can be a little like children who refuse to see things through anyone else's eyes," which correctly assumes that a bachelor maintains his own *modus operandi*, his own ways of proceeding, always a dangerous characteristic, and one that ought properly to be subjected to scrutiny and gradual correction. Granted. Any further advice?

Yes. Don't rush into a *relationship* (one of our cherished words) because it may well cause a bachelor to vanish for reasons not immediately apparent. But remember: time can change all such behavior, especially with bachelors who, as we all know, have "not had to answer to anyone in their entire lives," a daunting thought if ever there was one. What not to do is ask precisely what his intentions are, even though we may have our suspicions.

What then? Begin immediately to offer advice. That's a damned fine idea, but we'd have to know to what the advice pertained, although again, we have our suspicions. Other advice? Don't be the slightest bit surprised if he doesn't "do something you might expect a guy to do," such as slurp beer and gaze at television screens. Be mindful that (chances are) "he's been eating canned food," with the serious implications that may come of it, such as his questionable ability "to act like and adult," even if he isn't one. Whatever happens, "always treat him with respect." We could hardly agree more. Be mindful too that the man of your dreams will emerge "from inside himself," if indeed it's there, which is probably isn't.

Whatever else you do, or fail to do, "Don't scare off your new beau by constantly bringing up marriage," which is to say urging it every so often, not every hour and a half. Now what to do? Simple. "Enjoy the person you're with, and accept them [sic] for what they [sic] are willing to give you, such as a lifetime of captivity. Next? "Don't chase the fellow off by questioning [him] about his commitment [that word again] to you and the relationship." We could hardly endorse this advice more, since we are *into relationships*, and celebrate them above anything else that we can fathom. The advice concludes with an endlessly helpful list of tips and warnings that may be useful when attempting to capture and (later) house-break bachelors, one of which it to request that the bachelor "talk to his male friends about relationships," which is a damned fine idea. Men are, generally speaking, authorities on relationships, a touchy subject about which they are more they prepared to dispense advice, as they say, at the drop of a hat, but all the same, "be mindful that they are still a different person [sic] than the one you are dating." Noted. Remember too that "if the bachelor you are dating is significantly younger than you," certain other precautions may well need to be *put in place*, primarily insurmountable problem of his being "significantly less interested in settling down," or in plainer English, being encouraged to bark and stand on his hind legs. The matter of settling down may in turn introduce other issues, as nitwits refer to them, especially (let's be frank about this) "there are some men who are ready to make a commitment at a young age [16 perhaps?] but for the most part they want to do some roaming [roaming?] before getting married, or even making that commitment [that word again] to a long term relationship."

Again we say that we could hardly concur more. These things aren't accomplished overnight. Prospective husbands, even the best of them, need desperately to roam around a bit, seeing disparate parts of the world, getting to know people of different hues and ethnic origins, maybe joining the Marines, managing a lingerie salon or taking up residence in a brothel. These are all maturation *issues* that demand time and maturity before a fellow begins to *find himself*, promote a sense of his unique *selfhood*, and learn a few lessons about life before he's at all prepared to *settle down*, quit worrying and allow himself to be guided by the whims of mercurial women, then surrender his identity, respond cheerfully to commands and learn not to resist routine castrations. The softest way to course through life is to agree with everyone, all the time. It leads a fellow into what, in all probability, he hasn't got. To get along, nitwits tell us, one must goddamned well *go along*. It's maturity of the sort that allows him, with ease and aplomb, to develop a certain chronic submissiveness of the right sort, and enables him to lapse, with unparalleled self-confidence, and without the slightest signal of resistance, directly into a *relationship* that will straightaway introduce him into the dangerous joys of modern matrimony.

Assuming that bachelors are all but helpless, which they are emphatically not, there is an eternal river of advice on a variety of bacheloric fronts from a variety of supposed authorities, some of them to be taken serious, most not. A site called simply *about.com* has introduced such timely avenues of counsel as "how to cook food" (rather than burn it) and another valuable piece entitled, "if it sprays, it can probably kill," another is called "anything can be grilled," "the code of men," whatever that might suggest, "laundry the manly way," "spotting a bad date' (one of the more helpful sites), "how to tell if she's interested" (if so, for what, when and for how long), "stay single and stay manly (which should pose no problem, and Housekeeping? Hire a Merry Maid; "it's worth the money." We do know that marriage isn't worth the money. *Psychology Today* (April 17, 2013) published a piece by Hara Estroff Morano called "Advice: A 46 Year old Bachelor" that relates a sobering anecdote about his five year misadventure with "a divorced mother of two" that proceeded remarkably well until he "began to feel as if all she cared about was financial security and would love whomever provided it." His male intuition came to the rescue. "We ended things," he reports, on a note of regret and continuing doubt, adding that "It's too late to save this relationship, but not the next one," which he seems to think will be more satisfactory than the last. Bachelors often move through a perpetual parade of women, followed by another parade of essentially the same thing.

On the womanly side, a site called "Amber's Cucina" advances a curious bit of council that begins with "I'm about to give all of you single, unattached men out there a very important bit of advice, so pay attention. If you really want to wow a woman, learn to cook," which contends that the straightest route to her heart (let's call it) is through her digestive tract, by way of his culinary prowess that prepares him to "cook pasta and maybe grill something," things that nearly any damned fool can accomplish without being lectured. But to continue: her advice is intended, apparently to render an otherwise unattractive man suddenly and stunningly handsome, at least, and exhibit some potential for taking enough care of himself to the satisfaction of any women who "don't want to adopt an overgrown child," so inept that he cannot so much as wield a mop or attend to his own laundry. She makes a damned good point, if you ask us, but of course there's more to it. He's being invited to propose marriage to a woman who, at least, has the enormous satisfaction in knowing that this fool can cook, maybe clean. Suppose that the same woman, is currently in a hospital "following the birth of baby #3" where at least she has the satisfaction of knowing that the cook she married can, besides boil water, change diapers, and swab floors, minimally certifying himself as an "attractive mate" but who may be little more than a shell of a man. For some women, it's all they can get, but at least it's a little better than nothing.

It's an uninspiring, if calculating, way to corral a husband who, chances are, will be assigned to wait patiently in the shadows for his next directive. In theory, it's one way to corral a bachelor, but not much of one. She concludes by averring that if a man (any man) can learn (stupid though he may be) "the necessary skills" he will become what she always wanted: a (presumably) "attractive mate" who will quickly (time being of the essence) believe that she's his Mrs. Right, presuming too that Mrs. Rights exist, right here in her cucina where her submissive husband has become a kind of bachelor-cum-victim, hardly a surprise. He will next find himself belittled, emasculated and dominated—as was clear from the beginning.

Gender brutality is much in the news these days, and much of what is understood about it can be advantageously discovered in the pages of an scholarly article called "Gender, Victimization and Outcomes: Reconceptualizing Risk" by Sheyl Pimlott Kubiak and Lila M. Cortina in the *Journal of Consulting and Clinical Psychology* in 2003. This is what it appears to be: an exhaustive (to write and to read) inquiry of what it promises, specifically the outcomes of gender victimization that "75% of American adults have experienced at least one act of interpersonal aggression and some point during their lifetimes," viewed as "apparent gender differences in those outcomes" some of which involved domestic violence. An unsigned article called "Men: The Overlooked Victims of Domestic Violence," appeared in a journal appropriately called *Domestic Violence Statistics* on May 16, 2012 and reported that one in four women (1.3 million) will at some time become a victim of domestic violence, but that 40 percent of those victims will be *men*. It also asserts that "almost equal" incidents are aimed at those same men, even though men are assumed to be physically stronger and "should be able to subdue a female attacker easily," it is often regrettably true that men's allegations of having been accosted by a woman are "off times received by disbelief and ridicule by law enforcement people and the general public." Reports indicate, furthermore, that men are 63 percent more likely to be assaulted by a deadly weapon, compared to 15 percent of women, on whom public money is frittered away on related research. There is also the perception that man can far more easily exit a violent situation, even when women become violent when under attack.

Another unidentified man reports that whereas he has never been violent toward women, he has regularly been accosted and has been quite able to defend himself physically, but has never done so, and to the contrary has had "a lot of trouble getting people to believe" him. "Perception is everything," he continues, "She acts the victim, says I have abused her and the children. I never have or will not do such a thing." Another man reports that he is "serving a two year probation for a simple assault" whereas he "was hit, scratched and more" by his former wife. After three years of separation, he continues, "she stopped at my home. I couldn't get her to leave." After ushering her out, he lost his firearms rights, his job, his credit and 90 percent of his belongings, then suffered the embarrassment of fines and jail time. "I have no history of violence," he says, although "I do have a new life." Still another man writes, "I am a victim of DV that was perpetrated by my spouse. I am a male and could quite easily cause major harm to her in any way. Now, 10 years later I finally broke away. I was beaten by a 2x4, stabbed, [had] hot foods poured on me, raped (yes, it happened...the 2x4 played a major role in that). Had I touched her at all I would have been arrested...." On it goes, being, as it is, generally within the context of married life, if such it can be called. When people call matrimony *unnatural*, they mean that it is, to put it one way, inconsistent with civilized interpersonal relations to keep a man and a woman bottled up for 50 years. It is hardly cause for celebration, when in fact not much good came of it. Bachelors and a few others are fully aware of this circumstance and stay well clear.

One often hears of something called the marriage penalty as it relates to the crooked IRS, but there are several other marriage penalties that are far worse. Notwithstanding, there is, believe it or not, a Journal of Gender lurking out there in the weeds where it is more than capable of enumerating the manifold joys of married life. It also invites our attention to phony marriages, as if we hadn't seen and heard enough of them. According to the J of G, we have a phony marriage when, well, there is just something that isn't quite right about it, but nothing that would cause us to look up from our Danish. We also learn, however, that, time was, when, under common law, folks of the (then) opposite gender might well consider themselves married, which is to say without the *de rigueur* squealing women in bridesmaids dresses. In the meantime, if any of us suspect that certain man-woman alliances are not officially married, we are under obligation to report same to the U.S. Citizenship and Immigration Services for prompt official action of some official sort or another. We are partial to the word official because, *je ne se quoi*, it carries a certain impression of finality and certainty about it. That's why we march around proclaiming, it's official, day in and out. Should any of us suspect that certain men and women are not married to each other, we should, and must, report same to the crooked *Department of Homeland Security* for further investigation, namely, after several months of bureaucratic committee-meeting indecision, they arrest offending parties and compel them to marry in the presence of the DHS in lieu of paying a $250 fine for pretending to be married when they really weren't. It gets worse. If you are not really married, but think you are, the DHS can bloody well see to it that you're "punished by up to five years in a federal prison" which, when you consider the options, might well be better than being actually married and risk the distinct chance of being soundly clubbed with a 2x4.

This leads us into a closer glimpse at other desperate acts, such as endless marriages. Yes. We were all disheartened to learn that a certain amply publicized couple was calling it *quits* after a 38 year wedlock (with the emphasis on *lock*) grace period. Many of us, if the truth be told, had a *good cry* over it, then resolved to gather ourselves up and carry on, regardless. Then we heard distant rumblings about Arnie Schwarzenegger's split with Maria Shriver. But take heart. The AARP, one of America's purveyors of the *unvarnished truth*, has looked long and hard at the intimate lives of folks 45 and older, and concluded, as one spouse put it, "that extramarital affairs happen for only a relatively small number of couples, and that marriages fall apart for other, unspecified reasons," such as the couple's being totally bored and sick of each other, which is what we'd all suspect. The AARP says that marriages don't so much explode as *deflate*. Imagine such a thing.

By this time, husbands wish to hell that they had never married and were bachelors once more. *Bachelor*, recall, primarily denotes a marriageable man who may or may not have been married. In other words, the definition has been broadened (that word again) to include the whole universe of unmarried men. By whichever sense of the word, a bachelor is among the more fortunate of adult men. Married men regard them as *lucky*, but luck has little or nothing to do with being independently independent. Only an independent mind can envision and enable the obvious: that operating singly, without the needless interference, and burden of a tag-along wife is a sensible way to proceed (without baggage) through life. There is some perception that, to the contrary, bachelors are as a rule a decidedly unhappy lot, longing for the miseries of marriage to (as it were) cheer them up. Charles A Waehler, a psychologist at the University of Akron (Ohio) researched the question by querying 30 white, never married, heterosexual men over 40, and concluded that they were, if anything, more than happy; they were real happy. Why? They were satisfied and successful. Waehler concedes that the sample isn't large enough to confirm that certain of his hunches and guesses are confirmed. Nonetheless it more than likely supports the impression among some unattached women that it isn't that 40 year old bachelors don't have the opportunity to marry; they don't care to. "Once a person reaches 40, there is only a 12 percent they [*sic*] will marry," says Waehler. At age 45, it's one in 20." His findings also undermine the impression that bachelors are dissatisfied, unhealthy and sexually deviant. Stuart Roan of the *LA Times* (September 25, 1991) reacted to Waehler's conclusions, commenting in a terminally warped sentence that "bachelors have long been viewed as women-haters, attached to a parent, unhealthy, disabled, fixated on lost love, workaholics and playboys." To the contrary, Waehler represents them as accomplished loners, not especially misogynistic nor necessarily anti-marriage—especially as it pertains to others, not themselves.

It has been amusingly advanced that "every man should get married sometime; after all, happiness is not the only thing in life," which is a warning that every man should deliberately expose himself to *extra strength misery*, as part of what it *means to be a man*. There is plenty of misery out there; no need to seek more. Oscar Wilde said (and he was neither the first nor the last), that "bachelors should be heavily taxed. It is not fair that some men should be happier than others." His comment is not entirely a joke. Pliny (the elder) suggested in his letter XCV that a penalty ought to be assessed upon bachelors and married men without children. Even today, the corrupt IRS provides tax advantages to men who support children. Men who marry without reproducing have been criticized as married bachelors for failing to send more innocent children into this fallen world, electing instead to devote time and energy to hedonistic marriages headed by hedonistic husbands. Bachelors can better accomplish the same thing without the burden of a wife.

Miriam Adahan, writing for chabad.org (May 24, 2009), commented upon the profound immaturity of bachelorhood, reminding us that rabbis have a long disapproved of it, but with little influence. She believes that married men have been somehow or another lured into the joys of singlehood, and are bloody well *making the best of it*. She goes on to say to say that such men are likely to be deficient in other respects, which motivated her to form a group called EMETT: "Emotional Maturity Established Through Torah," the assumption being that it is more than right and proper for a decent man to marry, become a good husband and all-around darned good American family man. Hence this married bachelor (she does not use the word) is given to such disreputable habits as taking loans with no notion of how to repay them, desiring to be the centerpiece of his wife's world, wanting his wife to be his mother, wanting a separate life without her knowing where he is or with whom he is or what he does with their money—all the while avoiding stress by engaging in such addictions as drugs, alcohol and the internet, showing his impatience at having to wait for his wife to primp; generally behaving like a bachelor, except that this bachelor isn't a bachelor—he only appears to be, having been weak enough to marry.

It occurs to this sap's wife that she's married a child. She begins to despair, in the knowledge that instead of marrying a husband, she's married an adversary. She begins to nag, if she hadn't long before. He spends even less time with her. In the meantime, as Ms. Adahan explains, she begins to riffle through his pockets, snoops his cell phone, finds out whether he's been driven to drink, been covertly visiting lewd internet sites or picking up any socially inappropriate diseases. She now begins to feel alone (a circumstance that bachelors, among other, treasure), fearing that she will be held accountable for this mess by having married this character. Remember: if a woman fails to marry, she is not yet (covertly) certified as a woman. She is partly accountable for this marital mess, but keeps it under her hat for fear of owning up to her botched role as wife. The problems exacerbate. He may not show up for work. She lies awake all night waiting for him to return, and nags him all the more.

Such are the joys of matrimony. He reacts by staying away all the more. What to do? She drags (appropriate word) him to a woman marriage counselor/therapist who attempts to make him abandon all of his deplorable habits "on a consistent and predictable basis." He now realizes that instead of having one harpy on his back, he has two. The therapist advises the wife to prop up what's left of her husband, and be pleasant to him. This is not about to happen. Eventually the therapist tells the wife that it is her sorry fate to have taken up with this most preposterous of men: a phony bachelor who will never so much as *cross the threshold* into adulthood. Sorry, old girl; you've married an emotional invalid. Make the best of it. Do what? *Make the best of it.* That's all that can be done. Make the best of it, knowing things will never (repeat: *never*) improve, unless maybe he will die an inauspicious death. That may work, but it hasn't yet happened. Good luck. The balance of Ms. Adahans's article addresses precisely how any decent woman comes to terms, or attempts to, with those scoundrels we know as *bachelors*. First, women have to acknowledge that they cannot possibly cause a man to *grow up*, implying that bachelors are as immature as children, and may be expected to remain that way because there's not a bloody thing to be done about it.

As we have been more than intimating, there is considerable antibachelor jealousy out there, much of it fueled by miserably married men, and unmarried or unsatisfactorily married women. So what's wrong with men? Evan Marc Katz who writes for "Understand Men, Find Love," asks whether there is something not quite right about a man in his 40s who has never been married." One woman respondent says, yes indeed, there's a whole lot wrong with him. "He's a player. He's a Peter Pan. He's a commitment phobe. He's too picky. He's emotionally unavailable, He's a heartbreaker. He's unrealistic." He's guilty on all charges, we'd say, and add that the poor bloke has a mind and will of his own that ought, in the name of modern maturity, to be discouraged, even deleted. He's a pretty fair bachelor, not to be readily harpooned. By *player*, we apparently mean one who (in the pejorative sense) plays rather than acts as a man should, in the opinions of some, must stop playing and start acting he way unmarried women believe he should. He may also be a peter pan, i.e., a character straight out of James Barre's play, who, *luftmensch* that he is, never grows up and exists in a fantasy world of his own creation. He doesn't come to terms with life as other people construe it. Chances are that he's uncomfortably aware of life's realities, but does not wish confront them. Being a commitment-phobe implies that, because he doesn't agree to marry some awful women, there is something terribly the matter with him. He has no intention of being a faithful manservant and faithful retainer to some hideous old bag. It could well be that he's more suited to spending his valuable time and energies in the service of something existentially else.

Relationship is a code word for being trapped, call it relation-trapped, as for example in marriage, an arrangement involving a binding kinship, possibly to something once enticingly, even passionately, romantic—something that once may have been, but isn't. It is with an understanding of this inevitability that bachelors are what we might call antirelationary, or more to the point antimatrimonial—and for damned good reasons, of which there are easily a truckload. This is every bit why bachelors are believed to be *dysfunctional*, a currently favorite expression meaning something that doesn't quite work the way we thought it would, because (if he's a dysfunctional person) he can't, or doesn't want, to fulfill everyone else's glorious expectations. Such a fellow might also be referred to disapprovingly as *de facto defective, de facto* meaning *sho-nuff* defective as husband material.

Hence, if he refuses to marry some dreadful woman, he quite frankly *isn't worth much.* Women like to call such fellows *losers,* the implication being that they passed up every confounded matrimonial opportunity. Ignoring those 50 percent of failed marriages, women like to believe that statistical probabilities don't apply to them. Even if (heaven help us) a bachelor (in a compromised moment) should agree to marry someone (of the opposite) gender, the time spent under that dreaded yoke (as he well understands) would better have been spent in flourishing in bachelorhood with its fun-loving, skirt-lifting, free living, self-serving, independent-mindedness. Chances are that men in their 40s who are enjoying the bounties of bachelorific life should (but often don't) know better than to forsake it.

Forbes correspondent Kiri Blakeley, in a review of Lori Gottlieb's *Marry Him*, begins by expressing the dangerous idea that women cease searching for Mr. *Right* and instead make do with Mr. *He'll Do*, admitting that Ms. Gottlieb frittered away 20 years searching for the *perfect man* while she, even had she uncovered him, fell short herself of being the perfect woman. Her slogan, whatever it may have been, was revised to say, "Ladies, you are not getting any younger. Don't dump that 8 who's not a 10 because, in a decade you won't even be able to catch a 5!" There is a chance, too, that the 8 will remain an 8. Gottlieb had interviewed two groups of women: one in their 20s, the other in their 30s and beyond. The younger ones were bent on developing careers of one sort or another and signing men up on the basis of their wit, illustrious appearance and limitless potential. The latter group that had dumped their suitors were about to settle on anything they could dredge up. It's essentially the difference between finding a young man who has launched a career and another who's about to be furloughed. Beneath all this is the fear that they will be alone, abandoned, lonesome, friendless and forsaken.

This terror is more prevalent among women than men, if we may say so, because men have a clearer estimate of what it takes to be self-sufficient. This is partly why bachelors have every confidence that they can be far along in life and still, if they choose, find other women who are at least presentable in some sense or another. Bachelors wear better, or think they can. An old saw says, be it mostly valid or not, that over time women decline and fall while men tend to ameliorate with age. This is a bit of an overstated myth (in the current meaning of the word), but there is a blossom of truth in it since men tend to handle age better, or are at least capable of it, and of course there are also wealthy widows out there stealthily stalking the streets for new matrimonial victims.

What's wrong with bachelors? To hear Bill Bennett tell it, quite a bit. We remember Bennett as a rather intellectually uppity Secretary of Education and later director of something called *National Drug Control*. Bennett feels that men are, so to speak, on the run, while women are (so to speak again) off the run, saying that in 1970 men earned 70 percent of university degrees that fell to 50 percent in 1980 and 43 percent in 2006. It should be cautioned, however, that large numbers of women took degrees (whether earned or not) in elementary school teaching rather than in intellectually challenging fields. Be that as it may, Bennett argues that women surpassed men in the number of diplomas they carted off. So too, in 1950 an estimated five percent of working age men were unemployed, whereas by 2010 the number expanded, for a number of reasons, to 20 percent. Bennett, armed with shaky government statistics, also reported that in 2011 the out of wedlock birthrate had climbed to 40 percent, compared to a 1960 rate of about 10 percent. In 1960 at least one in ten children lived apart from their fathers, compared to 27 percent in 2010.

Meaning what? Bennett wonders under what rock all the decent single men were hiding, suggesting that there was a *maturity deficit* that is ever worsening. Hannah Rosen in her essay called "The End of Man," argues that a colossal change in role reversal is afoot, and that it finds its origins in the shift of modern labor from *backs to brains*, the latter of which she assigns to women, allegedly the weaker sex that we explored earlier. She also claims that men in the 18–32 age group spend more of their time playing video games than boys 12 to 17. Ms. Rosen concludes that there is some reigning confusion over what it means to be a man, a question as ambiguous as it is complicated. It would be easy and obvious to suggest that they've been in one sense of another emasculated, meaning that their virility has been undermined and weakened, their potency compromised and castrated—rendering them more cowardly, compromised and effeminate. Accordingly, Ms. Rosen asks, "do we even need men?" wondering as some coaches and drill sergeants do, "what kind of man are you?" She also presumes that "the founding fathers believed that "industriousness, marriage and religion" are the keys to "male empowerment and achievement," also concluding that a young man must "get off the video games five hours a day, get [himself] together, get a challenging job and get married."

Did Hanna say "get married"? Yes, and not only that, her essay ends with the message that "it's time to man up," suggesting and more to the point insisting, that to be a man is to be married," a contestable concept. One might just as well say, "man up and be a gentleman." To the contrary, she is arguing that, to her, marriage means responsibility, which in this context has merit to it, provided that marriage survives for more than a month or so. Thoroughbred men can marry, and even rise above it, suffer through it and armed with manly composure and fierce determination, see it through, even though it is one of the otherwise pointless barometers of masculinity, don't we know. Real men are tough, they're determined, they're trustworthy, they're intractable, they're brave, they're feisty, they're dependable and they're undaunted. They're ideal marriage material because no lesser man could begin to manage it—and still survive. Such a person is hardly an example of masculinity's decline, but in spite of all his virtues, he may be a bit soft in the head. Sociologists have a name for that. It's a mesomorph, a body type meaning a handsome fellow, athletic, muscular, large boned—

and stupid. Mesomorphs are ideally suited to playing football because of their well-developed, powerfully package of bones, muscle and connective tissues. A powerful man is well equipped to protect himself and anyone else he chooses. When we gaze into the fellow's eyes we discover to our dismay that they're terminally dull and uncomprehending. Whether he would make some dopey woman a good and proper husband is questionable. He's a potentially dangerous dope, a sleeping giant with an IQ in the lesser double digits. He may, in a random moment, and quite by accident, mind you, *break her neck*. There's nothing personal in it, since it's all accidental and quite unanticipated and therefore unpremeditated. It's just, as mesomorphs say, *one of them things*. Could a mesomorph become a bachelor?

Technically, yes; in practice, no. He's not the right stuff; that's why. As mesomorphs also say, it's considerably *outside the realm of possibility*. And why is this? It's all too obvious. They haven't that subtle sense of tact and propriety, that extreme sensitivity to women's elusive *feelings*, generously celebrated in song and story. We're referring to women's infinitely subtle turns of whim and random notion. A mesomorph is hopelessly unable to conduct himself gracefully and courageously, through the most awkward of situations, moral, sexual and philosophical, that bachelors oft-times encounter. Mesos are deficient in sophisticated erudition for one important thing, since, chances are, they've never so much as cracked a book and as a result are unequipped to associate gracefully with the more or less literate classes.

Nonetheless there are women who prefer, nay crave, their attention, if only because they pose no intellectual threat, real or presumed. The Britannica emphasizes what it calls an extreme mesomorph, as a fellow with massive hands, a broad, masculine chest and shoulders, a large heart (literally), heavily muscled arms and legs and minimal body fat. There are such things as female mesomorphs of the sort who teach girls gym classes, and sport, as nitwits say, what's been called a firm chest not without feminine curves, and can walk on their hands, smart as you please, across a basketball court. Let's put it this way: if such women were to become men, they would bear a striking resemblance to *Hulk Hogan*, a sporting, athletically-inclined sort of chap, lean (by all means) compactly built but not with the combination of features one would ordinarily classify closer to barbarism than bachelorism.

What have women to say about the average bachelor as we generally envision them? No telling. There is a certain woman who facetiously calls herself the neighborhood shrink who claims forthrightly that if a bachelor wants to man up, the best place to begin is by asking a woman what she wants. No less a person than Geoffrey Chaucer entertained that question through his Wife of Bath in the *Canterbury Tales*, declaring that women want to control their husbands and that they want to see and be seen. We're given to understand elsewhere that they want to feel like a woman, however that may be interpreted. If a woman doesn't feel like a woman, she may feel like a gorilla or some kind of a ghastly Hollywood ectoplasm. Let us posit for the time being that a woman wants to feel like women are inclined to feel, or in our prescriptive times, are *expected to feel*. Bachelors are well advised to complement women whether they feel inclined to do so, or not. We understand by now that women like men to be decisive, trustworthy, candid, honest and all such wonderful things. What not to do is be truthful. Many a man has uttered the truth and thereafter relinquished whatever it was that he'd been promoting. Another thing not to do is to direct attention to another woman's features, specifically any of her potentially erotic regions. To do that is to cause a woman to feel like other women customarily feel, such as insecure or irretrievably uncertain.

What's wrong with bachelors? Not necessarily anything, except that they may rub women (literally or figuratively) the wrong way. Our neighborhood shrink lists the potential problems and rewards for men assuming any of several familiar roles such as 1) Mr. Nice Guy, 2) the Bad Boy, 3) the emotionally disturbed bloke. They all possess, be warned, *certain attendant problems*. Presuming that men want to humor women, all of the aforementioned roles can (shall we say) backfire and even blow up. Mr. Nice Guy, presuming that he's an easy-going, durable, endlessly agreeable and good-natured jackass, is not likely to offend and upset, ever thinking of ways to humor some harpy whom his has the misfortune to have on his hands. Harpies are, in the words of classicist Edith Hamilton, "frightful, creatures with hooked beaks and claws who always [leave] behind them a loathsome stench, sickening to all living creatures." In the normal course of interpersonal relations, bachelors inevitably encounter them, and it isn't (as some folks say) *pretty*. A man's first and primary impulse is to get the hell rid of them in the cleanest, quickest, most efficient and decisive means that may cross his mind. This could involve rushing them to an airport and dropping them hastily at the curb, then motoring smartly away. Lives there a bachelor who has not done precisely this? Were he (God help us) married to this beast it would introduce certain vexing problems, such as how to dump her, and how fast. Even Mr. Nice Guys, agreeable, durable and good humored though they be, can find themselves searching for ways and means to rid themselves of such creatures.

Mr. Bad Boy is, as the name denotes a boyish, rather undependable and immature, selfishly and playfully unpredictable—anything but a bachelor in the sense that we've been using that designation. He's simply not the *real article*. Women may find him amusing in the short run, but not the long. As to *emotionally distant* men, it's the same thing. Emotional distance doesn't travel well. There are loads of emotionally distant men littering the landscape, but they're of no use to women because they're distant, disconnected, detached, uncoupled. Women have short patience with them. The long and short of it is that such men don't know what they want, aside from a few fundamentals. Women obviously don't want anybody quite that unbacheloristly off-putting. The sensitive men we cited earlier don't wash well because they're less than masculine. An unidentified correspondent to "People Skills Decoded" remarks that while women say they're searching for one thing, they often settle for the opposite, possibly because the one thing can't be found, and if it could it would be the wrong thing. Certain men are, strange to say, monkishly-inclined in the sense that they're more exponentially reflective and inward looking, benignantly self-confident. These are manly characteristics, but not all men have them. Bachelors, the real ones, are likely to be self-assured and self-confident without being arrogant, but hordes of women who are bent upon making them over. Self-possessed men will exit such women at the earliest possible instant, and look elsewhere for feminine company, if any.

As "People Skills Decoded" remarks, women like (or appear to) what are generally recognized as *masculine traits*, among them confidence, self-reliance, firm voice, decidedly good eye contact along with a sense of who they are and where they're going. They show no signs of needing protection. So-called *social skills* are important to some women, although men's social talents in social circumstances may cause women to fade back to the point that they're part of the wallpaper. Men move on to other women, variety being the spice of vice. While this is going on, or failing to go on, we might venture to propose the obvious: that a man is who is, what he is, where he is, where he'd like to be and why he is. Such things identify his identity through the steel armor of bachelorhood. By armor we mean (in a metaphoric way, of course) a sturdily defensive covering, a protective layer amply capable of protecting against onslaught of any kind, be it external or (so to speak) internal. It's a defensive shield, polished and at the ready for any bacheloristic inevitabilities, most of them instigated by women who have cause (or think they do) to challenge having been, say jilted, meaning that they've been unceremoniously dumped, albeit it by accident or intention, capriciously or overtly with not so much as a by your leave, suddenly directly, overtly capriciously, irrelevantly, redundantly, intentionally, finally, irrevocably, giving rise to another of the world's abundant inventory of goodbye girls.

Sad? Maybe, but it happens. Bachelors have been known to shuffle their rosters of women who ordinarily *don't take it sitting down*, if you know what we mean. They're every bit capable of returning fire with a formidable arsenal of conspiratorially vicious insults and other screaming exchanges intended to occasion psychological devastation. That's exactly why bachelors are amply protected, *ad hoc*, for the worst. Think of it as amatory housekeeping: something that no bachelor likes to do, but likes having done. This comes as no surprise. *Jilting* is merely one of a dazzling array of snags that bachelors routinely encounter and resolve. It's particularly troublesome, which is why they must be, in the manner prescribed, armed with the things just cited, along with a protective helmet to ward off any unforeseen and unanticipated attacks (real or figurative) when women can turn quite anticipatedly and launch a volley of mostly pastel cannonballs. For him, there's only one thing to do, namely move on to the next woman or women without so much as a *how-do-you-do*. The original meaning of *jilt*, by the way, aptly applied to a woman who, without having given it much thought, surrendered her honor and had come to get it back.

Bacheloric *honor* (we'll call it) is an anything but an uncommon target among both jilted women and less than bacheloric men—we'll call them *bachelors manqués* (that's the French *manqué*, not "monkey," and means *to fail, to lack*). In this context it means a would-be bachelor who hasn't quite the *right credentials* that we cited a few pages ago. He is something that might have been, but wasn't. He is in this respect defective with something somehow lacking, spoiled or missing (if we may say so) in action, hence a failed bachelor, *a* would-be who couldn't, Bachelorism, we hasten to add, cannot apply to just any bloke who fancies that he can play the part. Bachelorism properly applies (we've said it before) to a select few, in the sense that not all men are marriage material, not having been cut from the right (if unfortunate) bolt. Would-be bachelors may well arise out of nothing but jealousy, and therefore find fault with genuine bachelors out of spite. This is why bachelors need armorial self-protection as may be required for certain unanticipated *emergent occasions* in the way one might well keep a grenade within reach for in emergent circumstances. This is every bit why bachelors maintain as their motto *non semper erit aestas*, "It will not always be summer," i.e., one must *be* prepared in more senses than one.

It has been reliably and unpleasantly reported that there are such things as *married bachelors*, the meaning of which have at least two oxymoronic forms, one of which is to be married but prefer to think of themselves as quite the opposite. There are huge numbers of these men *at large*, especially when they're away from home. Another are married men who have the audacity to represent themselves as a bachelors, although they're *bachelors manqué*, impostors. There are millions of such men prowling the thoroughfares, pausing to assure women that they're not really married; they only appear to be. Impersonating bachelors is an adulatory gesture that extols the bacheloric existence by impersonating it. It's a gesture of high endorsement and extraordinary flattery. Everyone knows that excellent things happen to bachelors, presuming that they're among the leading ranks of *conquistadors*.

An excellent word, that, and a manly one, representing him as one who possesses a gift for executing conquests by conquering (sometimes by feats of arms) and helps himself to whatever is up for dinner, if you see our drift. He identifies his victims (so to speak) then storms them. As Shakespeare wrote in *King John*, "better conquest never canst thou make/ than arme thy constant and thy noble parts." Being a conquistador is to vanquish and overcome with a mind to winning whatever he's after. It's all quite wonderful, while it lasts, but what it really means is taking whatever one wants, presumably without being arrested. On a more polite level it means determining what one wants to do, and doing it without having to explain one's self to a jury of his hostile critics. It's all quite urban heroic, but it's still feasible for the right sort of independent man.

We're discussing bachelors here, and bachelorism means among a flurry of other things, a self-aggrandizing and fully independent lifetime of going where he wants and taking all he sees that's fit to seize and maintain, while arriving at his own occasionally bizarre decisions. It's a splendid option, and a life that few men take because they haven't the will, meaning that they allow others to order them about and point them in directions they don't wish to follow. There are men, great numbers of them, who merely want to fulfill their own ends, not everyone else's It should be the right and duty for every adult, and some children, to conceptualize and realize the kind of life they divine for themselves which, in a certain sense means resolving their existential dilemma, namely clarifying and proceeding with the kind of existence (hence *existential*) one has selected after painstaking consideration and soul-searching. Obviously no one can become anything that crosses his imaginative mind. Still and all, the existential dilemma for everyone is to discover where to go, what to be, what to do. These are among the most significant decisions of a lifetime.

Above all, one would normally elect to be unfettered, unshackled, unconfined, and free to proceed in one's own direction. Not to pursue one's existential options is to settle for heredity and environment to dictate his destiny. The traditional meaning of existential has been captured in three easy words: *existence precedes essence*, the message being that we exist before we settle upon the *ultimate nature* of that existence, or to say it more simply, we're here before we understand why we're here, and to what purpose. What is one to do with himself, and why? In one sense these questions are mysterious and elusive; in another sense they're fairly simple. To what does one wish to commit himself philosophically, morally theologically and so forth? One can devote himself to building, in all senses of that word; he can also devote himself to healing in all senses of that word. One would presume that he devotes himself to something that is (again in some sense) productive and generally beneficial. Bachelorism is not necessarily inconsistent with these ends. Viktor Frankl in *Man's Search For Ultimate Meaning* tells us that "Despair is suffering without meaning." Aristotle in his *Nicomachean Ethics* reminds us too that that whereas "There is pleasure with respect to every faculty of sensation," one discovers it too in "thought and contemplation," by venturing into solitude, the best of all places for comprehension and understanding, things that often encourage one to go his own way and on his own terms.

This in turn demands a greater than ordinary commitment not to marriage, but to an uncommon belief in one's self and his possibilities and a healthy respect for one's judgments, capabilities, prospects and a better than average ability to encourage a level of self-discovery never before contemplated. It means also that one does not wandering into the trap of necessarily doing what others have always done, and with the same dismal results. Real men are masters of themselves, their own critics, their own sources of encouragement, their own best company and, to be sure, and their own best and most loyal friends. That entails going it alone, developing a reclusive life mostly devoid of ordinary companionship so to encourage self-reliance and acceptance of one's self as his primary counsel. Such people travel alone without others understanding their identity, and move about in anonymity. It's all great fun without having to feel, as others might, helpless, ignored, passed over, neglected, unloved, rejected, uninvited, over ruled, outsmarted, left in the lurch, lost in the Hebrides, dumped, duped and disengaged. The ability to thrive among all these demons tells us that one has his life securely under control, one of the prerequisites of true bachelorhood, one of the pleasures of which is to navigate one's own ship. Bachelors of the sort that we've been discussing are generally unprepossessing fellows, unmarried of course. They're not quite what we'd call a *professional bachelor*, but more an *independently minded* sort of chap, abundantly self-sufficient, decently well educated at some ivied university where he took the customary bachelor's degree and is able to summon his charm and skills at persuasion, subtly secure in his understated self-esteem.

He's one of our *bountiful bachelors* who has applied his learning and his understanding of ordinary psychology to his own (some would say nefarious) ends. This, obviously, opens the door to jealousy, that curious and understated word with even more curious implications, connotatively and denotatively assumed to mean *covetous* (inordinately desiring the wealth, possessions, talents, achievement belonging to someone else in a manner that is greedy, acquisitive, avaricious, lacking in restraint) but also characterized by a certain wrathfulness, a furious desire for, say, the love of another. Such a person is possessed by the notion that what he covets is in the possession of someone else.

From what we have said and shown about bachelors, it is perfectly clear why what we'll call *ordinary men* are inclined toward a suspicion of jealousy toward other men who have committed themselves to bachelorhood as a rather suspicious way of life. Husbands, after all, have gone to a great deal of arduous trouble finding a wife, among them coming to terms of the ocean of portentous conflicts that marriages bring. They've done what they could about making the best of a badly flawed decision (matrimony), they are uncertain about their ability to survive it, much less make it in any sense successful. Then there appears what was out there all along: the option that bachelorism offered, the obvious advantages of without the burden of monogamy, sexual monotony, financial worries, children to raise and possibly to send off to universities, having to resolve every kind of unanticipated and unmanageable dilemmas common to marriage and domestic life.

Bachelors have a few problems of their own, but of another sort, such as where to turn when they're sick or injured, although one of their willing women may be all too happy to nurse a bachelor back to good running form. Another problem, if he wishes to consider it a problem, is how to handle what we'll call normal people who don't know quite what to make of bachelors and other independently-directed individuals who don't always observe the usually accepted and customary rules of civil engagement, things that are normally summarized as love and marriage. A bachelor must surmise who, besides himself, is going to clean his quarters, how well and how often. If he is socially inclined, as he probably isn't, he will notice that only couples are invited and not singles. The thought, if any, behind this. is somewhat elusive, but it has something to do with recognizing and accepting people only in tightly bonded comfortable pairs, that in turn may be a gesture of inviting guests who, since they're in couples, are presumed to be persons of presumed stability, psychologically and otherwise. Then too, nobody quite knows how a single person is going to react, since ordinarily he has no one near to edit his remarks and thought processes. Then too, he may or may not have all the women he wants, but not the one he wants on the present occasion. This may strike the average, normal adult as frivolous, which it may be, but it hardly compares to the dilemmas that married men routinely face in the best way they can. One can only count himself fortunate when he's spared the boredom of marriage that others face.

Bachelors, when pressed into it, can lie with near impunity. Since they haven't the obligation to report their prevarications to anyone but themselves, there are exquisite occasions when they utter remarkable untruths merely for the effects they occasion. They need not answer to anyone. Married men sooner or later will have to report to their lovely wives. Thus it is that bachelors are the objects of frequent, unremitting and pronounced jealousy, which has its favorable and unfortunate sides. It is flattering to become the object of someone else's jealousy, since it may be assured that he's doing a few important things with more than ordinary success. If one enjoys jealousy, he deliberately does things to occasion still more of it. Those who are jealous would go to great length and great expense to trade places with a bachelor for just one erotic weekend. Since this is a little on the impossible side, he seethes with frustration and boils over with jealousy. It's a joy to behold, and, as we all know, it's the highest manifestation of flattery. Jealousy! We adore it, knowing all along that it's the most insincere of praise, but all the same it's one of the more preferred forms of delicious self-deception.

CHAPTER III. THE FOOT-LONG WELTANSCHAUUNG

The modest book you're clutching is entitled *Bachelors Abounding*, mindful that *abound* has various voluble denotations and connotations, such as moving in waves, plentiful, wealthy, copious, overflowing, rife, abundant and teeming. John Milton in Book III of his *Paradise Lost* (1667) included a line that reads, "In thee Love hath abounded more than glory abounds." It also has been taken to mean being at large, fully sufficient. A true bachelor is one who abounds, has a plentiful existence. One might venture to call it spiritual affluence. John Donne insightfully commented that "every laborer is miserable and beast like" compared to "idle abounding men." Hence when we say bachelors (with or without an apostrophe) we are referring to that stripe of gentleman who moves freely, identifies himself with plentitude, abundance of spirit and (possibly) extraordinary resources, approaches life and destiny through a *macro* rather than *micro* perspective, greets women and the rest of life as what he is, quite frankly, a *bon vivant*. By this we mean a lively, active personality, freely expressive, irrepressible, forward moving, sometimes gleefully sociable, erudite, an elevated product of what we'll call unhesitatingly the good life that he presumes to embrace for a good long time. This presumes that he can maintain his robust health and youth, all the while viewing life (some folks say) as his oyster, or in some instances what seasoned Bostonians call an *erster*.

Thus far we've shown why men ought not to marry, or to put it another way, never to marry a woman, especially if they're what we've been properly calling bacheloresque men who believe fervently that they have better, more abundant destinies outside of matrimony. That's why it strikes us as discouraging to encounter a bachelor at an altar with what appears to be a woman in a wedding gown that she's been storing in a musty closet for just such a dramatic, if sinister, occasion. We're presuming that it's a woman; these days we can't be certain. Our friends at a redundantly titled site called *Happy Bachelors* remind us that older men should not fall prey to matrimony because they may possess property and other assets that may too easily, shall we say, fall into inappropriate hands. They may by this time have been exposed to a gaggles of women, some of whom have been emotionally entombed long enough to resemble Egyptian mummies, while bachelors (if they have played their cards advantageously) have been out there having a generously good old time of it. We happened to have been acquainted with and older gentleman who not inappropriately breathed his last in a brothel that, if one considers it, may have been as good a place to expire as any. Then too, he might just as well have departed this life while (presumably) regaling himself.

We have also been reminded that men of lesser means should not marry because, even if they should marry wealthy women, it's still not advisable, except possibly in the *short run*. Visionary men ought not to marry because marriage will undermine those same visionary possibilities, derailing them and turning their visionary ideas into vacant thoughts of a vacant life. So too, religiously-inclined men shouldn't marry because, if nothing else, marriage has little or nothing to do with holiness and because Jesus himself, whom we'll encounter in Chapter V, for whatever mystical reasons he may have entertained, remained single. In the meantime, the folks at *HB* believe, as we do, that churches aren't especially accommodative to men and because they keep the divorce statistics alarmingly high by willy-nilly marrying people left and right who, as any damned fool can see, have no business marrying in the first place. For that matter, even the government, among its miserable loyalties and other abysmally poor choices, actively encourages marriage. That being so, matrimony is one of the more enormously popular of piss-poor options.

But all this negative talk pales when there is the bachelorific life for a gentlemen who doesn't know the meaning of loneliness because he's perfectly contented being with his *best friend* who isn't his wife; it's himself or, failing of that, it's his dog. Besides that, the single life is, as we have gently suggested, is an ideal and economical way to *move about*, in any sense of that expression. Bachelors can, and do, travel light and move fast, cultivate a life that is by all odds best for a bachelor. It's private, discreet, ever open to whatever they can manage to open, thanks to their being their own agents, their own butlers, their own footmen. Of course bachelors are often seen with women of the sort who are attracted to bachelors because bachelors are mostly a cut above ordinary men and because they represent a certain cultural challenge. There is a curiously British site calling itself *CrossFit: Forging Elite Fitness* that, despite its somewhat vaguely misleading title, contains a compendium of bachelorific voices (we will protect their privacy) representing international bachelorhood, by publishing some rather outspoken comments. One fellow, for example, claims that he is every bit at liberty (we deploy the word appropriately) *to work out* whatever matters are at hand, without securing permission from what some boneheads call his *better half*, because, without fear of infamy (as Dante tells us) he will henceforth leave his "exercise equipment about," which at first strikes us as irrelevant, and yet addresses s life lived free from female supervision.

Another good fellow tells us, with barely concealed joy, that his apartment evidences what he calls a certain *lived-in smell* that certain others may well comprehend, since this same fellow has all the freedom in the world to "stay at home, alone, on a Saturday night if [he wants] to, even though he's quite "free to *have a date.*" Another well-intentioned fellow tells us that he "gets tested [we leave the implications of that to our readership] with each new girlfriend," while still another bachelor with an enormous sense of confidence informs us that he consumes his "zone meal straight from the fridge...one block at a time." Of course it scarcely ends there. Another chap advances the idea, quite frankly (we admire that), of not having "to share with anyone" (we know the feeling) and that "all my money is spent on me!" We can scarcely imagine. Other liberated voices come forward, again without fear of infamy, such as the chap who says that he's entirely free to "work 50+ hours a week...save out 30K and take over 2 years off traveling the world," doing, we have every reason to presume, any bloody thing he wants. That's the good part, as any bachelor *worth his salt* will openly attest. As another fellow aptly summarizes, "don't hold back!" Indeed, why should he? There is little to nothing to prevent his holding back or, as yet another bloke says, just before he goes, he proceeds to "raise a little hell," that we may as well concede, may playfully (no more than that) involve women for recreational (mind you) purposes, so long as a bachelor holds his tongue at the appropriate times, and above all knows what, and what not, to say. We all understand, of course, that what not to say in one circumstance is quite appropriate in another.

Ask Man, subtitled *Become a Better Man,* however that's to be taken, comes to our rescue, and could not have arrived at a better time. We will quite openly submit that some of those never-to-ask questions are clearly off the mark and are certain to destroy what women call a *relationship.* For example, never ask a woman about her *track record,* something that can lead to insoluble dilemmas, whereas if you ask a fellow how many women he's been with, chances are that he will respond with a more or less accurate estimate and be ever so completely prepared to name names and describe the circumstances. Another problematic question is how, if at all, to conclude the evening without seeming too direct, even when addressing a woman who, on a level of sophistication not exceeding ten, comes in at a one. The same thing applied other touchy questions that modesty inhibits our reciting. One can conceivably repair and resort to bacheloric freedom symbols, as for example the common bicycle, where the *bi* refers to two wheels, not a bicycle built for two. One fellow, in a moment of inspired rapprochement, traded his wife for a bicycle, since the latter affords more possibilities for liberty than the former and because bicycles are excellently low maintenance items easily stored in a large closet where they remain silent until deployed as a more than welcome means of conveyance—except that, like a wife, they need their tires inflated every so often. Even so, one can park his bike far easier than he can park his (former) wife. Bicycles can be stolen, which can be a relatively minor dilemma, whereas having his wife stolen can be a blessing.

A fellow known to us only as *Harry* has authored a piece he calls "Don't Be Ashamed to [*sic*] Being a Bachelor," possibly to avoid and evade some witch's taking him to task for expressing his opinions, which reminds us nevertheless that as a bachelor "life gets better as one gets older," something that we've all heard before but have yet to verify. Harry confidently goes on to say that "women have it ridiculously easy until their late 20s," after which they exhibit signs of deconstruction, when their careers (if any) fizzle out. Between the ages of 30–35 the number of women who vacate the workforce becomes a mudslide, mostly because they have an irrepressible desire to have families. In the meantime Harry discloses that "women in their 30s are throwing themselves at" bachelors. Harry also reminds us that bachelors can travel more freely and infinitely better than married dopes with their wives who are perpetually scowling "at everything under the sun." Another unidentified bachelor earnestly advises us to "disregard females; acquire currency," a damned fine morsel of advice, since it is ever so much better to be single and flush than married and debt-ridden.

Jeremy Singer of *askman.com* has observed that whereas received opinion advises men that it's their destiny in life to be married, "It's time to put that 'white picket fence' influence to rest." Presuming that Singer's readership consists mostly of lone wolves, it behooves them to proceed through life "as an adventure" rather than to see it as a dismal lifelong expectation of decades with women in tow. He also with characteristic earnestness reminds us that traveling is far better done singly than in pairs, the point being that "canoeing in Northern Maine" alone easily beats "taking your spouse to see her parents in Florida." He adds the unusual observation that a bachelor is more inclined to be philanthropic, since he's often to be discovered in the company of single, attractive women whom he's trying (whether consciously or not) to impress through his apparent generosity and abiding concern for those less fortunate than bachelors. That is what some nitwits would immediately call an interesting observation, although Singer has more to say, namely that bachelors sleep better, but not for reasons one might presume.

To the contrary, bachelors most often (contrary to general perception) sleep alone and therefore, being mostly self-absorbed chaps, feel no pressing need to share a bed with anyone else. Singer emphasizes a University of Chicago study that single women and men, for reasons that go largely unexplained, have the *inside track* on uncovering choice employment opportunities, albeit that those same singles account for 90 percent of jobs lost during the 2009 financial crisis, as compared with 22 percent of marrieds. That said, singles do financially far better than marrieds, since they're living less financially-demanding lives supporting (presumably) one person and are therefore not paying for twice of everything, nor are they (heaven help them) suffering (yet) through the stress and expense attached to divorcement. Moreover, as Singer reminds us, singles are far more likely to remain in exemplary physical shape, partly because (whether they admit it or not) they're trying to make themselves attractive in the estimation of other singles. The same does not hold true of marrieds who see themselves decades from now in a select adipose colony called Fatville.

Speaking of inclinations, Singer claims that *sleeping around*, a tendency among bachelors and other singles, is ironically *beneficial*. Says he, men "get to meet and sleep with as many women as [they] choose," assuming of course that those women agree to it. The point is that men who live in (let's call it) *perpetual sin* allegedly report fewer symptoms of depression. Small wonder: they have less to be depressed over since, as he observes, "Every night out can be a new chapter." By George, yes, it possibly can unless, of course, something goes terribly wrong. Lest we forget, singles may well be, and probably are, more productive. Why? Consider what marrieds have on their minds: bills to pay, promises to keep, appearances to maintain, neighbors with whom to keep up, dogs to bark, and so ludicrously on. Being single, possibly having achieved full four-star bachelorship, affords the distinct advantages of coasting through life with relatively more breeziness. Singer assures us that singles, all in all, coast through with (on average, mind you) comparatively little stress because they (for one thing) engage in fewer arguments and no marital conflicts that can inexorably lead down the road to any of three possible arrests: cardiac, developmental and police.

Were we not about to address the delicate and critically sensitive matter of confirmed bachelors, we would be seriously if not ridiculously remiss, by which we mean negligent in the daunting tasks looming before us, all the while careless, perhaps, even guilty of inattentiveness to our solemn duty as an inquiring and ever searching gender commentator. Women, for one, are more than leery of confirmed ones because they are what they say, confirmed, by which we (and they) mean solidly fixed in their pernicious ways and not bloody likely to alter them. To put it still another way, they can be expected to persist as bachelors to the point where they are safely beyond retrieval Moreover, while this persistence continues, they enjoy (while they can) the pleasures that occasionally attend a few married men—while they last, which is not long after the honeymoons of their truncated lives. Nevertheless, women persist in viewing bachelors as *scoundrels* who expect something for nothing, if you understand our drift.

Jennifer Brown Banks tells us that "confirmed bachelors are clever creatures! They often have good taste [we're all too fully conscious of that] and choose women who are the cream of the crop." We understand Ms. Banks' consternations, but all the same, bachelors, even confirmed ones, are and ought to be accorded some latitude in matters of love, marriage (that we've pretty well obliterated) and divorcement. She goes on to say that "some women have questioned the use of ultimatums, and whether they contribute more toward "getting a guy to the altar," but then again, as she concedes, does any woman want to deal with man hauled against his better judgment to that dreaded altar? We say that if he doesn't march forward by and on his own volition, then he ought not to go there. If he were bloody well convinced that it was a good and proper idea, he'd venture there on his own. In the meantime he may possibly consort with any of a dozen or so other women, presumably one at a time. Suppose, for argument's sake, that the tables were turned, such that the same chap so wanted to stick his head in a noose that he had no choice but to plead (on bended knee, mind you) for any of those several dreaded women to meet him at a dreaded altar for some dreaded purpose? What then? They would all soundly refuse, and for good and sufficient reasons, having in an uncharacteristically lucid moment realized that their suspicions were more than justified.

In the meantime, women have become impossibly insecure in the company of bachelors, which a woman compared to seeing "a cat that comes around, shows affection and [then] disappears." That's hardly surprising, since bachelors may or may not take what's immediately available and then (by the time the *check* arrives) they're long gone and earnestly taking up with some other lovelorn female. There are, to be sure, odd situations when neither the bachelor nor his victim (let's call her that, for the nonce) has any remote intention of getting him *anywhere near* an altar. Still and all, there are bachelors who have been accused of recklessly subsuming the best years of a woman's life (and their own), except that bachelors intend to be what they are until their bells toll. In the meantime, however, regrettable things sometimes occur. One woman explained recently, "It wasn't my choice to be single. I wanted marriage, but I fell in love with a man who lied to me."

The Catholic Church apparently doesn't view couples in quite the same way, declaring with holy outspokenness that "historically, the majority of people born into this world marry and have children." Mind you, priests and monks are rather a different story, but nonetheless, "rare is the vocation to the priesthood, religious life or [even rarer a] consecrated single life," consecrated meaning devoted to some high-toned, sacred purpose, to declare oneself devoted (in this case, we presume) to the adoration of God, with all requisite dedication and solemnity. The Church, however, holds that "all men should pursue marriage until they get a [collect] call to serve God and His people as a celibate Priest." What has all this to do with confirmed bachelors? They're to be considered and approached as "excuse maker[s] waiting for God to speak directly [to them] in words of direction," in other words, direct direction, unless and until they are determined to continue with their wicked ways, that, the Church argues, have other unfortunate consequences, to wit: every woman who in a moment of weakness submits to these ruffians 1) disrespects women in general, apparently compromising the *spotless honor* of the entire gender, 2) eroding their ability to love, honor and respect a woman for the requirements of marriage, and 3) refraining from contraception and divorce. In other words, bachelors aren't properly filling their obligation, which is to marry, reproduce and make the best of it, which is—to say the least—an outrageously presumptuous thing to propose.

The Church isn't the only party to endorse this position. One anonymous chap writes, "I think women find them [bachelors] creepy and undesirable for two reasons," one of which is that they "never met the right woman" and the other that they are apt to bring with them "a lot of old [salty] habits...and be resistant to change," both of which easily qualify them as blockheads and wandering bipeds, no more. Another problem with these creeps and rogues is that they're impossibly single-minded in more fatal ways than one, meaning that they regrettably want to remain single and on their own, and (more significantly) prefer to navigate life by placing themselves fully in charge of themselves without taking orders from some outside (purported) authority. Such persons have been more or less politely described as *introverted*, but that is far wide the mark. *Introverted* has the connotation of being self-centered to the point of caring for no one else. Introspective is a considerably more descriptive term meaning inclined toward self-examination, critical self-evaluation with a mind to taking personal inventory of what he has been, is and may well be, subject to periodic adjustment as deemed reasonable and half-assedly appropriate. Any bachelor not sufficiently introspective would do well to consider its manifold *consolations*, all the while challenging the notion that God wants them to be married, a borderline preposterous assumption.

Suspicion of bachelorhood is always with us. Eleanor Harris of *Look* magazine authored a memorable November 22, 1960, piece called "Men Without Women," a title borrowed from Ernest Hemingway's 1927 collection of fiction masterpieces. Her article has as its gist the testimony from an undisclosed number of bachelors about how they happened to be the dreadful misfits they are. At that time there were an estimated 18,022,000 men, among them 2,161,000 widowers and 1,093,000 divorced. All told, the number was estimated (by government bureaucrats) to be above a quarter of adult men. What's wrong with this picture? A bunch of things. Harris reached five primary conclusions, the first being that any man still unmarried at age 35 probably *never will marry*. Second, she concluded that whereas such disgusting fellows considered, but decided against, marriage, some of them subconsciously thought better of it, while men who are fated to marry have taken a wife before the age of 30. She further suggests that, considering the "increasing mobility of our population," marriageable men have been uprooted by military service or other commitments to the point being that "they seldom remain in one place long enough to be well enough acquainted with a women ever to be married." Moreover, as she puts it, "The single man's interest in sex is often as intense as his married brother['s]," as if to find these disclosures somehow surprising, albeit a "revolution [read *relaxation*] of sexual standards has made them less of a problem for the bachelor than it would have in the early years of this century." She concludes by venturing that, although the bacheloristic life is perhaps less satisfying than it may appear, "a substantial number" of bachelors "have worked out a pattern of existence [nothing more] that they find thoroughly satisfying."

The article treats bachelordom with a certain dank aura of disapproval, not to mention skepticism of exactly how satisfying it may be, adding later that "happy, well-adjusted bachelors" remain, when all is said and done, a miserable "minority" since they [presumably] devote their hopeless years "in search of a mate." This may or may not be a rational assumption, even though she assumes that a single man, in spite of himself "inches in the general direction of marriage," suggesting that it's one of life's inevitable (and dismal) inevitabilities, like death, dropsy, dyspepsia and dead batteries. Harris further suggests that, when an unmarried man meets and unmarried women, "he regards that as an unexpected bonus" of some undisclosed sort, although women pointedly turn up in situations "for the definite purpose of finding a husband," another contestable assumption. Bachelorhood, she concedes, allows such a man to march into any old bistro, and order up any old thing that any decent 60s woman would never even consider. What is a poor bacheloristic bloke to do? Harris advises us that "the lonely man" will inexorably resort to "the personal columns of newspapers," i.e., those that freely publish "frankly erotic" messages. She recommends instead some "scientific" solutions to the pathetic lives of "some unmarried men," the object being that they be expertly directed toward what we all know, presuming that marital bondage is the best, nay only, solution for such poor wretches, misfits and backwater roustabouts. It bloody well serves them right, and at the very least possibly keeps them out of brothels and taverns.

Oddly enough, there was precisely such a scientific response to the menace of bachelordom, and it was endorsed by such invincibly spiritual luminaries and more or less unhappily married saints as the Reverend Norman Vincent Peale, Methodist Bishop Gerald Kennedy and Rabbi George Fox who collectively recommended this experimental 1957 *Scientific Marriage Foundation*, located (if anyone had a sufficiently detailed Indiana map to find it) in Mellott, in the west central part of that state, the one where a doctor shot himself and his bride after only 12 hours of marital bliss. The *SMF* was for a time under the guidance of scientifically-inclined Dr. George W. Crane, physician and psychologist, who wrote a syndicated newspaper column entitled "The Worry Clinic: Test Your Horse Sense." He jotted a little scientific essay called "Why Men Are Superior to Women" and proceeded on the scientific assumption that he would single-handedly arrange 5,000 scientific marriages on the scientific theory that marriage failures were to be placed at the scientific doorstep of what he called *boudoir cheesecake*, along with other life-preserving scientific principles, to wit: 1) "you are not your mind," 2) marriage is the uniting of souls, and 3) marriage is the highest human relationship, along with other speculative scientific assumptions like "over identification with either the mind or the body...creates pain, suffering and hopelessness," and especially the surprising scientific observation that "we have the innate ability to know our self [*sic*] by withdrawing our consciousness from the body and mind." All this assumed that a bachelor would foolishly agree to marry someone, then return a questionnaire with references and photographs to the Worry Clinic, *aka* the *Scientific Marriage Foundation* for scientific review, following which they were to show up for a get-together with a local minister who, in turn, would write his impressions of the groom and bride, and passed them back to the *SMF*. If he was one of the Chosen Ones, the *IBM* sorting machine would find him a scientific wife. There was nothing to it.

Ms. Harris thought it a grand idea, noting too that the currently maligned King Kong of sex himself, Dr. Alfred Kinsey, said in a 1955 report (underwritten by the *Planned Parenthood Foundation*) that America's ever-evolving *sex code* was "the chief product of the concerted attack on prostitution." This declaration had its good side in that men turned to civilian women (as Ms. Harris interpreted it) to "enjoy sexual relations with them outside of marriage, thanks partly to the new frontiers of contraception that the Catholic Church so detested, but which may have led to more marriages and fewer bachelors. The dark side to all this was that bachelors were gradually *going crazy;* specifically 50,000 to 75,000 were believed to have surrendered to psychiatric counseling, something that could have been short circuited and avoided if only they had the good sense to marry and thereby obediently surrender the bleak balance of their lives to a state of bountifully blissful bondage.

Precisely what were these bacheloric psychiatric disorders? Consider: since these men are bachelors, it inexorably follows that they are therefore *fixated* on their mothers, even to the point where they continued to live with them until those mothers died or otherwise vanished, possibly because of their sons' refusing to leave home and, somewhere down the road *man up*, if that's not to too much to ask, since they were perceived (anyway) as a race of wimps and *milquetoasts* of questionable, of dubious, sexual orientation who, without motherly love, cast about for the rest of their ridiculous years. Another conspicuous dilemma that bachelors were perceived to face was their lightly veiled misogyny coupled with their almost terminal *irresponsibility*. What to do? Assign them to become *the head of a family*, presuming that they ever had the chance to marry and therefore make it what nitwits call *a reality*. Result? Ms. Harris envisioned their pathetically spending "a lifetime evading marriage," while in reality they are actually seeking it, *but don't know it*. The poor fellows die a slow, not to say *painful death*, wedged between a *yes* and a *no*, never (alas) to be resolved because they were too much the coward to arrive at any decision. But the dilemmas don't end. There's more.

Mindful of having been raised to "be a man and be independent," they can never become either one since, as Ms. Harris rightly says, "some adult males become confused over the conflict between their determination to be truly self-reliant, and the need to lean on a woman for love and comfort." In other words, it's confusion over whether they're to be inner directed or outer directed (in the parlance of sociologist David Riesman), a serious dilemma if ever we heard one. Real bachelors, as we have observed, are decidedly the former, chaps in charge of their own lives, who assume responsibility for their own problems and dilemmas, thus having no need to lean on a woman for even-handed guidance and counsel on anything that compromises old fashioned manly self-reliance.

But to continue Ms. Harris's list of bacheloric catastrophes, she raises the unpleasant subject of *latent homosexuals* who, to the best of her understanding, comprise "five percent of our total population." Such fellows, she had determined, may conveniently be divided into telling classifications, beginning with the "neuter" that, she has cunningly observed, "practice no sexual activity of any kind," and are to be discovered "working in boys' schools and boys' organizations." *Neuter*, we recall, is generally taken to mean "neutral," which is to say *neither one nor the other*, as for example a spayed or castrated animal, which explains why neutered men spend most of their time pursuing and deflowering women. That leads us to a second bacheloric dilemma that Harris called the *Don Juan*, a pejorative term taken to mean a professional *seducer of women*, an *unparalleled cad* and despicable womanizer, so skilled at his confounded roguishness that women find him, yes, irresistible, falling (as women do) at his feet in expressions of erotic surrender. That, Harris reminds us, is something other than what it appears to be, namely a scoundrel of the lowest order, "so threatened by his fears of unacknowledged homosexuality that he engages in affairs with women to validate his masculinity." Finally, the truth is upon us. That same sort of person rightly belongs among our "nation's confirmed [not bachelors, but] homosexuals, many of whom flock like pigeons to morally compromised places like New York where, in her day there were as many as "100,000 male homosexual prostitutes," all of them, needless to say, confirmed bachelors who were out there on the streets exhibiting their true colors. Consider too, that were they real men, they'd be amply well married, possibly even what's been exaggeratedly called *Scarsdale Galahads*, all of them true to their wives, of course. Still and all, there is ample reason to take heart, inasmuch as "while emotional problems are [all too!] common among single men, a number of un-wed men adjust completely to life without women, find a thoroughly satisfying existence alone" and cope with life by discovering "a sense of completion by rounding out their business by taking up a hobby [needle point, perhaps?] or something "in the sports field."

Bachelors, as Ms. Harris assures us, are five or six times more likely to *come down* with influenza and *succumb* to pneumonia than are your typical decent, house-broken married chap who, in the main, practices healthier habits and consumes Old McDonald-approved three square meals a day, while divorced men, widowers, bachelors and all such riff-raff are far more at risk of being murdered. Yes, murdered. Married men don't ordinarily share that problem because on Saturday nights they're at home on Jackass Hill listening, *all ears*, to *The Original Amateur Hour* on the radio with their lovely wives. Nonetheless, Harris concludes on an encouraging note, at least among those who actively promote marriage and discourage everything bachelorish and its way of approaching men's' grown up life. She cites two supposed Yale researchers (unidentified) who had written, "of all personal *relationships* [we love that word, and repeat it probably 60 times an hour] in our society, marriage is at the same time the most rewarding and most demanding," to which she adds, "unmarried men who believe that, should be encouraged by the "one point authorities agree on: if you really want to get married [we think not] it is never too late, one of the objects being to espouse many of those millions of dubious women and, more importantly, repopulate the world. There is also the implied intention of controlling (we mean *controlling*) men by determinably putting them in harness like so many beasts of urban burden waiting to be tamed and reduced to submission: carrying rubbish out, repairing drippy faucets, acceding to conventional pressures promoted by heretofore unmarried women who are searching for some man to bring the bacon home.

Some have raised the question of whether confirmed bachelors are what they are because they're admitting defeat, which begs the question of *what in blazes defeated them.* Some have also suggested that they've been defeated because they spend what resources they have on themselves, instead upon wives and children. Remember too that the operative word in confirmed bachelor is *confirmed*, which means to strengthen, remove all doubt, establish, verify, authenticate, present evidence in such a way that allows for no uncertainty. Such are aspects of manliness, implying strength, veracity, masculine vigor, not to say a passion for kindness, generosity, courage, independence, frankness and fortitude. Such a man is scarcely to be coaxed into matrimony unless of course he submits to it, which is contestable.

Our bachelors, on average, show by their inner directedness that they have confidence in their ability to estimate and discern their way through life, receiving strictly professional advice, The folks at *Psychology Today* provide us with a high end glimpse of narcissists who, they assure us, "cut a wide, swashbuckling figure in the world" envisioning the narcissist as a delightful B movie "self-loving...charismatic leader with an excess of charm, whose only vice [may have been] his or her *amour-propre* [self-esteem]." Even so, they remind us of other narcissistic interpretations, such as those who see them as they are, "manipulative and easily angered," especially when they seem to think they're not receiving enough attention," being, as they are, overflowing with *self-esteem.* Elsewhere they report that "too much intelligence, wealth or good looks can include narcissistic habits," and comment too that your boss is probably a narcissist. Suffice it to say that those psychological types are, on average, people who know a thing or two about narcissism *don't much care for it,* claiming that it tends toward *megalomania.* A site called *Feminist Power* mentions that "men can have sex any day of the week with zero effort," apparently one of the advanced benefits of narcissism that allows them to advertise themselves and take it from there. All this is to suggest that narcissism, for all its liabilities, can be, on balance, an effective bacheloristic weapon that, at least, beats the daylights out of having low self-esteem. It's been noted, however, that one can pass a goodly part of his life fixating on narcissists without interpreting their self-centeredness as abnormal.

In the wake of all this more than bad press, brave sources at *The Urban Dictionary* (January 27, 2008) come predictably to our rescue, bravely redefining bachelorism as "a prudent, sensible and wise life enabling decision to remain single, remain a first class citizen," not to mention thoroughly enjoying a "relatively high degree of personal freedom, prosperity and self-determination, not to say "most significantly avoiding a very dangerous, hostile, abusive, deeply exploitive and life-crushing, enslaving marriage" that herds men into "the deeply anti-male legal system in a likely, arbitrary, possibly unpredictable and life-crippling divorce." Separation, moreover, carries with it "the constant threat of emotional and physical abuse and arbitrary and unjust arrest, homelessness, imprisonment, ruin [and even] indentured servitude ...without legal protection, recourse or respect" in the face of the "exploitation and sacrificing of a used, disposable man's life for the unilateral entertainment and seemingly derisively, disrespecting vicious wife," whereas "bachelorism...is "freedom-ensuring, sane, safe, financially healthy."

As if to surrender her arms, Suzanne Mac Nevin comments in *Feministezine* that, to the contrary, men "have been essentially become brainwashed by the *philosophy of bachelorism* and thus cannot *commit to a relationship* and likewise would probably make horrible parents and would likely become "adulterous husbands," which very well could happen, since some men fall into matrimony without understanding its dark consequences. Such circumstances leads them into what we've been calling the *war between the sexes* otherwise known as the *gender war*, meaning that the genders cannot get very long with each other. As one anonymous man commented recently, "Women are angry because men have finally gotten smart and no longer wish to be slaves," while another fellow asks, "Has anyone noticed... that it's okay to stigmatize fat men, but it's a giant crime to make fun of fat women?" Another fellow responds that there existed a "whole tax-payer funded celebration by NOW called 'Love Your Body Day.'" Says still another, it's "time to stop pandering to these bitches, guys," in response to which somebody else comments, "Women actually instinctively like being put in their place by a man...I have five girls interested in me. Women like a man with conviction, not just a charming one."

The same Suzanne Mac Nevin, this time writing in *The Feminist eZone* (January 2008), responds by enumerating what she calls the "tantalizing prospects" for bachelors, among them the non-obligation to commit to a relationship" (haven't we heard that somewhere before?), no need to marry, no hesitation in sleeping with "many different women," no hesitation in group sex participation, no participation in child-raising, no need to support children financially, no hesitation in about living "the wild lifestyle of a bachelor." Moreover, she perceives what we have long suspected, i.e., that "there are after all a fair number of men who because their personal beliefs, do not make ideal husbands or fathers," concluding with apparent conviction that "as men get older they will undoubtedly notice the loneliness and feel like they are missing out on something," predicting too that "they won't be able to party like they once did and will be lonely on Christmas and Valentines," but after all, "one of the fundamental beliefs of bachelorism is that women are to blame for divorce."

At this time another feminine (more or less) voice lobs a threat directly at bachelors, saying forthrightly that, "I'm a bitch-princess from hell, and you're not fit to polish my tiara. No one tells this girl what to do..." A man writing a piece called "Curing Feminist Indoctrination" accuses feminists of characterizing bachelors as "a disease, an affliction, and a disability." As the battle continues to rage, one fellow claims to "have an acute bachelorism" and rather cynically pronounces that "career girls and single mothers believe that Mr. Right is just around the corner ready on one knee and holding out a ring when, in actual fact, Mr. Right is playing video games down at the pub with his mates, picking up casual women for casual sex and doing very well, thanks!" Someone else, unidentified, proposes not marriage but advises women "seeking a general relationship [that word again]" to respect a man and "treat him well," but says that "women just can't seem to do it," and in the meantime complain that "there is nothing a man can do, or not do, that feminism cannot define as 'power and control.'"

What to do? An article by Gavin O'Malley in the June 14, 2006, *Advertising Age* does everything it can to bring the sexes blessedly together and generate a few bucks at the same time by endorsing an ad in *People* magazine, imploring its readers to "join the fight against bachelorism." Here we went again. It had to do with "teams of anti-bachelorism 'activists'" who were about to take their august cause to the streets of New York and Dallas where they would distribute free t-shirts and orange awareness bracelets as well as informative *pamphlets* to folks interested in curbing the menace of bachelorism before it takes the planet over. The plan was instigated, apparently, by an outfit called *match.com* that was doing its level best to squander $19 million on "repositioning itself as being more serious about relationships," an urgent national problem exacerbated by what it believed to be 41 million bachelors prowling America's streets, looking for a home and begging from passersby.

A *Psychology Today* article by Neel Burton, M.D., July 2, 2012, called appropriately "Hide and Seek," begins by pointing out the obvious, namely that "the larger male of the species is biologically superior to the female," but, on balance, those "biological advantages and disadvantages are more or less equally distributed amongst the sexes." Nonetheless, "men are physically stronger than women who have, on average, less total muscle mass, both in absolute terms and relative to total body mass." Men's greater muscle mass, however, is the outcome of what Dr. Burton calls "testosterone-induced muscular hypertrophy" meaning "denser, stronger bones, tendons and ligaments." Women, on the other hand, "produce more antibodies and at a quicker rate than men, and have more white blood cells," meaning, among other things, that "they develop fewer infectious diseases. Men, meanwhile, have greater cardiovascular reserve, with larger hearts, [perhaps figuratively speaking], greater lung volume per body mass, higher red blood count and higher hemoglobin, not to mention higher circulating clotting factors," which means that they heal faster.

In the meantime, women have generally lower blood pressure before menopause and are less inclined to cardiovascular disease. Dr. Burton also notes that women are less inclined toward "alcoholism, antisocial personality disorder and psychopathy," along with autism, while men are inclined toward higher IQ scores, whereas women on average have fewer learning difficulties. Men can still, in old age, father children, while women's reproductive capacity ends at menopause. Furthermore, men can virtually father any number of children, while women can bear a limited number. Allegedly, the all-time reproductive gold medal belongs to none other than *Sharifian*, the last emperor of Morocco, although we haven't reviewed the exact figures. We are told, however, that Mulai Ismail (1646–1727) is believed to have fathered 800 babies, with a little help from his harem of 500 or so apparently willing women who were probably not bedeviled by such things as color blindness, hemophilia and muscular dystrophy.

Dr. Burton concludes by gently reminding us that men are, on average, about six inches taller than women who have longer life expectancies partly because they "engage in fewer risky activities" aside from perpetual pregnancies. Life expectancy in *civilized* countries tends to stabilize because men have ever lessening probability of engaging in hard labor while, at the same time women are succumbing to such degenerative habits as smoking and heavy drinking. This tends to support Dr. Burton's contention that the sexes are, on balance, at a *dead heat*, which happens to be the name of a board game, the apparent purpose of which is to determine which of the genders is indeed superior. Not everyone sees it that way, however. John Gray's *Men Are from Mars* (1992) argues that the genders are undeniably different, enough so that they may just as well come from different orbs. An article titled "The Tangle of the Sexes" by Bobbi Carothers and Harry Reis

(*New York Times Sunday Review*, April 20, 2013) estimates that 30,000 articles have been written on gender relations since 2000. Their own investigation, published in *Personality and Social Psychology* concluded, among other things, that "men and women overlapped considerably in science-related activities, interest in casual sex, and the allure of a potential mate's virginity," which, in the end, doesn't settle much, since other studies are more inclined to stress gender differences. Over and above all that, as one lame brained comedian pointed out, "nobody will ever win the battle of the sexes because there's too much fraternizing with the enemy," or as someone else said, "flirting with the enemy."

We do know that men donate hugely more to politicians, partly, no doubt, because they are in a better position to throw dollars to swine, whereas women know better. In 2002, for example, the highest percentage of donors who sent over $200, were 60.2 percent men, 30.3 women, although there appears to be a tendency to support candidates of one's own gender. In any event, the genders tend to view politics differently, which is the subject of a November 30, 2013 article by Jane J. Jones in the *National Geographic Daily News*, called "Battle of the Sexes: How Women and Men See Things Differently," concentrating, as she does, on so-called *hot spots*, images excerpted from popular motion pictures, with emphasis upon such body parts as eyes and hands. The conclusion was that "women explored more of an image than men did," leading one doctoral student at the University of Bristol in the UK to conclude that "risk aversion may explain some of the differences," in that "a direct gaze can be construed as threatening." It may come as no surprise, however, that "women may be attaching more risk to looking people in the eye," and therefore "gaze at a lower part of the face."

Be all that as it may, *Biology Letters* (August 7, 2012) dumped cold water on such seemingly irrelevant and clearly irreverent perceptions about perception when it published a Dutch study advising us "not simply [to] assume that when a trait is beneficial to one sex, that it has much to do with the other," and moreover "that genetic underpinnings beneficial to the health of one sex may increase the susceptibility to disease in the other." Endless gender differences prevail, and are likely not ever to be modified. In the workplace, for instance, *Career Builders* correspondent Mary Lorenz has presented evidence on how differently the sexes approach aspects of their working hours. Men, she reports, are 25 percent more likely to value prospects for career advancement, whereas 20 percent of woman place more emphasis upon the balance between their work and their private time. Meanwhile, employees who promote advancement are more likely masculine. Nurses represent a more female-oriented profession, and are especially conscious of reconciling their professional and private hours.

Engineers, interestingly enough, being a more male-oriented discipline, are generally less likely than most men and most women to place emphasis upon advancement for reasons not entirely clear, except that their work is more private and less public.

Such sometimes inscrutable differences spill into other complications, among them the differences between men and women as automobile drivers, something we casually cited earlier. Insurance figures tell us that no, women are no less a risk than men, or to say it in a more convivial way, men are no better than women, and that accidents appear to have not much to do with gender. Oliver Matlock's "The Battle of the Sexes: Debunking the Myth that Women are Rotten Drivers" (*autoinsurance.com*) reaches the same conclusions, albeit over the years there have been more men in the driver's seats, in more ways than one. Other evidence shows that men are predictably more aggressive in their motoring, and the accidents they have (3.41 as compared to women) are therefore more expensive than the motor accidents that women have. A site called *GirlMotor.com* sells auto insurance to women and runs ads in a screaming pink, blatantly showing us a woman in a pink dress brandishing an ignition key. An auxiliary site called "Increase Risk for Women Drivers During Pregnancy" tells us, quite frankly, that women in the second trimester of pregnancy are 42 percent more likely to experience "a serious road accident," compared to the same woman before pregnancy. A scientific chap named Dr. Donald Radelmeyer, explains that "Pregnant women often worry about air flights, scuba diving, hot tubs and other topics in maternal health, yet may overlook traffic crashes that are greater health risks," a point (if we may say so) well taken. Aside from all that, "pregnant women are generally more conservative." We've observed that ourselves, but nonetheless obstetrical literature adds that there is a certain "absentmindedness during pregnancy that is sometimes referred to as baby brain" that more than suggests that about half of pregnant women report "sporadic cognitive lapses." Even so, Dr. Radelmeyer has long been "urging pregnant women not to give up driving," having "compared their chances of an auto wreck" with men in that same age bracket who crash even more. He concludes by advising non-pregnated women to do some less than usual things, such as avoiding excessive speed, observing traffic signals, cutting back on "potential distractions" while of course wearing those annoying seat belts.

The editors of *Café Babel* published a provocative article on the alleged "101st Women's Day," that reports with barely controlled approval that there are ever "more women in places of authority," presuming that they survived the potentially lethal combination of motoring and being pregnant. Audiences reacted enthusiastically upon learning that there are hugely more women "heads of corporations and even heads of state," than ever, and were heartened to learn that the "Counsel of Francophone Women On the Bridge" was lighting things up by organizing a symbolic gathering [rather than a real one] ...while the County of Querelle [was contemplating] a "hair salon" in collaboration with a "debate...on genital mutilation," to which we say onward and upward! But to become yet more historical for a bloody change, the folks at *Café Babel* affirm that the Battle of the Sexes is, as we often hear said, "old as the stars." By George, yes. "Old as the stars," or anything that we take to be exceedingly old. We are also reminded of a person, completely unknown to us, mind you, who memorably said, "It's common for a woman to look at a [prospective] husband like an old house with lots of potential. The idea is to relieve him of whatever conforms to her expectations and specifications. One can just as well call this a perilous deconstruction, to be followed by reconstruction. All of this is an insidious process that customarily follows a wedding ceremony.

We've heard it said that "women have been remodeling their men since Eve enticed Adam to bite from the apple," a remarkably sharp observation and one with Biblical authority outspokenly supporting it. The writer, whose name we have yet to uncover, attributes this sort of thing to girls' fascination with Barbie Dolls, who eagerly await a fellow named *Ken* who in turn "arrives on the scene" whereupon circumstances begin to implode. Years later these girls discover living Kens. The process repeats itself when they uncover another naive bachelor (there are a few; let's be honest about it) who unwittingly gets himself caught and is left to devise a means of untangling himself before he's been completely devoured. In our enlightened times, some lapsed bachelors have worked out a compromise, wherein they marry for a specified period, say three years, after which they have the option to re-up or, better still, *get out from under*. Mindful of this, Matt Richtel composed an article called "Til Death, or Twenty Years, Do Us Part" in the September 28, 2012, "Fashion and Style" section of *The New York Times* about marrying (if one must) for a limited time, noting that "prenuptial agreements are on the rise, as is vowless cohabitation," adding too that "the ages at which people marry have hit record highs, 28.7 years for men and 26.5 for women." Mexico City, in the meantime, recognized short term, renewable marriage contracts with stints as brief as two years, mindful that marriages that "fail about half the time." This was not universally endorsed, since an archdiocese deemed it, "absurd," in the knowledge that matrimony, God help us, has a "short shelf life," thanks in part to the nuclear war between the sexes, although older, better educated couples do better at remaining together than younger couples do. Researchers at Ohio's Bowling Green University found that people between 50 and 64 have doubled their rate of divorce since 1964, which may also be less than surprising, since married men have learned that it's not necessarily *cheaper to keep her* after their Ozzie and Harriet marriages bottom out, although children from broken marriages suffer less from the shock of divorce than from the "disruption of their rhythm of life." Couples are also reporting that the cohabitation is less than unanimously successful, since studies show that a mere 36 percent are so much as "very satisfied," compared to 57 percent of the marrieds queried. To complicate matters, Stephanie Coontz at the *Counsel On Contemporary Families* reminds us that *'til death do us part* is a bigger challenge than it used to be, in view of extended life expectancies. Another *New York Times* article cites a comment from Virginia Rutter, a sociologist at Massachusetts' Framington State, who has suggested a "ban on all performative weddings."

Fantasy? Yes, and certainly bachelors, being bachelors, emphatically don't buy into it, either. There is little comfort in hiding, although Rip Van Winkle, almost terminally henpecked by his termagant wife, reacted by dozing off for 20 years (which happens to be the amount of time Odysseus was parted from his faithful Penelope in Homer's *Odyssey*), and is delighted to learn that his wife had gone to her *eternal reward* after she "broke a blood vessel in a fit of passion at a New England peddler." Rip's was an instance of being saddled with a foul-tempered hag who had, mercifully, expired in a rage. Until he lapsed into a profound anesthetic slumber he was terrified by her, a situation not uncommon in our time.

Ex-Army, a site designed around men who served in the military but still fear women, ran a May 9, 2014, piece called "The Dagwoodism of Sweden," that remarks on schools where students are forbidden to deploy words like *he* and *she* for fear of offending someone not altogether gender articulated. Sweden is where psychologist Geert Hofstede tells us femininity stands as a preference for wonderful things like "cooperation, modesty, caring for the weak and quality of life." The wonder is that a nation that came from the Vikings, "the finest people on earth," has been taken over (some say) by women. Hofstede concludes by telling us how, only 300 years ago, "Sweden was warlike enough," although the Swedish people "were not necessarily warlike themselves." Another commentator remarks that Sweden's flagship university was determined to attach a certain "gender certification" to its courses of study, especially through its Department of Gender Issues, the faculty of which consists of 89 percent women.

Speaking of Blondie and Dagwood, that was the popular 1930 Murat Bernard "Chick" Young cartoon that satirizes a wife's less than comical domination over her dunderheaded husband, the disinherited son of a multimillionaire, who married Blondie Boopadoop, worked for a perpetually irritated boss named Mr. Dithers, had a son named Baby Dumpling and a daughter called Cookie, and kept Daisy the dependent dog—all of them in one sense or another Depression Era types. It's all about American marriage and the gradual erosion of the American Husband who, in spite of himself, has been pretty well emasculated and trimmed down to manageable marital material that eventually deteriorated into the Blondie and Dagwood eight page bibles, pirated Tijuana pornographic parodies of the original parody. Whereas Dagwood gets roundly cuckolded and left to blunder through life with his once flapper wife, the poor fellow is more confused and confounded than the day they met. Blondie and Dag are of course gender stereotypes, she the married floozy, he the helpless sap caught between a grumpy employer and advantageously proportioned wife to whom he cannot seem to relate. He's an entrapped buffoon who, if he weren't trapped in a comic strip, might have done better for himself were he single, although he obviously hasn't the characteristics to become much of a bachelor. Were he that, he wouldn't have married Blonde in the first place. He would, were it possible, have done better to have taken her for a joyride through a psychological tunnel of love and been done with it.

Whatever else we say, women and men do not perceive in the same ways, which is all but certain to create nagging problems, preferably while they're not yet married, so to make their exits quite a bit more graceful and less expensive. Michael Connor, a "clinical and medical psychologist" at Oregon Counseling has remarked upon what we may have presumed all along, namely that "problems arise when we expect or assume [what] the opposite sex should think, feel or act whey way we do," and that "our failure to recognize and appreciate these differences between men and women can be difficult.

And while Dagwood is left to handle Blondie in the best way he knows how, which isn't very well, a bachelor can walk away and find himself another women, stay put until the same problems re-arise, then walk off again. If, as we were repeatedly told, the genders are wired differently, there's no real way to reach a detente. It begins early in life when boys and girls don't quite understand each other. A site calling itself *SixWise.com* has methodically assembled a convenient table of gender differentials and how genders react to them. It observes, for example, that when problems arise, men "retreat" (more accurately retire into solitude), the better to resolve difficulties, while women chatter to others and resent men's having reentered their caves: dark, silent, peaceful zones reminiscent of a monk's dismal cell. When the question of revenge enters the picture, men tend to seek satisfaction by (as it were) evening the score and savoring their opponent's misfortunes. Except during sex (and maybe not even then), men are far less attuned to closeness and tend to refrain from kissing anything except their pets, their guns and their golf balls. Women, as we all know, adore closeness with accompanying emotional intimacies. We recall seeing a pair of newlyweds together on a couch, with the woman exhibiting overt signs of amorousness, the man showing pronounced signs of irritation, hence the pattern of miscommunication has been relaunched.

Of course there are entertainment palaces where men and women literally battle it out. Women have tried their luck at the Indianapolis 500 auto race, but men have so overwhelmingly outnumbered them that it is difficult to arrive at any conclusions about who races faster, better and longer. Similarly, women have long competed in thoroughbred horse racing, but not in statistically sufficient numbers to draw many conclusions. We are told that three fillies have won the Kentucky Derby after about 142 years of that equestrian contest. Apparently male horses prevail because they are bigger, stronger and faster, but not necessarily more durable.

Hollywood, however, has traded long and hard on gender conflicts; the lists of films are long and getting substantially longer. Consider, for example, *How to Propose* (1913), *A Kiss in Time* (1921), *The Battle of the Sexes* (1928), *Female* (1933), *Women Haters* (1934). *Marry the Girl* (1935), *Hats Off* (1937), *College Swing* (1938), *Lil Abner* (1940), *Lady Eve* (1941), *Woman of the Year* (1942). *Don't Trust Your Husband* (1948), *His Girl Friday* (1940), *Adam's Rib* (1949), *The Happiest Years of Your Life* (1950), *The Lady Says No* (1951), *Pat and Mike* (1952), *Woman Hater* (1949), *Cat Women of the Moon* (1953), *Marry Me Again* (1953), *The Pajama Game* (1957), *The Desk Set* (1957), *Designing Women* (1957), *Pillow Talk* (1959), *Lover Come Back* (1961), *The Ladies' Man* (1961), *All in a Night's Work* (1961), *If a Man Answers* (1962), *Carryon Cubby* (1963), *Kisses for the President* (1964), *Billie* (1965), *In Your Dreams* (1996), *Taming of the Shrew* (1967), *Carnal Knowledge* (1971), *What's Up, Doc?* (1972), *Belle Star* (1979), *9 to 5* (1980), *Squeeze Play* (1981), *Maid in America* (1982), *Educating Rita* (1983), *Blue Skies Again* (1983), *The Bostonians* (1984), *Firefighter* (1986), *How to Be a Woman and Not Die in the Attic* (1990), *Spies, Lies and Naked Thighs* (1991). *Speechless* (1994), *All Tied Up*, (1994), *Burial of the Rats* (1995), *Booty Call* (1997), *Pride Divide* (1997), *How to Be a Player* (1997), *Men Seeking Women* (1998), *Body Shots* (1999), *What Women Want* (2000), *The Closer You Get* (2000), *The Perfect Man* (2001), *Two Can Play That Game* (2001), *Secret Ballot* (2001), *The Other Brother* (2001), *When Billie Beat Bobby* (2001), *40 Days and 40 Nights* (2002), *Clean Sweep* (2002), *Roger Dodger* (2002), *Risk/Reward* (2002), *Women Vs Men* (2002), *Down With Love*, (2003), *Intolerable Cruelty* (2003), *Bachelor Party* (2003), *A Miami Tail* (2003), *The Anchorman* (2004), *Bachelor Man* (2004), *The Stepford Wives* (2004), *With or Without You* (2005), *Dave Barry's Guide to Guys* (2005), *Her Minor Thing* (2005), *Trust the Man* (2006), *Toy & Moi* (2006), *The Pigs* (2006), *Caffeine* (2006), *Kettle of Fish* (2006), *Failure to Launch* (2006), *Be My Baby* (2006), *Cease Fire* (2006), *What Love Is* (2007), *What Happens in Vegas* (2008), *The Pink Conspiracy* (2008), *He's Just Not That Into You* (2009), *Alpha Males* (2009), *Women Do It Better* (2009), *Doghouse* (2009), *Let the Ex-Games Begin* (2010), *My Bloody Wedding* (2010), *The Heart Specialist* (2011), *Madrid* (2011), *Without Men* (2011), *The Great Divide* (2012), *Men, Money and Golddiggers* (2014).

It's safe to presume in all such collisions that women win (out of magnanimity) since the kosher thing is to allow it, although men may or may not be more generally rational, women prevail anyway. Our film list, merely a sampling, is Hollywood's response to gender misalignment. It shows that there's always a market for it, especially as comedy—although there's nothing fundamentally amusing about these scenarios.

Bachelors have an *easy out* because they've stayed out of matrimony and need not engage in battle with a woman about anything. Jim Philip of the *Brantford Expositor* (April 24, 2014) tells us with the rarest of candor in his "ABCs of the X–Y Battle of the Sexes" that "as a long-suffering male of great experience in the battle of the sexes, I am very familiar with the jibes and taunts of the female of the species" and assures us that he is no stranger to the "testosterone poisoning argument." Nonetheless there obviously is "a lot of competition that goes on whenever men and women get together in a social situation [where] my sex often seems to be on the losing end." He ultimately traces the seat of the problem to the genetic code that he finds in chromosomal misalliances that cannot be remedied. That, of course, is discouraging, if apparently rational. Hence, if nothing can be done to reconcile the sexes, it remains for men to take women or leave them.

Motion pictures are more than capable of finding amusement in marital conflicts, but that is Hollywood talking, not Main Street. Some of the naturalists among us are all too familiar with brown-headed cowbirds mentioned by London's *Western News*, claiming that certain feathered varieties have females that perpetrate conspicuously fewer errors than their male partners, as for example, by executing more direct paths to a given destination than their males, leading us inexorably to conclude that the female is indeed the more rational, but there's more to it. Female cowbirds lay their eggs in other birds' nests rather than building their own, something that, to be quite honest about it, we've observed before in other (shall we say) contexts. These same birds have an unscrupulous tendency toward "hijacking host's nests before sunrise," a phenomenon with which we are more than familiar. Participants in that more-than-routinely interesting disclosure may assume (and we don't quarrel with it) that these females have a superior notion of direction, more literally rather than figuratively, but we will decline to press this presumption.

We are also in receipt of a missive telling us (*SmartPak.com*, January 12, 2014) that it was a woman (yes, a woman) who stole the show at Wellington, Florida's, Palm Beach International Equestrian Center's "Winter Festival Nespresso Battle of the Sexes" horsing events, lending some credence (we submit) to the assertion of women's innate knack for *directional acuteness*, whereas we regret to say that a chap named Todd Minikus was "the only man to jump a clear a six bar round," illustrating persuasively that men are less than *directionally inclined*, especially when on horseback. By Jove, we'd rather not wish to witness that disgrace.

The battles of the sexes have been showcased at all kinds of sporting contests from the bowling lanes to the golf links to track and field contests. We must not omit to mention that gender collisions have also surfaced in offices, a matter discussed by Lauren Weber of *The Wall Street Journal* (May 14, 2013) in an article accurately titled "Battle of the Sexes: Office Edition." The genders are generously represented in such places, but between male and female workers who, as it develops, are altogether different in nature. Weber also cites another book by Barbara Anis and John Gray, fondly remembered for his *Men Are From Mars, Women Are from Venus*. Their book is entitled *Work With Me: The 8 Blind Spots Between Men and Women in Business*, which illustrates that women are disgruntled in the workplace and men don't *know why*. The result is that women feel less than *appreciated*, which is not something that men take more or less seriously. In any event, women want to be *involved in conversations*. When engaged in a conversation, it is necessary to exchange ideas with *someone else*, although conversations with one's self are not unknown. One of Weber's readers asked why women did not make more of an effort to investigate *how men think*, as if all men think in the same way. A woman responded that in an office, better communication with women is *imminently possible*. A man suggested that too much communication with women will unquestionably lead to "harassment/discrimination claims," ergo, it's better to hold conversation to a prudent minimum, especially when it has to do with frank, up-front cards-on-the-table full disclosure that may somehow end up in a courtroom, whereas men can trade contrary ideas without duking it out in a court of law. Therefore the secret to talking with women is to tell them *what they want to hear*. That's the kind of communication that provides what appear (only that) to be *sound results* in conversations with women. Bachelors, at least, keep up the mirage, the appearance, the impression that circumstances are the way women would like them to be. It comes with the bachelorific territory.

Ask Deborah Tanner, Ph.D., the author of a book called *You Just Don't Understand: Women and Men in Conversation*. She opines that "for males, conversation is the way you negotiate your status in the group and keep people from pushing you around; you talk to preserve your independence. Females, on the other hand, deploy conversation to negotiate *closeness and intimacy* which beams more high wattage light on women's alleged communication in offices and other places of business. Men don't communicate with women mainly because men are not women. Let's leave it at that. It is such women who are ever seeking an elusive *closeness and intimacy* and wish to take men with them. Men listen to their problems, size them up and offer a solution that women interpret as being dismissive. Men, for their part, don't ordinarily discuss their problems, if any, with other men. When they do, they're after a solution." As Susan Sherwood, another Ph.D., says, "Women communicate through dialog and discerning emotions; he's all action toward achieving something, the outcome." Women identify through other communicative perspectives, among them "non-verbal communication as a means of expression: eyes squinting, legs crossing, hands fluttering." Men, she explains, have decidedly more conservative body movement, and tend to sprawl while "women tend to bring their limbs closer to their bodies."

Dogs, by the way, seem to be surprisingly good at interpreting hand gestures and are keen on *intentionality*. Tanner also tells us that women in discussion sessions tend to arrange their chairs in a circular manner, the better to view each other, whereas men in their discursive modes "sit at angles to each other" while viewing other things in the room, such as flower pots and ash trays. When women are in an argumentative mode they make a case by raising questions, whereas men, as Sherwood points out, are "often simple and direct." Men appear to view women's questions as merely threatening. Women apologize to *secure communication*; men are wary that apologies will consign them to an inferior position. Women are quite free with compliments because they're a means of securing relations, whereas men are more likely to render some sort of muffled expression of approval.

When addressing problems, it's the same game. Men isolate issues and resolve them in the best rational way they can. Women want to discuss everything to death, apparently feeling that out of *earnest discourse* may arise resolution. Sherwood also discloses that "men don't understand why women don't want to solve problems" and why "they seem to disregard direct corrective assistance." Apparently they would rather chatter about those problems with a mind to solving them through emotional intervention that men are likely to regard as absurd.

Our friend Henry Higgins raised the essential, the inevitable and eternal question, precisely, *why can't a woman be more like a man?* His query makes sense to men, if not to women, who are of a mind to *getting their way* once again by attempting to bring rhetoric to their assistance, talking their way to success, while men may interpret this as mere *manipulation*, something that Sherwood claims the genders deploy in about equal dosages. The same applies to medical visits: Men succinctly convey their real or imagined ailments; women want to discuss them in a predictably roundabout manner. Women physicians are perhaps more patient-oriented and discuss the interconnectedness of health, emotional and social relationships, extending visits by about 10 percent in the process.

Hence the failure of communication undergirds the eternally ongoing battle of the sexes, even if, in an ideal world, there might be perfect communication, whatever that might conceivably be. Consider the prospects for accurate and effective communication with one's dog, if that's anything remotely close to an analogy. Communication prevails on some level or another, but beyond that a person remains a person, and a dog a dog. Possibly in the life to come, all creatures, dogs included, will communicate with pristine clarity. For the time being, however, the chances of male–female connectedness remain remote.

The February 2011 issue of *Communication Currents* addressed this point with a few contrary observations. Example: What happens when women are in positions of authority? Suppose a woman police officer arrests a male suspect? What, if anything, comes of this chance encounter? What happens when a woman university professor addresses an all-male class, especially since (as we're told), men are from Mars and this woman has lately arrived on the night train from Venus? What happens when all Brazilian women and Brazilian men happen to come from Brazil? The point here is that men and women do communicate differently—sometimes. How so? Women may be, as the article suggests, *more flexible*, that allows them to adjust their rhetoric, "depending upon the roles they are playing in a specific relationship," whereas men "are more consistent across situations," whatever that may tell us. Nonetheless the pitfalls of communication are only one baffling aspect of eternal gender battles.

There now appear to be incipient signals that women prefer effeminate men, apparently in an attempt to answer the ho-hum question of "why can't a man be more like a woman?" By selecting less than masculine men, certain woman may be on to something resolutionary. For a bachelor, this is completely out of the question and a frontal assault upon healthy masculinity. To this point, there appeared an article in the March 18, 2010 issue of *The Economist* (of all places) titled, "A Disease Free Society Helps Effeminate Men Attract Women." Oh? The piece refers us to a study by Ben Jones and Lisa De Bruine on the subject of strong women and weak men in (also in, of all places, the *Proceedings of the Royal Society*) having to do with health matters including child mortality. "The healthier the society, the less women valued masculinity," meaning among other things that "hygiene and wimps seem to go hand in hand." In still other words, when researchers sought to clarify "the relationship between women's preference for masculine and feminine men, as related to national health issues," they discovered to their amazement that "effeminate men are just as competitive" as your average village mesomorph.

Whether or not this makes any sense, Jena Pincott of *The Wall Street Journal* (March 27, 2010) reminds us that as "women are the choosier sex because they take on most of the risk and burden of reproduction and child rearing. While a man can sleep around with 100 women in a year's time and have 100 kids, a woman who sleeps with 100 men in a year will have only one baby (baring multiples)." What has this to do with masculinity? Women covertly identify masculine men as "uncooperative, unsympathetic, philandering and disinterested in parenting," traits not necessarily associated with effeminate men, who may be of quite the opposite temperament. It has been established that men with higher testosterone levels are 43 percent more inclined to divorce, 31 percent more likely to leave home because of marriage problems and 38 percent more likely to philander.

It is more likely that some women prefer less than masculine men because they're easier to control and dominate, like our beleaguered friend Dagwood, whose living legacy to civilization was a huge Dagwood sandwich. This of course does not make such women attractive to bachelors who, as we have repeatedly seen, intend to run their own affairs rather than proceed through life like herds of emasculated goats who aren't (as they say) *getting any younger*.

Should this trend continue, which it won't, we can foresee a blossoming generation of wimps, that, even now, one can perceive faintly in the distance, banging their muffled drums softly so as not to awaken their mothers and their termagant wives. The next thing to happen is their marrying each other, a trend that today is heartily encouraged and applauded in our nation's corrupt capitol. Still and all, human progress in these times is as much accountable to brains as it is to brawn, which seems to some people like a good idea. One would decidedly not much care to see a nation under the control of brutes, as can be amply witnessed in other *less developed* regions of the globe.

It has been suggested by one visionary that women who love cats love weak men; women who love dogs love strong men. In the meantime there are those who believe that the feminizing of America signals a distinct downturn in our national character that will render the nation weak and unprotected. Feminized men will become what women have long applauded and sought, namely the *sensitive man*, a fellow who wears his heart on his sleeve, can readily be brought to tears, paints his toenails and composes heartfelt love sonnets on the backs of Cheerios boxes. His sole mission in life is to keep women happy, even though they themselves have no idea how to accomplish it. The *submissive man* is one who denies his manliness and promotes an androgynous nation, which is to say a neutral culture, neutered and compromised by poor leadership.

Rex W. Huppke, writing in the January 21, 2014, *Chicago Tribune*, complained about what he called "the ongoing persecution of men in America." He cited an Australian author, an "uber-manly-man Nick Adams," who supposedly wrote that "the very fabric of our society is in danger because women are no longer allowing men to be men," although in reality women have insufficient leverage and authority to be much of a threat to men. Even so, Adams astutely commented that "we have all seen their attacks on men. It's a very hard time to be a man in today's society." Elsewhere, *The Chicago Sun Times* featured a Gerry Garabaldi article called "The Feminized American Classroom—and How it Hurts Boys," explaining that since boys were presumed to be heard too often in schoolrooms, school administrators (products of America's hopelessly stupid colleges of *education*), resolved that they were to become girl friendly to the point where boys were substantially marginalized, a problem treated in Christina Hoff Sommers' *The War Against Boys*.

It's doubtful that the feminizing of America has any direct impact on the bacheloric life, although it is an expression, as we have made clear, of the unending war waged between the mutually distrustful genders. Nonetheless, Will and Arial Durant in their famous 11 volume *Story of Civilization* (1935–1975) blamed single men for the fall of ancient Greece, averring that while "sexual and political authority continued to decline...bachelors and courtesans increased in fashionable cooperation," implying what we have witnessed before: that they identify bachelors with playboys and freelancing *Goodtime Charlies*, while decent and proper men were faithfully performing their social expectations by marrying, raising children, joining PTAs, Rotary clubs and attending church regularly—which is to say becoming thoroughgoing, head-over-heels family men, preservers of wholesome living. We find no fault in such things, although they are not characteristic of the somewhat subversive edge of bacheloric life.

The term *family man* calls to mind the more elegantly expressed Latin *paterfamilias* (family head), one who leads a domestic household, a person more than comfortable with lazy-boys, family life, applauded every year on Father's Day, and probably makes a damned good obedient husband and father who is also a good and generous provider, solid citizen, clean-living chap, a regular at high school athletic contests. Such fellows mow their lawns and sweep their clippings, play softball and are anything but feminized, except to the extent that that they have been housebroken and attended oodles of fairy kingdom weddings. Husbands are supposed to keep children in line and out of trouble, while managing to get along with their wives, all the while keeping their cars in repair and in fuel. They are supposed to fix clogged drains, carry trash out, deck the shrubbery with Christmas finery, open jar lids, work 40 hours a week, take family vacations, eschew pornography, refrain from flirting with women, call plumbers, balance checkbooks, donate to charities, follow baseball, embrace commonly-held notions of middle class morality, advance Christian thought via Sunday school's peerless honesty, embrace exemplary work habits, nuts and bolts education and support *community standards* of moral behavior.

In short, he's been defined as a provider, a teacher, a coach, a friend, a lover, a disciplinarian, a go-to guy and a more or less fulfiller of roles and other functions such as mechanic, nurse, bus driver, launderer, cook, vacuum sweeper, animal groomer, marriage counselor and amateur lawyer. He's just about everything that a bachelor is not. Those bachelors, probably not particularly *family oriented*, are without any need to be. The more accomplished and professional ones are substantially less likely to settle into the middle class that is common among most family men.

We are not referring here to *middle income*, something that politicians consistently confuse with *middle class*. Middle income has little or nothing to do with it. Middle class, as some say, is a *state of mind*, most of it pronouncedly mundane. A bachelor, if he sprouts from the middle class, ought well to conceal it, if that be possible, which it is probably is not, since it is close to impossible to represent himself in any other way. Being middle class, to put it in a snobbish way, isn't something to flaunt.

We begin with some census numbers that say "most Americans consider themselves middle class," which at least the census-taker describes as "those aspiring to be part of the middle class," hence using the word to define itself. The government (such as it is) ventures to say that middle class people "want economic stability, a home and a retirement. They want to protect their children [part of the time] and send them to college" from which not more than five percent will ever be graduated with a bachelor's degree, primarily because they are fundamentally anti-intellectual and therefore not motivated to undertake much beyond what little to nothing high schools had to proffer. They want to drive, if not own, impressive cars and take impressive family vacations. Be all this as it may, the idea is that they all want to realize their dreams and expectations, should they have any, all the while working and saving, which won't happen.

We can rely upon the following information because it comes directly from the bureaucrats at the U.S. Department of Commerce Economics and Statistics Administration and was prepared for (are we ready for this?) the vice president of these United States, his nibs Joking Joe Biden, himself a middle class dunce and married man who bobbled to the top of his not always admired profession in the District of Corruption without being born in Kenya.

The report drones on for 15 pages devoted to what being middle class really means, or, failing of that, what Washington bureaucrats *want* it to mean. One thing does stand out from this morass of pleasant sounding platitudes, and it comes from a 2008 *New York Times* survey and is therefore to be taken seriously. Only one percent (yes, one percent) of respondents described themselves as upper class and (equally astonishing) only seven percent viewed themselves at part of the lowest class. Everyone else believes himself part of the middle or working class. Such estimates, of course, don't originate from people properly schooled in sociology, and they may very well be irrelevant. They do, however, seem to feel that being a middle class person is not only appropriate but *pleasantly respectable*, if pleasantly ordinary and pleasantly pleasant. In other words, they seem to be altogether comfortably situated in the middle of things, i.e., the middle of the middle class. It's also hard to say just what circumstances would be necessary to assign someone in Dante's frozen hell or, for that matter, to assign someone else to the simple pleasures of the upper class. We're guessing that they too, like tinhorn Washington bureaucrats, identify themselves to their social class according to their annual incomes; however, to do that would be assign some professional basketball player a secure place among the most select of social ranks. Our Family Man, whom we only recently had the pleasure of meeting is (we'd all have to agree) securely situated in the mid ranks of the mid class, simply because he possesses all of its tell-tale characteristics such as slurping *burr*, Simonizing his car and taking Miss America contests seriously.

Commentator Craig Ford has concocted a chart that separates what he calls poverty, middle class and wealthy that we will take the liberty of relabeling lower, middle and upper—the conventional social class breakdown, each of which is sometimes divisible by three. Beneath his middle class category he addresses ten subcategories, the first of which is *possessions*. What does a middle class person have in his possessions? Things, that's what: loosely meaning, we suppose, just about anything, as long as he's got it firmly in his grip. Some people would call it junk, and even trash, those leftovers from his less than distinguished past. Second in category, and of unusual significance to a middle class person, is money. To a lower class person, it is something to be spent, and not very prudently spent, at that. To a middle class person it is something to be managed, even perhaps designated to any of several purposes such as home and auto payments, groceries, tickets to middle class entertainments, dental visits and so forth. An upper class person, having just about anything he ever wanted that money can buy, doesn't spend it; he *invests it*. Over time, he has invested a great deal and, to a large extent, lives off of the interest and dividends that he accumulates and even then invests. He may well drive an old and decidedly not prepossessing automobile, while a middle class person will spend $50,000 that he doesn't have on a new car. An upper class person will invest the $50,000 and wear quality clothing he purchased years ago. A middle class person possibly buys the best quality he can and is impressed by the supposedly prestigious labels on his possibly prestigious shirts. A lower class person wears what he thinks will showcase what he believes is *his unique personality*. He tends to judge food by its quantity, not so much whether he likes it (a middle class approach).

Mr. Ford also introduces the subject of time as it applies to social class, and he observes that for the lower class, "time is the right now, this instant." A more middle class tendency is to assign more emphasis on the future, assuming he has one. An upper class type is more likely to be retrospective, with attention to tradition and to crucial decisions made during his murky past that, in turn, have fashioned his murky present. Social considerations are, of course, extremely telling. It is perhaps a lower class tendency to surround oneself with people he seems to like, whereas the middle class individual is socially more self-sufficient and (truth be known) is pleased with his own company. This is more an upper class approach since it borders on *exclusion*, which is to say winnowing people out of his roster of acquaintances, always with a mind to assessing the quality, the essence, of those with whom he associates. Ford's attention to language is similar, in that a lower class individual considers words a tool for survival, rather like a can opener, while a middle class idea is more devoted to negotiation, bargaining, getting along, whereas an upper class sort may regard it as a lever to develop and maintain critical connections, i.e., correctness, coherence. Family structure? With the lower class it's matriarchal, mother-centered, since she is probably the most reliable person in the household, whereas with the middle class household it's more likely to be patriarchal, father-centered (like our Family Man), the solid citizen we mentioned, the go-to fellow, the family mainstay.

There is a foot-long upper-cased German word spelled Weltanschauung, which means world view, which means what it says: the way one views the world at large. It is a lower class tendency to see the world at close range, nearby, in clear evidence. A more middle class approach is likely to be far broader and more comprehensive, an upper class view still larger, or in more practical terms, internationally comprehensive. Finally, Mr. Ford introduces us to what he calls one's driving force, which we take to mean his animus, his motivation, his impetus. For the lower class it's mostly survival, with some emphasis upon his pals and his tastes in entertainment. For the middle class, it's one's work and what that work has or wants accomplished. For the upper class, it's the drive to be judged by financial, political and social connectivity and leverage.

Our subject, lest it be overlooked, is bachelors, especially bachelors abounding, not something that emerged out of the wreckage that lower class existence invites nor something appropriate to the middle class mentality, by which we mean some of the rather vague but still telling considerations we've been citing. Unlike Mr. Family Man, Mr. Bachelor has a few discretionary dollars in his pocket, but that's rather beside the point.

If being middle class is a state of mind, so is being upper and so is being a bachelor. Bachelordom is not a social class, but something more aptly viewed as a way of life quite apart from any other. The Norwegian-American economist Thorstein Veblen in 1899 introduced the notion of *conspicuous consumption*, the idea being that one spends lavishly to impress his middle class neighbors who of course aren't worth the trouble to impress anyway. Historically, to be among the middle class one must properly belong to the *bourgeois*, a French word meaning *burgess*, a citizen, a commoner (not a nobleman), a civilian (not a soldier), a master or mistress of an establishment, an owner of something like a house or a sailing vessel, a freeman—but one whose manners aren't quite up to snuff, maybe a bit vulgar. What's called the bourgeoisie refers loosely to middle class citizens of a small town. Such a person may be a shopkeeper, possibly to be identified by the disparaging term *proletariat*, one of the laboring classes who, lacking the skills necessary to produce something, sell their labor, occasionally also characterized as a philistine, meaning a person of poor taste, lacking a sense of proper manners and propriety, someone who is materialistic and unimaginative. In other words he's a deficient person whose tastes are commonplace and (shall we say) prosaic. Hence it is all the clearer that such a person, though he be worth a king's fortune, remains whatever one may properly call him, variously middle class, working class bourgeois or what have you. It's all quite pejoratively deprecatory, disparaging, belittling, et cetera), but we hasten to add that a middle class person is not, as they say, half bad, usually stays within the boundaries arbitrarily prescribed by law, pays his bills on time, shovels his snow, walks his dog, fills his tank and rows his boat. He occasionally reads a newspaper, but never reads a book of any description, such as the one you hold lovingly in your hand, but he drives a newer car than you do. You'll have to give him that.

That said, he clearly hasn't the right stuff to become a bachelor in the sense in which we've been using the term, partly because he hasn't the necessary social imagination to carry it off, and is insufficiently inner-directed (as we said before) to carry bachelorism off with finesse and authority, routinely to march himself toward the bacheloristic battlegrounds, or take on those gender conflicts with any authority and come out the better for it. A middle class fellow, good man that he may well be, is too conventional and ill-quipped for the task of living that sort of peculiar (so it appears) life with its not always honorable designs that we'd rather not enumerate at this time. To reiterate: the middle class fellow may even be virtuous and (by all appearances) abundantly well-intentioned. Recall that none other than Aristotle earnestly tells us that "the middle class is strong, as only the middle class can mediate between the rich and the poor," another point pointedly well taken, if we may say so, although in some circles the middle class remains under suspicion of being constitutionally smug in a way that no upper class person might be inclined. Whatever else one says, the middle class is controlled, if not dominated, by a certain elusive notion of respectability that has remained vaguely ill-defined but which has something to do with church-going and middle of the road respectability as evidenced by such things as working hard (whether by appearing to work or actually laboring), knowing how to shake hands, foster appearance (whether real or assumed), orating before Rotary Club luncheons or campaigning for a position on a school board. Withal, he's a public ally recommending tolerance and piety and keeping his blinds drawn to prevent the impression that, as one (unidentified) woman commented recently, the middle class is more than likely to be "hypocritical, staid and boring."

She may, we have to admit, have been on to something, since hypocritical usually refers to a person who falsely appears to be religiously, maybe virtuously, inclined, otherwise some scoundrel who appears (only that) to endorse a high order of morality but which, may well be ordinary middle class standards. Such a person is a fraud, a pretender, a person who feigns some feeling or another, who assumes the appearance of something that he emphatically is not. It's not a pleasant word. Combine it with the lady's use of the term *staid*; it's even worse, since it means what it appear to mean: *stayed*, which to say is fixed, constant, permanent, unchanging. In other words, it's striking an assumed pose and, by George, grasping it tenaciously. The outcome may well be boring, but it's thoroughly false and intentionally misleading, not to say pretentiously offensive. Such behavior, repulsive though it assuredly is, becomes a parody of genuine (we won't necessarily say upper class) convictions held by people who mean exactly what they say, and deliver on it.

We've said little to nothing about the implications of higher education upon the middle classes. Understanding what we do about Pygmalion, we have a tendency to believe that, if certain conditions are met, a person can conceivably become pretty well anything he desires. Given enough of the right sort of education one can to some degree (if you'll forgive the pun) extricate himself from his present circumstances and make of himself what he will, provided that he has the desire and the ability. The class system is not by nature a caste system, meaning that a person is locked into a certain walk of life because of his station or race. Caste is a Hinduistic designation consisting of words meaning both feminine and masculine, in turn meaning pure, chaste (hence the word castigate), literally to remain pure by being forever captured into a certain hereditary social rank secured by a rigid, virtually permanent social stratification with conferred prestige that may even involve occupational restrictions. There is no question but that there is a class system in American (and nearly everywhere else), and that this system has a great deal to do with one's identity, prospects, choices and so forth.

Socially, people used to talk about knowing one's place, and staying in it, which may be less severe than it sounds, since ordinarily in social and other matters, like tends to attract like, especially in matters related to social mobility. Bachelors, being as they are a social subcategory, may not so much associate with other bachelors but instead gravitate toward women mostly of their own station, a word we've been using that refers to one's state, his position as compared with everyone else's, his standing, his stopping place, meaning where he finds himself, his situation and such like. Whether or not the right sort of education can appreciably elevate one's social class is a moot (arguable, contestable, debatable) question. If this *right sort of education* is pursuant to joining any of the professional ranks, it would seem more probably to improve one's social rank, but even then one's class plays into the equation.

Finding a good liberal arts education at a good, well-seasoned university that refrains from indoctrinating gullible students (whom we used to call "young seekers after truth,") can appreciably liberate a young person from ordinarily mundane middle class habits of thought and expression. With such obvious life advantages one may conceivably improve his station and may (who knows) grow up (or down, as the case may be) to be a libertine, one who lives a dissolute, normally compromised, free-thinking, free-drinking sort of culture that may rise to the level of a bachelor, which is where the fun begins, what with the freedom to pursue vulgar thoughts and vulgar habits, the nature of which we would (in the name of modesty) prefer not to disclose. In the meantime one may see fit to jettison, or at least disguise, his middle class heritage (if any) and be at perfect liberty to cruise through life in a more or less uninhibited manner.

One could do worse, and become, say, a politician, a snake charmer, a roving jackass or, as Shakespeare used to say, "an eater of broken meats," that has recently been defined in *No Fear Shakespeare* as "a knave, a rascal...abased, proud, shallow, beggarly, three-suited hundred-pound, filthy, worsted stocking...one trunk inheriting slave." Perchance if this bachelor wanted a real job, at least he's been liberally-educated to the limits of possibility, part of the object being to enable him to hold his own with evident authority and without so much as a trace of pedanticism, to speak to a wide range of topics common to cocktail party chatter and other forms of babbling, all the while knowing that he's a gentlemanly-appearing chap exhibiting evidence of having passed several alcoholic semesters behind the ivied walls of some amply aged university where he had the rare privilege of trading ideas with some of the finest minds for miles around.

Laugh if you must, but we persist in believing that every such elegantly educated gentlemanly appearing (at least) figure will in time be that weathered face at any convergence of the wealthy and the handsomely appointed, associating with well-tailored minds of the right sort, if you know what we mean. The well-informed bachelor (we'll say this up front) is broadly (forgive the pun) the sort of chap amply prepared to manage, nay thrive, in any comfortable environment involving persons of quality. This is not merely a talent; it's the product, the outcome of these years in university libraries in the presence of other young scholars who will, in years to come, prove invaluable at assisting former classmates through the thickets of cultural confrontation.

Our subject to this point has centered upon the touchy subject of middle class life, its pitfalls and pratfalls, its pernicious pit bulls and perplexing perplexities. We have said what we could about striving to comprehend the mysterious middle class, and (by all means) evading it. We conclude this third chapter on this point: unless the potentially career bachelor has not culturally prepared himself to address the challenges that will without doubt pose themselves, he may just as well abandon the whole idea, find some apparently nice girl, marry her and disappear from sight and mind. It means surrendering to middle class mediocrity (if this not be redundant) shaped by generations of working class men and women who, in lieu of having prepared better destines for themselves, instead surrendered, body and soul to a morbidly depressing existence, nothing more than that. Every right-thinking young man plainly sees life's bifurcations and has not neglected to opt for the primest of prime options.

Chapter IV. Bachelors in Paradise:

If life were best lived as couples, we'd all be Siamese twins

It all began (and ended) as we find mythically explained in *Genesis* (chapters two and three), when an agrarian-oriented God planted an allegorical garden east of Eden and gathered every tree that was pleasant to behold and life-sustaining, most notably the tree of the knowledge of good and evil. He placed there Adam the first man, on the proviso that he, on pain of death, must not eat from that tree, then (in a seeming afterthought) declared that "it is not good that the man should be alone," after which there appeared "every beast of the field and every bird of the air. Adam lapsed into a coma, a kind of Biblical anesthetic, after which God relieved him of a rib, out of which God created a woman, although this is not the only Biblical account of womanly creation. They naked were, and were also (in so many words) *married*. Eve, as she came to be known, allowed a serpent's guile to persuade her to eat the fruit of that forbidden tree, after which she and Adam were regrettably introduced to the nature of good and evil and thereby relinquished their innocence. They were hereafter cursed, rendered mortal, made to eat dust, and were subjected to a number of terrible things, among them *mutual enmity*, meaning intersexual strife. From that moment forward it was *paradise lost* for them and for the human race. *Genesis* is the *work of many hands*, which is to say it is an endlessly ambiguous and mythic fragment of folklore, at once simple and complex, cunningly expressed and widely scrutinized, if not as a theological lesson then as an anthropological puzzle.

The title of this chapter is "Bachelors in Paradise," something that can be construed in different ways. Adam was, for a regrettably short time, our archetypical bachelor. Today there are folks who speculate seriously upon whether bachelors can anticipate any Heavenly expectations, since a good many bachelors are viewed as common scoundrels, if that. There is a heated debate on just what metaphysical prospects these scoundrels (if scoundrels they be) possess, to be found for popular example in a site called *Create Debate* that on July 14, 2014 carried a provocative essay redundantly called "Can An Unmarried Bachelor Has [*sic*] Hope in Heaven," which we take to mean either has he any prospect of finding it or, having found it, have any prospect of enjoying the multifarious amenities believed by some to flourish there. Other perplexing matters enter the controversy, to wit: granted that if Heaven exists (an *a priori* assumption), whether these blackguards can justifiably be considered *eligible*. One reader cogently asks, assuming that they make it through Heaven's heavenly gate, *will anyone marry them*? Other perplexing matters arise, and will arise again. *Can they be saved?* We'd rather not venture an opinion. Yet another voice asserts with evident authority that "nobody wants to marry them," or possibly if they can be married, they repair to some other place to have the ceremony accomplished. Another citizen comes to the fore, saying that since all marriages are made in Heaven, *it's a* decidedly *done deal*. But other controversies continue. Still another person asks whether, if married couples can partake of heavenly bliss, can unmarried couples do the same. On that too, we prefer to defer to more speculative minds than ours, for fear of offending someone and for fear of embarrassment.

Says another citizen with apparent confidence, "there is no marriage in heaven," as if to assume that any damned fool knows that, but on whose authority? Yet another fellow takes the floor, shouting: "Whether you're married or not...it really doesn't matter" since "a marriage certificate means nothing." A different voice enters the discussion, attesting that "I do know in Heaven there wouldn't be any marriages, nor would anyone really care to get married in heaven." Why? We'll tell you why. "If you're feeling like a million dollars [strolling over] streets of gold" you don't need matrimony. Another citizen dismissively tells us that "heaven is for escapist[s]."

If Heaven doesn't materialize quite soon enough, there's always Brazil, overwhelmingly recommended by a chap calling himself *Sancho*, published in the September 10, 2013 number of *Brazil Dating*, where we're assured that Brazil "is definitely a place every single man must go once in his lifetime," averring that one visit is quite enough to sate his insatiable bacheloristic lusts since, according to "men who have traveled the world in pursuit of women," it is the *Brasileiras* who "are simply the best sexual performers on the planet." Nonetheless, be advised that "if you've never been with a Brasilian woman... you will be convinced it's love," that's probably not exactly what a bachelor has exactly in mind. Lust, after all, is as Sancho concedes "a common feeling to have when around Brazilieras." We're beginning to get the idea. "It's all lust." We like the sound of that, so long as we don't feel obligated to get married. Sancho cautions us to be wary: "Many men fall in love here...because it's so easy to do." He ends his comments with a rousing "God Bless Brazil!"

Herman Melville composed a narrative entitled, "The Paradise of Bachelors and the Tartarus of Maids" in 1853. The title says it all: that bachelors may, with the utmost confidence, look enthusiastically forward to bliss while women in this tale look forward only to a Tartarean blizzard. Melville's bachelors are, for some reason or another, hoping some day to become lawyers who live in a state of earthly bliss that he calls their *Temple*, a site of complete capitalistic chaos. The narrator has come from a New England paper mill staffed by young women, all of them dehumanized, everlastingly faceless drones, while the bachelors apparently represent the capitalist ideal of elegant living, being, as they seem to be, well educated and well fed. The long and short of it is that bachelors have all the advantages that lead them to self-indulgent liberty in this earthly paradise.

Recent figures tell us something quite different, that on average, the younger bachelor is not necessarily the wealthiest, most privileged sector of America. Theirs is an after tax income of $32,300 compared to an average of about $51,330, and they're 50 percent more likely to join the army, oddly enough, than spend a week living it up with Brazilian girls. Instead, they work 42.2 hours a week and are paid less. Few young bachelors occupy penthouses, but about 42 percent occupy single residence homes. If they're renting, it's costing about $1,160, which is about $270 less than average. Bachelors, being bachelors, are partial to pools of the kind that hold water, and folks of their profile represent about 12 percent of the adult population. They drop $400 per annum on clothing, compared to married men who drop about $280. The average bachelor, if he's not entirely reclusive, spends about $2,100 entertaining himself, which is about $500 less than average, but he also spends 6.8 percent on spirits and 7.4 for tobacco. He is likely to be a homebody but allocates about $1,200 to getaways, about half what the average American adult allocates.

If a bachelor is serious about migrating to Heaven but thinks it a touch on the improbable side, he may nonetheless be *looking into it*. Chicago, for instance has bachelor-preachers, one of whom claims to have been *praying* since the age of 18 for the right sort of woman to tumble unaccountably out of a cloud. What, then, do such bachelors mean by *Heaven*? Nearly anything they want it to mean, since (despite newspaper reports) no one has been there and then returned to reveal its mystical mysteries, presuming that there be any to reveal. That said, the more imaginative of us envision it as that indescribably magnificent place where the sun, moon and stars form a huge canopy that arches majestically over the world. Those who claim to have seen it report that it is engulfed in clouds, beneath which lies firmament over which birds fly and where God and angels reside. Dante Alighieri reveals all this and a bunch more in his *Paradiso*, advising us that it is the domain of the *virtuous*. In Jewish thought, we are availed to seven heavens, the highest of which is the abode of God, the lesser of which is a place the most blessed regard as home, or whatever else they choose to call it, if indeed they call it anything. We've been told that marriages are made in Heaven, the implications of which are various and, to say the least, ambiguous. It apparently means that the earthly pairing off of genders is orchestrated from *above*. To some bachelors still in the midst of their *halcyon days*, Heaven may be as close as such impossible places as Brazil.

It's been frequently observed by better minds than ours that a good many of the personalities we've had the privilege of knowing have been consigned, however erroneously, to Hell, with its customary temperatures, the corollary of which is that a good many of the less than engaging persons with whom we have at least have shaken hands, have been assigned to Heaven. Your average Eskimo, having passed his frigid days in the comfort of an igloo, may, to a point, warm up nicely to temperatures of about 70 degrees Fahrenheit, or may, in the nether world, prefer to consider it an eternity of frigidity. Dante, the world's foremost authority on Heaven and Hell, assures us that sections of Hell are, yes, frozen over, as befits the cold-blooded atrociousness of those condemned to pass eternity in that region locked, as it were, in an ice cube.

Bachelors, in the meantime, have been known to practice the dastardly practice of unabashed *womanizing*, about which we will have a good deal to say. By *womanizing* we don't mean turning men into women. We use the word hesitatingly to mean (we blush to say it) those who play upon and abuse the disarmingly sensitive psychological tendencies that women possess. And what precisely is seduction? It's the disgusting practice of luring women through the astute application of psychological manipulation, with a mind to encouraging them to *surrender their honor*, then to wander regrettably astray (in the moral sense of that word) for the erotic and dastardly amusement of some rogue, not necessarily a bachelor, although yes, there have been bachelors reputed to have participated in this ungentlemanly chicanery. We are not personally acquainted with such unrepentant and unprincipled caitiffs. No. We at least acknowledge, if only through intuition, that they're out there, and that they're up to their customarily coarse stunts, snares, tricks and ruses, motivated by their lechery and their vile lewdness and unabashed debauchery. We won't call such men gentlemen, given that they assuredly are committed to their unbridled baseness and sexual incivility that involves unremitting woman-chasing, and all but hydraulic skirt-lifting. We refer to such men as *Casanovas, Don Juans* and *Lotharios*, lady-killers, libertines—disgusting philanderers all. Worse still, they're not above preying upon ostensibly upright women, claiming all the while to be *in love* with them, of all preposterous things to assert. They're fellows who, chances are, maintain a gallery of unassailably fine women, even ladies, to whom they have directed their stale, amorous lies. There are even fellows who would, more than anything, *aspire to become* womanizers, but haven't quite got what it requires to succeed in that shadowy activity through the customary trial, error, dishonor and common legerdemain. There are men out there who actually idolize these ruffians to the place where they're jealous of them.

If you're a woman in the market for a husband, you can more likely satisfy yourself by taking up with a hydrant or a dead tree rather than coming to terms with a womanizer who may otherwise be your best (if only) bet. Bachelors, we've made abundantly clear, as blockheads say, aren't much interested in matrimony and, to be quite candid about it, are just not into doubling up. If ever they did allow themselves to be lured into romance, they would be out there philandering at the earliest opportunity, for a brace of purported reasons, central among them that they *don't much care* for confinement and would *just as soon* like to present themselves to a dozen or so other conveniently approachable women, depending upon the phases of the moon. Will womanizers be welcomed into Heaven? We don't know whether there are womanizers currently in Heaven, and we can't say whether there is even one. Personally, we'd rather not take the question up; we do know that the average womanizer remains a promising candidate for admission to the *Bad Boys Club*; we'll give them that.

What, we may ask, do women who have victimized by womanizers have to say? Listen to this: "I dated N for a year, and clearly a commitment from him was not happening." That's not the best of signals for a woman; we agree. Why not spring for several psychiatric sessions to discover what in blazes ails him? It might be worth the investment. Next? "To really hurt a narcissist [i.e., a womanizer] you must injure them [*sic*]." Whips? Chains? Next? "Can a womanizer be reformed?" We wouldn't bet the farm on it. Next? "What are the signs of a womanizer?" Women can't get enough of him. Next? "What is a serial womanizer?" Redundant. Next? "Have there been any well-known womanizers?" Remember Jack Kennedy? Next? "What is a *roué*?" It's a word employed to describe the Duke of Orleans that's come down to us, as beanballs say, referring to a man's having the requisite energy to perform some of the vile things we just described, meaning that he's out to satisfy his beastly self.

Womanizers operate in predictable, even familiar ways, many of them neatly summarized in an unsigned (we can't image why) document explaining what it takes to succeed at it.

It's called "Womanizing Techniques" that matter-of-factly elucidates the fine art of seduction as one might explain the finer fundaments of fly fishing, which, in a way, it is. Might we repeat some of the more salient points pursuant to ravishing women? No. We emphasize that it is neither our objective nor our intention.

Let's continue by saying that accomplished womanizers (or at least *some of them*) foster what's been called a *clean-rich* theatrical presentation, regardless of whether the scoundrel is either clean or rich. We assume that by *clean* the intention is to represent him as free from anything that is sullied, one who is apparently neither defiled nor debauched, but remains (dents and all) in reasonably good condition, free too of any sort of wretched filth, common dirt or other defilement. The fellow wants to appear guiltless, guileless, altogether innocent, above suspicion, having no treacherous intentions, faultless, chaste, with no darkly sinister motives.

Were we to guess, we'd have to say that bachelors are not necessarily the most morally upright of chaps, but then again we don't necessarily know who the more probable candidates are for Heavenly *presentment*, as it's been sometimes elegantly called. It might be the eventual abode of barnyard preachers, rope-dancing rogues and other random rubbish. While we're on the subject, there are those well intentioned people, even what most well-meaning of them, who not infrequently asked whether dogs, being as they assuredly are, morally superior to womanizers, have any realistic prospects for a blissfully eternal destiny. That question has long bedeviled some of the more spiritually gifted, not to say most *theologically sophisticated*, scholars of our enlightened time or any other. We have little doubt that philosophic recognition of this learned sort continues, even to the present hour.

A site called *Clarifying Christianity* assures us that, to the best of anyone's knowledge, there are angelic dogs. This begs the question of whether at the moment of death certain dogs and people become *angelic*. Others have asked whether newly-minted *angels necessarius* are elevated, or perchance elevate themselves, to the highest of all places in the divine cosmos. Another oft-raised question is whether anyone (we mean *anyone*) who without fail has obeyed the Ten Commandments (that assuredly excludes bachelors) enjoys the fast track to the Great Beyond. Still other citizens have asked (and asked often) whether folks who frequent a church, any church, have the inside track to salvation, and whether one might joyfully anticipate more church-going personalities in the life to come. These are issues (we're partial to that word) that, even in our more lucid moments, we find ourselves utterly incapable of uttering any kind of considered response. In the meantime there are those who, quite rationally, raise the perplexing question of whether, having kept score (as it were) of one's less than becoming acts are less frequent than his holy acts, he might, as they say, plea-bargain his way securely into the Great Beyond. For a response, we defer to more elevated intellects, and that's an end to it.

While such metaphysical questions rage on, there are women, some of whom (let's say for the sake of argument) who have been complicit with those naughty boys who may (or *possibly* may) be en route to their supposedly *divine destinations.* We regret to bring women into this controversy, but it's something that we all need to confront. Question: Do women, even the best of them, advance to those same heavenly destinations as unrepentant rogues? One wise guy responds, *no.* "They stay behind [to] clean and cook and do the laundry," a snotty retort if ever we heard one. The sorry fact of it is that we simply and totally don't know, and therefore suggest that we ignore, or maybe drop the subject entirely, since contemplation leads only to quarrels and other forms of intellectually divisive discord. Next? There isn't any *next.* The case is closed.

Wait a minute! What about more enlightened prospects for those dogs and possibly other beasts like coyotes, dung beetles, raccoons, fruit flies and such? Have they no theological possibilities? No. Dogs, and we mean all dogs, are forbidden in Heaven. Why? We don't feel prepared to say *at this time.* For the time being, it's no dogs. Don't forget it. We won't have dogs roaming at will around Heaven pissing on hydrants. We won't have it. That's an end to it. A recent Gallup Poll (we take Gallop Polls with the utmost seriousness) reveals that 80 percent of those polled believe that people (some of them, anyway) proceed up to Heaven when they die, and we don't mean to Scott Fitzgerald's *select Episcopal Heaven*; we mean the less select Heaven appropriate to ordinary church-going folks, upright guys, window-washing, bird-feeding, lawn-mowing *solid citizens.* Whether bachelors have standing (as lawyers call some entitlement for certain people to do this or that, while others don't) for heavenly election, remains uncertain.

We do know that Western Carolina University undergraduates who have a whole lot of *standing,* made a few observations about the odds of their passing through the *pearly gates* without a *pat-down.* According to them (and they're nobody's fools), dogs have a 57 percent probability, while cats (we're referring to house pets) trail, but not by much. Fish, bless 'em, come in third at 49 percent, rats at 48 percent, mosquitoes 45 percent, while earthworms crawl behind. If we had to say, we'd say that bachelors, the best of them, mind you, have only about a 43–45 percent probability, mostly because they've endorsed things that other men probably haven't, and therefore right-thinking people of all descriptions take a decidedly *dim view* of them. We have a tendency to urge others to *fall into line,* if you catch our meaning. Bachelors, though they have been known to *fall in love* (until they thought better of it) but have seldom *fallen into place*. They pay a steep price for this disobedience, as well they should. What right, we ask, had they to seduce women while other decent men are variously available, willing, prepared and undone to volunteer as husbands? We rest our case.

Henry Thoreau wrote in his Brook Farm journal that he'd far refer to keep what he called a *bachelor's room* (whatever that may have been) than "go board in Heaven." We'd rather not want to know that his *bachelor room* was, but we hasten to add that Henry, God save him, was probably one of the world's greatest bachelors (and proportionately one of the world's ugliest men) if not in Heaven, but in the next chapter. We don't think (and we've looked into the matter) that Henry *cared a whole lot* for women, and to be sure, had a mind and a will *all his own*. So well remembered is he that his conspicuously modest tombstone carries the name *Henry* on it. In the meantime a scribe named Yabke Tauber has written an article called "Bachelors in Heaven" for the July 7, 2014 *chabad.org* that raises some provocative questions, to wit: with men, women never quite know that they're getting into. "You meet the man of your dreams," she says. "It's love at first sight; you practically fall off your camel the first time you set eyes on him." Sound good? What does it *bode* for marriage? The word is more than enough to send most bachelors into hiding. Will he, in the end, find some select bachelorific home in Heaven? For the nonce, he's busily minding his own *affairs* with one disreputable person or another.

We quite comprehend in principle what *being wealthy* is, since the word does not occasion much elaboration, except to say that if one is wealthy he is somewhat more likely to be overbearing, opulent, overrun with possessions, amply prepared for nearly any outrage, extraordinarily abundant and readily abounding in some exquisite sense or another. If women were to choose between poverty and wealth, chances are that they might opt for wealth and whatever amenities and strategic advantages attend it. A woman is also likely to articulate the crucial words marriage and maternity, since to the feminine gender marriage is precursor to reproduction, even when there isn't any. Women receive the word future, even if there is little to no future awaiting them until a man intervenes and deploys the word we (cited earlier) as a feminine expression not necessarily outside a man's vocabulary, but essentially so. We mean doubling up, pairing off, marrying, closing ranks, and fostering (we nearly said festering) that awful word togetherness. There was, and possibly still is, a television channel called WE, meaning (on the surface of it) "women's entertainment," a clever title. A man then waxes fast and loose with earnest words of endearment and becomes just as fast and loose with expressions of endearment. It has been suggested that professional womanizers begin applying the language for the obvious purpose of hastening their seductive objective, all the while speaking women's alluvial rhetoric, leaning upon the correctly sentimental nothings and current clichés.

Others have posited that a bachelor falls (as it were) into the category of sociopathology, meaning for example one with a certain personality disorder (such as a preference for seducing women instead of marrying them the way a normal man would unhesitatingly do), all the while exhibiting alarming anti-social signals and related behaviors, but not without surrendering his fiendish manipulative and egocentric characteristics similar to ordinary sometimes happily married folks are with their serial lying and their occasionally deceptively seductive charm. That said, there are men who cultivate the skills pursuant to communicating (more or less) with women on their own baleful terms. They engage in this because it's fun, erotic and even *sporting*. It's just another psychological gambit. Men who participate in this sort of thing feel, *to a man*, that the grass is always greener a few doors up the street, which it usually is, or shows every sign of being. They are perfectly aware that their disgusting gambits will fail over half the time, but that does nothing to dissuade them from experimenting within their theaters of emotional engagement.

Mara Tyler of *eHow* offers the following sensitive advice to sensitive women who (ironically) happen to prefer womanizers even when they *remain* womanizers. She writes, "If you're interested in dating a womanizer, you should be prepared for a long and possibly difficult road to commitment." *Commitment!* There's that word again. We haven't seen it in quite a few pages. Mention commitment to a womanizer and he'll bolt, down a fire escape, out of town and out of sight. Tyler continues her counsel by suggesting that a man who has a womanizing reputation needs to be approached "much differently [from] other men." Has she any suggestions? Yes. "Since he typically stays interested only if there is a chase [good point, for once], it's important to always [split infinitive] keep him on his toes and require him to pursue you." How, we ask, might that be achieved? Best of luck. At this point another women leap rhetorically in, claiming that the best strategy is to decline his offensive proposals for a while, since womanizers supposedly enjoy *the hunt* (as just mentioned) and then persist, theoretically. And oh yes: don't accommodate him any old time he proposes something lewd, unless of course it's marriage. This rather begs the question of relationshipping, presuming there can be any, between women and womanizers. The answer, a good bit of the time, is yes—other times *no*. Let's leave it at that.

At least one apparently reliable woman places bachelors into a different, more approachable, if overly optimistic *subset*, believing, as she seems to, that this *someone* she finds will not only need to be tamed *like a stalking a pet mouse*, but potentially will be a very promising partner in a *relationship*, that dreaded, recurrent term that *resonates* (as jackasses say) among certain persons with rhetorical disorders. She continues, "His heart will be formed only on the woman who was capable of taming [that word!] his heart, and he'll be in heaven," the one with oodles of free-ranging, eternally roaming bachelors and pissing dogs.

We'll see, but let's not allow optimism to run away with us. As long as the good times prevail, a true womanizer will be there, womanizing for all he's worth (which may be nothing) and all she's worth, and then some. Eventually the potency of her persuasion exceeds the extent to which the womanizer is prepared to exert his. It's then best for him to take on another moving target, or better yet to target a woman with a compromised inclination for resistance. Bachelorism, remember, isn't a sickness; it's a robustly healthy state of perpetually revolving between pleasure and the impression of it. Nor is it necessarily anti-social, except that there are those who claim that (unless one joins a cloistered religious order) the only normal life happens after a man is married. This advice, as we have repeatedly seen, is the purest of illicit rubbish. One woman, whose patience was exhausted, tells us that one accomplished womanizer is so in demand that he'll take women only by appointment, similar to what one would discover in a popular gynecological clinic, except that it's less hurried. He accommodates them at, let's say, 2:00, 4:00, 6:00, 8:00 et cetera, after which he's pretty well depleted until the following day.

Another excellent womanizing strategy (let's call it) is for the perpetrator to represent himself preposterously as, of all ridiculous things, a virgin. The nerve! There are chaps out there who are not entirely entitled to be represented as forthright. It's one of the world's best kept secrets (as dipwits call them), but it is nonetheless not unheard of (as other dipwits insist upon calling it), but it's an outstanding example of what depths these rounders will stoop to.

Rounders do not much bear that burdensome cognomen on their shoulders anymore, but perhaps ought to be so branded once again. A rounder is a chap who *makes the rounds*, which may be well and good, but in this context it *assuredly isn't*. It refers to one who makes the rounds of such detestable places as alcoholic saloons, prisons and workhouses that cater (so to speak) to drunkards slackers, loafers, itinerant berry-pickers, politicians, women of compromised virtue, blackguards, dog walkers and all such riffraff, not excluding the vilest of womanizers.

We've reviewed one woman's guidance on how to extract a commitment out of a womanizer, but to elevate the matter to a securely higher plane, how is one to transform this rogue into an obedient husband and family fellow?

Personally, we are less than sanguine about the possibilities. Others, of course, embrace other points of view: man can be *brought to book* (as morons used to say) with a pleasant disposition; men of this stripe are deucedly difficult to uncover and recover. Another tack will be to happen across an aging womanizer (we'll have more to say about them in the next chapter) who has devoted some thought to being looked after in his maturer (we don't intend that in any pejorative sense) years when he may well have forsaken womanizing in favor of that old time religion of morbid monotony. Another woman (we presume) tells us that in general it is folly to make much of marriage anyway (a point especially well taken) if it's necessary to subdue men. There are some professional womanizers who, instead of marrying, close in upon mother–daughter combinations and are therefore among the dregs of their horrid occupational subset, such as it is. They're clearly in obvious need of psychiatric overhaul. The shortest way is to march them (blindfolded) before a firing squad and await the countdown.

Another thing that this type of rogue may attempt (although we're inclined to question it) is to assure some helpless woman that she is his candidate among the myriad other women of his intimate acquaintance, and that he might (*might*, mind you) agree to enter into holy matrimony with her, except that (there's always a catch) she will have to represent the highest of personal characteristics, if you get our drift. Any fool can see that what he's proposing is improbable, if not outright curiously outlandish. We've heard of a few cases where the tables are exactly turned, when a woman teases a womanizer into marriage with a mind to farming him out (at a price, of course) to the lonely and lovelorn. This means that she has a despicable womanizing husband on her hands, but at least he turns a profit. We applaud this prospective wife and admire her resourceful ways of humiliating a scoundrel while making a little bread and butter money on the side. Now, that's an original idea that deserves some not-too-serious consideration. Desperate women (and there are some, but we can't think of any) can actually enroll in a sort of rent-a-rogue in untamed places like Alaska, where one woman vulgarly put it, "men are men and caribou are nervous." We think we've heard the message.

Women, at any rate, and of any legal age, are combining to give it a try, as boneheads customarily say, and at least it accords a hearty Dionysian effort (we'd rather not be specific) for the benefit of these cheerfully participants, and wish them well in encouraging something of a lascivious nature that may attract the attention of women of a certain age (as Henry James called it), and thereby avoid being at home after the sun sets, if you see our meaning. We wish them well and presume that they remain within certain generally understood limitations.

Speaking of a certain age, young bachelors may very well evolve into older bachelors, depending upon how committed (look out!) they may be, not to women, but to running off with a mind to recovering the sort of lads they once were: free-wheeling, self-sustaining inner-directed stout-hearted younger blades. It's proven satisfactory before; it may just as well prove out again. Sam McManus of *The San Francisco Chronicle* (January 26, 2003) correctly observed that older bachelors obviously refuse to marry merely because it's expected (in some circles) of them, just as it was in their 30s, 40s, et cetera. Through it all they escaped being entangled in any matrimonial net. Nor are they covertly homosexuals, a common charge used to undermine them. Nor too have they miraculously discovered what women call the love (of one's) life, which is of course utter romantic balderdash. It's also repeatedly alleged that women are commonly suspicious of older bachelors, probably for good financial reasons. They are not likely to be hoodwinked, nor are they likely to be hustled into circumstances contrary to their better judgment, such as blundering into marriage early in life before they're even dry behind their ears. Then there is the matter of an older bachelor's being *set in his ways*, another pejorative expression, inferring that they've been trapped into life's ravines, unable to help themselves through, buying into current, foolish, passing trends and demonstratively abominable fashions.

He by this time knows what works and what doesn't, and he's not about to experiment. "The marines," an old marine colonel once told us, "aren't for everyone" and neither is matrimony. If a man is incapable of monogamy, then he has no business stumbling into matrimony, especially when he's not exactly marriage material. Such things happen. Besides all that, late life bachelorhood is an advantageous adventure all its own. If you're not married, we've been reliably advised, chances are that you're not overweight, although with advancing years one becomes aware of life's hideous meltdown and with it the possibility of unanticipated mental collapse. With it, however, is a keener sense of who one is, where one came from and where one has gone, or more likely failed to go, with his ridiculous life. The pattern of existence now begins to fumble into place with greater clarity and pristine understanding; it's no time to take on a marriage or any other high risk. To the contrary, it is a time for a bachelor to refine his bachelordom, which is the ideal older age arrangement, especially if it continues to be cleverly managed. One also has the challenging prospect of identifying new illicit objectives and (when feasible) realizing them.

By this time a man has an even clearer comprehension of women and how to identify with them accordingly without the customary grief, bewilderment and dismay. There are short term bachelors out there who seem to think that they'll strike out for themselves and find another wife and discover bottomless bliss. Such fellows have been called none too kindly bachelor goons, i.e., bachelors who never were the sort of fellows who keep their shades down, so not to be bathed with sunlight. Judson Culbreth in his "I Don't Want to Get Married" illustrates, evidence to the contrary, why over-fifties women don't want marriage, and asks why, at this miserable time in their lives, they would seem to promote it, this echoes what older bachelors have been saying for generations, although a goodly proportion of them never seriously entertained the idea during their adult years. Mr. Culbreth argues that, for one thing, they've got loads of company, and if they don't they can damned well find it. Time was when such women were the objects of pity, treated condescendingly like old maids, female throwbacks that no men claimed as wives, women who survived well beyond the customary age limitation (so it was once commonly perceived) for marriageability, whatever it may have been. It is still obviously true that some ostensibly presentable women remain, shall we say, as unclaimed freight in marriage after a succession of men astutely recognized them as premarital hazards, and left them decidedly alone. The term old maid, we further regret so say, pertains also to a certain bi-valve mollusk, and to a card game that demands the removal of a queen (interestingly enough), from the deck. Old maids have also been called spinsters, which brings to mind women hunched over a spinning wheel, in preparation for weaving the fabric for some younger woman's bridal gown. Spinster has also been applied to a spider or other sinister creatures given to spinning webs. Mr. Culbreth ventures that some of these women have variously been married or been taking care of others, and are now ready to put all that behind them. Besides that, bringing a husband on board (so to speak) is far too complicated and too problematic, especially when such women are financially sufficient. The same line of questionable thinking applies as well to certain older bachelors who demur in complicating their lives after all these singularly single years. It's not likely to work.

Then, truth be known, such people secretly, or not so secretly, wish but to prolong their philandering youths. Call it immaturity, if you wish, be we find no fault in preserving some of their 20s and 30s. It's not half so foolish as it first sounds. One need not surrender to acting his age. There seems to be a prevalent feeling that bachelors can be statistically quantified with vital information, such as how many times a month they dine, so to speak, with women. One need also not submit to acting out other people's expectations,

There is growing perplexity in Israel about pairing eligibles off and getting them married, that strikes us as a questionable, if well-intentioned, campaign. Judy Siegel-Itzkovich, writing for the July 14, 2014, English language issue of *The Jerusalem Post*, comments at length on that ever-expanding trend among religious singles who can't seem to form up matrimonially together, even though "building a Jewish home and family is the modern Orthodox ideal from childhood." So seriously is this taken that for "thousands of young and not-so-young in Israel and beyond," a counseling service has been established to, as it were, fix them up, on the apparent assumption that marriage is to be regarded as an obligation, even though early marriages often result in matrimonial uncoupling, but still has among its objectives "the importance of romantic love as being nature's selection process of finding a suitable partner" at any age.

The perceived seriousness of over abundant Israeli bachelordom also finds excellent expression in Lilach Weiss's "Life Story as a Therapeutic Process Among Israeli National Religion Singles," illustrating that "the community" considers bachelorhood a problem primarily "because in spite of religious prohibition, "singles are susceptible to engaging in pre-marital relations," and furthermore, "bachelors without families of their own do not belong to community institutions" since they appear to represent "self-fulfillment by virtue of their bachelorhood."

The menace of bachelorhood seems to have left its footprint (as idiots say) upon Japan, too, according to Andrew Miller in the January 19, 2013, *JapanToday*. "The number of men and women choosing to marry later in life," he writes, "is on the increase and has reached a figure that no longer can be ignored," which conveys a ring of desperation supported by an ostensibly simple survey that asked men two ostensibly simple questions: "Have you ever thought, 'marriage isn't for me.'?" and "Have you ever thought, 'I prefer the life of bachelorhood'?" The results were a mite on the unanticipated side, to wit, 39.7 yes, 60.3 no. The men who responded with a yes were invited to comment. Their responses were unequivocal: one man remarked. "When the boss grumbles about his family, it makes me think that I'm better off single." Another commented, "Just looking at my married friends and how day by day they become more and more emaciated, makes me think that I'm lucky to be single." Yet another says, "Hearing about the way cruel wives treat their husbands turns me pale with fear." Another: "To me, married men just don't look happy, and the more time passes, this look of unhappiness becomes apparent." Another: "hand[ing] over all your earnings to the household and being given 'pocket money' by your wife leave me muttering, 'you've got to be kidding!'" Another: "Rather than having your wallet squeezed of its last dime, spending your earnings as you please has got to be the more appealing option." Another: "All your hard earnings, in the blink of an eye, disappear into oblivion. That is housekeeping!" Another: "My job's not a fixed contract; so I can't imagine that bringing up a family would be a bit of a struggle." Another: "My pay check is too low to support a family." Another: "Keeping relations with your partner's family is bothersome to say the least." Another: "Putting up with the nagging from the other half's parents takes its toll." Another: "I like my free space and I can see that if I were to get married I'd lose a little of my free time." Another: "Going on dates is admittedly a lot of fun, but I've lived the single life for many years now. I don't think I could bear someone else entering into my space." Another: "From impressions alone, marriage means throwing my hobbies out the window." Another: "I like drinking and gambling, but tying the knot would surely mean an end to all of this." Another: "After the stress of my work, being able to unwind alone in peace is what it's all about for me." Another: "When things get busy with work and you're not getting home until late, the last thing you want is to keep company with the other half." Another: "Those living the single life seem to retain their youthfulness longer." Another: "Just looking at my relatives and how peculiar they are, makes me think that having any offspring would be a mistake," Another: "I've got too much of a mother complex. I can't see myself breaking away from my mother for the sake of, say, a partner." Another: "I can cook better than most housewives and I'm not afraid of housework either. I'm also pretty good at my job. Bringing someone into what is a more or less perfect lifestyle is simply unnecessary."

They confirm, among other obvious things, that to prolong bachelorhood indefinitely, especially for a lifetime, obliges them to assume roles that have ordinarily been within the province women, i.e., meal preparation, routine laundry, fly-swatting, housekeeping tasks, grocery and other household purchases and decorating decisions. There is nothing necessarily gender related about any of them, and if there were, it wouldn't matter. Since Adam's once golden days, men have managed surprising well on their own without fretting about what's for dinner and when to mop what requires mopping. Those are easy tasks that men handle without much adult supervision. That, by the way, rather diminishes notions of what purposes wives have in the more or less civilized world. We've all heard of house husbands and stay at home boys, awaiting the miraculous return of a wife to glide, sans souci, through the front door, paycheck in hand. Meanwhile, the house husband has enjoyed an especially less than flattering life, clipping coupons, viewing soap operas, pushing sweepers, telephone gossiping, folding diapers, ironing unmentionables, awaiting the ceremonious reappearance of the family breadwinner, maybe gussying up a bit, inquiring about how things went at the office, paying a few bills, swatting a few more flies, reporting on what's for dinner. A few men find that they're not (as they say) cut out for such domestic assignments, but to be quite forthright about it, such a man aptly represent the result of domestic taming and housebreaking.

Kate Hahn, a *Details* commentator, mentions one New York matchmaker who "gets calls from hundreds of single women asking for setups." For supposedly promising young men under 35, her fee is a modest $25,000, and for men over 35 it hikes up to a reasonable $50,000 that sounds like a cross between a slave market and a stockyard cattle auction. For some men it means "being bonded to one person for life" if it results in matrimony and in the process "losing a huge part of [one's endangered] identity," concluding that such matrimonial "overreaching is typical of the unmarried chap in his early forties who tends to think that nothing is good enough for him—that perfect partner isn't right around the corner."

While this is transpiring , bachelors remain under a heavy mortar attack, which may be as flattering as it is threatening, since it raises the hideous prospect of surrendering their lives to some matrimonial circus—anything but a pleasant social spectacle, unless one is a woman who craves weddings especially when they're hers. A bloke calling himself *Midas Mulligan Magoo* at a publication calling itself *WallStreetOasis.com* observes that young men's bachelorhood, while it survives, "is the most prized period" in their lives, having, as it does, "an air of debauchery, rebelliousness" and other such deliciously footloose vices that are also about to fall under full siege, except that, (in his view) the encounter *has been lost.* At any event, our fellow may or may not have had the masculine stamina to ward off what he knows to be something not, (as we say) in *his best interests.* If he has surrendered, it might signify that he never was the best of bacheloristic material from the outset. Other men would have fared better under such matrimonial pressures. The bacheloristic life isn't for everyone, because it requires will and determination to overcome certain lethal social and cultural pressures. There are certain men who are not about to *commit,* which sounds eerily like a suicide attempt, something that in many instances may be preferable to marriage.

There is no need for men to make excuses, although our favorite one is to protest (at any age) that one is not *old enough* for matrimony. One can easily find probabilities and impossibilities, such as that boys who have a high school diploma begin to consider marriage when they're about 23 or 24. Men with substantial (rather than flimsy) university degrees begin to give it some circumspect thought at about 26, whereas men who enroll in graduate colleges don't on average reflect much about it at all, because they're apt to know better and because they'd rather study medicine or jurisprudence than turn themselves over to a life of domestic domination. In other obvious words, the more education a man accrues, the more unlikely he is to under sell himself, partly because more education means more of life's prospects and possibilities. Bachelorism is particularly attractive to the professions because it confirms that professionals make the right rational sort of decisions that demonstrate maturity and self-realization rather than a lock-step adherence to patterns dictated by the mob.

Bachelordom is for a lifetime, and a conspicuously abounding one. When an arrangement with one woman begins to go under, he quickly paddles on to the next, without being fatally swamped. It's what we call *perpetual bachelorhood* that might (who knows?) extend (as we conjectured) into the next world where all the fun experiences (we'd also conjecture) keep on being fun, possibly *more fun*, with nary a wedding day nor a divorce in sight. Such is perpetual bachelorhood. Some might call it, ominously, *chronic bachelorhood*, which sounds like some venereal disease, but it can last for a hell of a long time without ill effect, and is, in most circumstances, an especially good thing. Think of it as a life lived outside of jail, where one may variously be locked up or locked down. For those who feel more secure being held under lock and key, we heartily recommend marrying the first woman who waddles by.

There are men, lots of them, who consciously opt for this. A possible bachelor may at this time review the implications of surrendering (we use the word advisedly) to military life, such as it is, with its regimented lockstep, endless badgering and order-taking, without once complaining, but such a man is emphatically not bachelorist material. He might, as we used to say, have made somebody a good wife. The fellow hasn't the right sort of temperament.

It is Nature's (upper case N) way, i.e., the normal, orthodox means of proceeding, the customary method of acting and reacting, for a healthy, good natured, responsible fellow of the right stripe to close ranks (let's put it that way) with some female, and do the natural thing, to wit: remain in the same quarters for the balance of his insufferably monotonous life, and reproduce, for the presumed good of the economy and the human condition. When he passes into the life to come, he does so with the immense satisfaction of knowing that, yes, he's left persons (optimistically speaking) behind, the better to reproduce his own likeness who can proceed to fumble through life. For this sort, marrying means being cooped up together and replenishing the earth and shutting up about it.

There always remains that lingering problem of having to coordinate one's tastes and inclinations with someone else's before reaching a compromise on the most trivial and insignificant of petty decisions. If life were better lived as couples, we'd all be Siamese twins. A man's eligibility for marriage rests on the extent to which he can, at some woman's whim, be deconstructed and reconstructed whether he needs or requires it, or not. *Expert bachelors* don't react well to having themselves rebuilt to suit some wife's current tablet of arbitrary specifications. It's better to be guided by *self-determination*, which means what it says: arriving at determinations by and for one's self without the interference of others who would enjoy nothing better than to supervise somebody else's impossibly ridiculous life. There are young men of immense potential; the last thing they need is someone policing them and forcing inappropriate choices on them. When this becomes clear to our heroes, divorce follows; and following their divorce, a goodly part of their property predictably vanishes.

Some once respectable universities are currently geared to feminist indoctrination, whereas *by their nature* those same universities were once institutions that encouraged the free exchange of civilized ideas, received or otherwise. In such an environment single men are less socially accepted, apparently because they're perceived to be a bit too independently inclined, something that, in modern civilization is to be discouraged, since most matters are determined by committees and other know-nothing assemblages. New efforts are afoot to publish extensive and even lengthy politically filtered columns of words that citizens are *forbidden to utter*. Married men appear to be easier victims because they are submissive to their wives (mostly one at a time) and their employers (mostly one at a time) until that fine day when, it ever arrives; they set sail on their own. Group activity is all the thing.

One bachelor of our acquaintance offhandedly mentions that "I see 95% of my married friends have put on a lot of weight...while I'm planning my third trip to South America." Another fellow says that he's taken up with "30-something women [who throw] themselves at you without a grain of salt," but in the meantime you must "always keep investing in yourself." Precisely, Bachelorism provides for constant renewal, reinvigoration renewed self-investing. It's the imperial archway to lifelong refinement without constantly having to justify oneself or accept unsolicited advice from those ill-equipped to advance it. Apropos of that, we cite another anonymous comment that reads, "There are a lot of men, the majority, I suspect, [who] prefer everyday boring people with no sense of adventure, no intensity of desire...no interest in experiencing the world." Similarly, "If you're a woman whose overwhelming, driving ambition is an eternal passionate love affair [,] you're in big trouble."

Every real man is his own best friend; every real man is secure in his self-knowledge. This is why we refer to them as *bachelors abounding*: at large, at the ready, in control, under nobody's guns except their own. All considered, bachelors should be happy, and more than that, happy that they keep that provoked, solicited jealousy coming. We've never known an unhappy bachelor unless perhaps he's under padlock somewhere. We've known bachelors to be dissatisfied about various unpleasant things, but not about being a bachelor. One of its joys is becoming an *affront*, which is a kind of veiled, quite frontal assault, deliberately conceived and adroitly delivered with a tinge of insult to taunt (for the sport of it) other men by intimating that "I play a different and far superior game than yours. So there." We are by now into the petty sin of bragging and ought not to carry the gambit excessively far.

There is a confrontational site called *Superbad's Excaping* [sic] that outspokenly recommends a life populated by seriously happy-hearted bachelors who are more than pleased to explain their good fortune, some of which they're about to credit to good luck. An older fellow speaking to a younger fellow says straight out that it's crucial to avoid and evade what he calls *the matrix*, a word we won't pass over without a closer examination. It directly refers to a mold, a die, something that duplicates. In Latin it denotes a pregnant animal, one used for breeding, perpetually self-reproducing like an old ditto machine. The message is directed toward would-be, might-be happy bachelors, advising them on a number of fronts, one of which is to "forget the game plans of the typical American" and sidestep all of the *matrices* by, for example, seeing to it that there are no marriages, no pregnancies, "things that we are pretty familiar with." And financially? "Find a job. Save every possible penny, spend none of it on women, buy an old Dodge truck, buy a home, plant rows of apple trees." The intention is to become what's now known as an *uber bachelor*, that is to say a universal, self-sustaining chap whom the world has but seldom had the pleasure of beholding. Such a fellow carries a license to be happy and remain so. Habits such a man needs to nurture include taking care not to attach his life to a woman's, to eat well and properly, exercise regularly, meditate, create solar heat, generate one's own power, save and invest, do without a mortgage, learn to fly, avoid acquiring what one doesn't need, hunt with a bow and finally speed learn."

Liberating enough? Superbad advises that we enjoy life, enjoy nourishment, enjoy the seasons, enjoy privacy, enjoy music, enjoy the rising sun, enjoy sleeping, enjoy waking, enjoy intellectual activity, enjoy selective learning, enjoy certain people. Do not, our advisor counsels, bother with other people's obstacle courses. Anything else? Yes. Understand that "the poor wish to be rich. The rich wish to be happy. The singles wish to be married and the married wish to be dead."

The objective is to be rational, one of the basic of bacheloristic characteristics. To be rational means to be reasonable, correct, right-minded, sensible, clear-headed, gifted with sound judgment which means that one does the things that make sense. As bachelors know, it means doing rational things that others don't seem to do or can't do or ought to have done. What other people think and do, since they're far less than rational, means nothing.

The right kind of man knows instinctively what to do, and sets about doing it while others stand mawkishly by, hands in pockets, minds in neutral, motor running, cell phones buzzing with voices better left unheard and not believed. The bachelor is entirely on his own. It's too good. It's just too good.

Bachelors need never run out of women, inasmuch as they draw upon a consistent, bottomless pool. It's rather like defying the aging process. Women, as they pile on the years, haven't quite the same advantage as for them, the pool of candidates seems to evaporate over time. If a man has a problem with one woman, he can reach for another (and in all probability encounter the same problem).

There's a father's day on the calendar, and there may just as well be a *bachelor's day* as well, such as there is (so we're reliably told) in China, every November 11, to recognize detached, presumably marriageable men. There are Oriental *goodtime guys* for whom every day is bachelor's day, generously full of valentinian excesses. There was once such a day set aside for women to adore one fellow, that being the allegorically named Rudolph Guglielmi Valentino (1895–1926), the short-lived Italian-born movie actor once apparently idolized by every woman on the planet. Valentino, *bachelor extraordinaire*, was a world class gigolo who had a hell of a time—while it lasted. The term *gigolo* (originally taken from *gigolette*, meaning prostitute, dancehall trollop or escort) correspondingly applied to a professional male dancing partner, from the Middle French *gigeur* (to dance), a kept man, a young chap supported financially by an older woman as a *house pet*. A gigolo, obviously, is not altogether to be regarded as a bachelor, in the sense that we've been bandying the word about, because he is presumably (or to all appearances) under the weighty domination of some shameless woman.

In 1922 the *Woman's Home Companion* disparagingly declared that a gigolo is "generally speaking is a man who lives off a woman's money." Another 1922 editorial voice called a gigolo "one of those incredible and pathetic male creatures who for ten francs would dance with any woman wishing to dance in the cafes, hotels and restaurants of France." In 1927, one newspaper reported that an "audience was delighted with granny's dance with gigolos— as lounge lizards are called." But what had Valentino to say about the throngs of women who craved his attention? "A man should control his life. Mine is controlled by me," apparently endorsing that indomitable self-reliant streak common to bachelors at large.

Over time, however, Valentino showed signs of losing his vinegar, saying that "I am beginning to look more and more like my miserable imitators." But what about all those panting women? "Women are not in love with me," he protested, "but with the picture of me on the screen. I am merely the canvas on which woman paint their dreams." Even so, Rudolpho was not above living the giggly gigolistic life in New York where he worked as a *taxi dancer*, a fellow who pocketed a dime after dancing with some swag bellied woman, and later cultivated the image of himself as a *Latin Lover*, although the impression he made as a gigolo was in real life was undermined by the sobriety of more than one marriage. At least he looked the part, fostering the bacheloric image which was more the appearance than the reality. Bachelors, real and happy ones, maintain a secure distance from older, possibly wealthy post-menopausal women. Because they're apt to be excessively controlling, which is the last thing they want. and because they have more sprightly younger options. There are, nonetheless, men who are more than happy to sidle up to such women for a combination of ambiguous motives, one of which may be to take them for a psychological gambit, possibly involving wealth. Meanwhile, the women participating in this game try their hands at emasculation.

Taking up with a succession of women is, as they say, all in the chase. As one candid (and somewhat lazy) bachelor says, "When I am chasing, there is no pressure to succeed," but when the chase concludes, he says, "I call it quits," a concise explanation of *the chase*, which is undertaken for its own sake. It's a game, a challenge, to be compared with pole vaulting without the pole. Or the vault. It has been claimed that, when there was greyhound racing, dogs were urged onward by the lure of a mechanical rabbit. If and when a dog caught up with the rabbit, he sniffed it circumspectly and raced no more. His racing days ended. So, too, there are men who love to pursue, to chase, even to stalk, but the game terminates as soon as his success is assured. Other men, having caught a fish, return the fish to the waters and continue fishing. Their object is to advance from A to B, but it stops there. If one receives a trophy, he gives it away and commences to secure another one. It's entirely possible that, if handed a women, he would give her away and set about finding another.

This game can, however, be interpreted as a means to exercise certain virtues such as bravery and courage, the way certain men volunteer for dangerous duty in dangerous places like Philly, why certain fellows walk a tight wire between two sky scrapers and why police seem to enjoy placing themselves in the direct line of fire (until they're fired upon). It may also be an activity chosen to determine just how much one can get away with, without being stung, nabbed, skunked, mugged, shot or arrested. Seen in a different light, the bachelor is a hunter and women are his prey, although it isn't quite so primitive as it sounds. It's also a matter of chasing the unknown. Any new acquaintance carries a trove of biographic revelations that the more curious among us have a passion for *uncovering*, maybe disrobing. Then, like the racing dog after it sees the reality of the decoy, it's all over.

This is type of curiosity is psychologically normal, but there are those who don't have it (and who are mostly quite stupid). Bachelors, by and large, are anything but dumb; and so, they are ever in hot pursuit of something. Inquiring minds want to know, find out and move on. This also explains why the better educated among of us have logged more years than four in massive libraries, perpetually investigating, and then having done so, turn our investigative passions elsewhere. So too, a bacchanalian adventure with every new women is a foray into unexplored psychological regions. That too never ends, although it's questionable whether women approach situations such as these with quite the same spirit, since they're more likely to nab their prey—*and run*, rather than routinely moving on to the next, presuming there is a next. By that time the bachelor will, if we may say so, have come, gone and conspicuously left no commitments in his wake.

Hence, chasing is an end in itself. Once we've won the game, we leave the playing field contemplating our next encounter. If this sounds like a football game, it is: just another more or less pointless male activity played for the amusement of playing, possibly now and again actually winning. Were women winning at football, they'd take the football home with them, bronze it, place it painstakingly upon a mantel, and *play no more*—unless the opportunity arose, which it probably won't So it is that instead of having one woman, a bachelor would rather have six. The objective here is to demonstrate to himself *it can be done*, that there are six, maybe a dozen others out there in the weeds, ready to play ball. The only way to settle the question is to test the waters. Every bachelor does it. It's similar to wondering if one could win a tennis title or even a tennis ball, assuming that that's what a certain person desperately wants at a certain time. The only way to find out is to find out; to see how far one can go without being permanently humiliated on a tennis court. Indeed, bachelors must learn to deal with occasional rejection since it comes, as they say, with the territory. It has to do with taking a chance now and then. The chase is all. Good night, ladies.

This raises the deeper question of bachelorific risk-taking as, for example, in financial investing, sports, military battles and all such challenging things. Freud speculated that men who participate in death-defying activities are acting out what he called their *death-drive*, meaning we suppose that in the minds of some men, risk-taking makes them feel invigorated, more than merely alive. They are otherwise known, not too sympathetically, as *sick takers*, as opposed to *risk takers*. Woman-chasing is, as they say, a far cry from lion-taming as an expression of risking too much for too little (more easily identified with bachelors than with the ordinary blokes one finds stalking in supermarkets). Taking a chance means that one runs the risk of losing, sometimes losing big. It's like placing a $1,000 on a horse's nose. Those with a sporting mentality make other men seem like submissive mice. To win is its own immense reward; one feels better about himself than before, having taken a big chance and made good on it.

Evidence indicates, to no one's surprise, that men are more inclined to assume risk than women, and for a number of reasons, some subtle, others not. Men are more inclined to reenact feats performed by their ancestors eons ago that have somehow or another come down to them by means of what's been called their racial memory, an inherited inclination that finds its origins incalculably long ago. It has also be posited that risk-taking is at heart a tendency among people wishing to create and sustain their own identities by distancing themselves from others, breaking free of those ridiculous societal habits and customs that we cited earlier. It's a means of separating themselves from the common run of common people.

We know by now that bachelors are intriguingly different from the common herd, and they derive surpassing pleasure from it. It attracts the right sort of attention, for one thing, and showcases things like their unusual risk-tolerance that distinguishes themselves from others, being more than usually prepared to follow their inclinations, not for the purpose of appearing different, but having responded to their natural inclinations to become what they are by playing from a different set of motivations and ends. Hence, bachelors are anything but risk averse; rejection comes with any ambitious person's territory and is, as certain people say, part of the cost of doing business. After all, they're constantly making rather outlandish (by common reckoning) proposals that have a high probability of being rejected as exactly that: *outlandish*. Every so often its outlandishness will indeed bear unexpectedly excellent results, even if it's (let's say) five percent of the time. Others will pass it off as good fortune, being lucky, no more than that. But the five percent is every bit worth the trouble, No one who takes rejection too seriously is going to be enjoying much *abounding*. Rejection is merely, to dredge up yet another cliché, all in a day's work, even for people who, like bachelors, are accustomed to getting what they want when they want it.

When that fails to happen, it has little or nothing to do with how happy or unhappy they happen to be for the next ten minutes. There are instances when being rejected even turns out to be fortuitous because it wasn't the keenest of proposals in the first place. It's also entirely possible that the person who did the rejecting made a huge mistake by turning something down that ought not to have been turned down. These things happen, but they're not to be taken too much to heart.

We know that bachelors have been customarily typified later in life as lonely, rejected, pitiful and impossibly eccentric old men (some of the time) whom no one invites to holiday dinners, alone and unloved, without the wife that bachelors are presumed to need and cherish. The poor fellow hasn't the advantages of a richly varied social life among chatty people who hover over his shoulder, attempt to boost his crippled morale and rescue him from the profoundest of depressions by cordially inviting him back into the human race. It's all quite melodramatic, and not commonly bacheloristic, inasmuch as bachelors prefer the solitary life to the point where they interpret invitations as *orders*. They're by inclination anti-social, meaning not that they're inclined to criminality but that they can't very well be bothered with socialization, preferring, as they do, their own excellent company rather than a room stuffed with jabbering, socially-addicted chatterboxes fawning over each other. A Michigan State University survey found that "at age 29 unmarried men had an average of 1.3 antisocial behaviors, compared to 0.8 among married men," the obvious point being that the marriage experience renders them more amenable to social relations, if only because they spend so much time with their lovely and accommodating wives that they'd rather chat it up with someone else for a change. It also has been suggested that by being married they have more to lose from antisociality. Bachelors, far from being socially dysfunctional, function perfectly well, although there is such a thing as a socially active bachelor, something that appears, at first blush, to be a contradiction in terms.

The bacheloristic personality tends to take a dim view of married men, probably viewing them as having surrendered themselves to a domestic existence that will do them unanticipated damage. The emotionally unstable English essayist Charles Lamb in "A Bachelor's Complaint of the Behavior of Married People" explains at the outset that "as a single man, I have spent a good deal of my time noting the infirmity of Married People, to console myself for those superior pleasures which they tell me I have lost by remaining as I am." He continues by saying that it isn't so much the quarrels that married have, but ironically that they "give the impression" that they "prefer one another to all the world." later noting pointedly that marriage to him is "a monopoly" that he finds "obnoxious." Obnoxious or not, it's enough to send a bachelor galloping toward the exit, as if he were exposed to some vile disease that he's bent on escaping. Obviously too, this hasn't gone unnoticed. Helen Dowd's "Plight of the Toxic Bachelor" (*theguardian.com*, August 10, 2006) goes on the attack of just this sort of renegade, pointing an accusative finger at "a generation of "toxic bachelors…risking their lives by drinking, smoking, taking drugs and playing Russian roulette with their sexual health," all dangerous tendencies that await treatment by marriage's therapeutic and civilizing influence that supposedly transforms such men into something more accommodating than they were as disgusting *street bachelors* and other such common riff-raff. It may come as no surprise that men are, at times, less social, a conclusion reached in *The Rath Institute Blog*, published on December 8, 2010 demonstrating that whereas men "with fewer nasty qualities," were more likely to "end up" (which sounds at first blush like their plowing into a brick wall) married. The article continues predictably by declaring that marriage has a rather *salutary influence* on men, rendering it easier to house-break them and subdue them to the point of being even socially presentable, at least in a minimally acceptable way, as evidenced by a one sample group's 35 percent drop in criminal activity, making them all the more like marriage material.

As we've seen, there have always been those who regard bachelorism as a crime, and to exacerbate the problem women are believed by some to be *fatally attracted* to them. The bachelors to whom refer were weed patch variety tough guys, drug dealers, wife battering predators, bullies, horse playing, psychopaths and such like who happen to prefer (however loosely) to be seen as bachelors but find themselves locked up in some god-awful matrimonial jail cell, possibly all the while receiving seductive messages from women who are apparently attracted to this sort of fellow, and find him ironically pleasant and receptive. There are some who refer to this sort of chap as *a bad boy* (to soften the blow) of which there are no shortages in jail houses. Evidently a certain kind of women finds a certain kinds of criminals an *amorous challenge*, although that seems improbable. Christopher Orler's "Bachelorhood and its Dissidents" (*The New English Review*, 2008) tells us that there is something vulgar, almost absurd, about a Ms. Plato or a Mme. Descartes or a Mrs. Wittgenstein on a honeymoon, simply because intellectually viable men as marriage partners seems wildly improbable. There are those who cynically repeat the cliché that "the bachelor is an undeserving guy who has cheated some woman out of a divorce." In Nairobi these days, bachelors aren't necessarily admired, but are commonly viewed as slackers who never married up and reproduced so that life might continue its dreary road to a dreary existence. Not to do so is to be viewed as an "oddball who [refuses] to the honorable thing and not [eventually] marry two or three times" or even take a serious fling at polygamy, to show the world that he's a right-thinking guy who sees his duty, and by George does it. Nairobi, quite needless to say, isn't some *bachelorific paradise* that we've heard about, but let's remind ourselves that such policies and customs as these are the products of unenlightened nations who haven't especially mellowed their thinking to 21st century confusion.

Rightly recognized, bachelors as we have identified them are in a social/cultural class all their own and have penchant for seductive habits of mind ought well be recognized and celebrated for the rationalism they've ordinarily endorsed, and the steadfast way they persist in being what they assuredly are. They offer us all refreshing glimpses at a life that many had never before imagined and examined. It used to be popularly said that behind every successful man was a woman, someone one who acted as his illustrious career co-pilot. Wives are no longer necessary for this purpose because they are merely to interfere and interrupt. Those discouraging marital statistics that we viewed with horror and dismay show us that fully half of those marriages disintegrate, and the other half somehow or another patch together for better, but more likely, worse. There are also those who say that wives follow their husband's leadership meaning, we take it, that one of his many tasks is to manage himself and his wife who apparently doesn't manage herself. This becomes just one more bother, and an unnecessary one, at that. We are also informed that wives, even the few good ones, mind you, sustain their husbands, assuming that they need to be sustained. Others say that it is her duty to maintain her husband in the particular way he was when she first enticed him.

Regardless of such tactics, marriages wear thin, differences develop and there is little probability of reaching compromises and other concessions. In the meantime wives are encouraged to treat their husbands with unbridled respect, at least until the honeymoon ends. They're also encouraged to communicate with then so that they have an understanding that survives for *nine whole innings*, which in all probability, it won't. Communication implies that a partner will presume total comprehension with the other, something that won't happen, even in the best of cases when partners appear to be glued by means of psychological ploys intended to secure them, something that bachelors clearly don't want and expressly don't need. Since married men are sexual prisoners, they're left to make the best of it without all those bacheloric advantages, especially the ones that foment all that extraordinary jealousy. Some of these are legal, in that marriages are a whole lot harder to get out of than get into, as those sadder but wiser 50 percent of former husbands will tell you in an unguarded moment. There may well be problems in getting along with one's in-laws and erstwhile friends. Beyond that there is a formidable list of potential snags that confront the unprepared and the unequipped. Ironically, however, married men seem to survive longer, even 13 or 14 years, than the unmarried. This was concisely explained in *Genesis* when it declared that "it is not good for a man to be alone," although the term *man* may be taken in its broadest (if you will forgive the pun) sense of the word. One may also, and without fear, infer that the single life, particularly the bacheloristic one, is appreciably more intense (in the best sense of that word) and therefore bachelors possibly *flame out* a bit sooner, having had fun *while it lasted*, as nearly everyone says with some regularity, even when they're not having any. Ironic too is the penalty of having a longer life, a situation that never seems to terminate. It is not uncommon for couples to fanaticize about the death of their spouses who appear to be experiencing if not enjoying, eternal life. One study tells us that marrieds live longer because it provides "emotionally fulfilling, intimate relationship[s], satisfying the [supposed] need for social connection," that strikes us as doubtful, although we agree that being married necessarily involves some pronounced *behavioral tune-up*, not always for the better, as for example prompting a *sedentary existence* that may therefore involve health *issues*, as dimwits call them, such as depression and major league anxiety. Our friends a WebMD counsel us that "there are many reasons to choose wisely when picking a wife." No kidding. We might add that there are a good many reasons to pick no wife at all. A psychiatrist (we won't name names) also counsels us that "selecting a spouse," if one must, "is more serious than choosing a house or anything." No kidding. Take this bit of down-home advice for what it's worth. There are plenty of people out there who would rather have a home than a spouse because, as the psychiatrist goes on to concede, "Marital strain can aggregate cardiovascular disease," We can just imagine.

Whether or not being married extends one's life (there are other reasons to challenge that assertion) married folks reportedly have a proclivity for developing diabetes. Swedish research report that married women have three times the probability of a second heart attack. True. Contentedly married people, if such exist, seem to make out far better, It comes as little surprise that in the rest of marriages, blood pressures rise (until partners are parted) then come back down. Evidence shows that couples survive marriage better if they're *real good* at managing stress. Others tell us that it isn't marriage, *per se*, that extends life; it's the quality of that marriage that tends to lessen risky behavior, possibly because pairing off palliates, housebreaks and mollifies men. The Canadian newspaper *The Interim* (December 21, 2010) carried an article by Pauline Kosalka entitled "Marriage Tames Men and In Turn Helps Society," that directs our attention to "the long term horizons of female sexuality [we weren't aware of any] since a man "has to change" and "settle his life" (We don't like the sound of that) because marriage obliges him to endorse "the mother-and-child bond," which means that the husband discovers himself reduced to childhood, and willingly surrenders to emasculation while submitting to feminist authority. Whether this helps society is at best questionable. Yielding to feminine control and domination is not likely to be in anyone's better interests.

A psychological paper by Satoshi Kanazawa at New Zealand's University of Canterbury argues that marriage actually inhibits creative genius in men. Yes. You read that right. This is essentially the same observation that Albert Einstein made in 1942, namely that "regardless of age the great minds who married virtually kissed goodbye to making any further glorious additions to their CV. Within five years of their nuptial vows, nearly a quarter of married scientists had made their last significant contribution to history's hall of fame." Kosalka concurs, citing the "dampening effect" that "directly affects their creative lives," whereas "unmarried scientists continued to make scientific contributions later in their lives." Part of the motivation behind taming men began with the observation that teenaged boys carry enormous deposits of testosterone that oblige them to seek and find sexual outlets, and that this situation calls for their taming, so to be brought under control like so many wild horses.

That said, men stay clear of marriage simply because it is too impossibly confining and because (as we have repeatedly said) the bacheloristic life is enormously more attractive, not only for the short run, but for the long. A fellow calling himself *Mack McMunn* has written that men are rarely happy in marriage because "the biggest enemy to a life fulfilled is routine and boredom." And what of men who have taken the matrimonial bait? They are "on display, a zoo animal that does what he is told, eats when told, works when told." There is, in fact, an article on husband taming in the June 8, 2010 issue of *BeyondJane* that proffers some sensible tips to wives with a mind to defanging rambunctious males. But why? three crucial reasons: 1) "to get what you want or desire," 2) "to feel secure and 3) "to feel a mixture of better and superior," hence fostering the impression, at least, of her being a better and more privileged person than her husband, rather than preferring to be more or less equal to him. The idea is to reconfigure husbands psychologically in the same way that military training transforms fat, drooling recruits into faceless automatons. We've been told that there are at least a dozen personal features not to be challenged when reconstructing a man, among them the poor fellow's upbringing and family background, his dump ditch education, his ridiculous peers, his pitiful income, his hopeless environment as well as matrimonial type, i.e., whether his supposedly amorous motivations arise out of love or whether they have been encouraged by a third party.

That much established, the taming process begins with emphasis upon seven factors. One of them is to keep him happy, after which it is important to feed him well. Having accomplished that, the next thing is to pamper him by giving him a bath now and then, followed by a perfuming and powdering, which implies that he's being feminized. Next, the poor sap is treated to a sanitary and tidy household, followed by doing something naughty, whatever that may entail, possibly by having his hands and feet massaged, and finally being permitted to "hang out with the boys for a beer" which means lengthening his leash, but not without establishing a designated time for his obedient return. The intent is to modify his behavior without seeming to order the poor devil around with military commands. The ulterior motive is to de-masculinize the goon without his realizing it. The fellow under reconstruction is clearly not bachelorific material, if only because he does not stand up for himself and not to consent to marriage or anything leading up to it, being aggressively manipulated to the place where he seems to like what's being done to him. Elsewhere there are large numbers of large women conspiring to *feminize their husbands*, dressing them in pink and even donning them in women's clothing, including lingerie. Unless there are children involved, the manly thing to do is walk out, never to return, never to marry. If he has the makings of a bachelor, which is doubtful, he will never be back. It's even possible that his domineering wife will be quite relieved to see him off, speaking of which we are reminded of the lovely Montana bride who saw her husband off by pushing him over a cliff after eight exotic days and nights of matrimonial bliss. This remarkable thing happened at Glacier National Park, after which a U.S. magistrate didn't take the second degree murder charge too much to heart, and chose to interpret her condition to heart, and released her on condition that she wear an *electronic monitoring device*, move back with her parents and seek a little help with her mental health problems "to alleviate any risk that she might harm herself," another point well taken.

In a similar case, this one in Tennessee, a woman was so fed up with her preacher-husband that she blew him away. Literally. This all transpired in the sweet little village of Selmer, population 4,500, more or less. She could very well have been sentenced to 60 years in the pokey, but instead got a three-year sentence which somehow became 210 days. The trouble started when the preacher allegedly insisted that she view some choice pornography right there in the parsonage and wear slutty costumes. Besides that, the poor woman exhibited inescapable signs of post-traumatic stress disorder, having pointed a shotgun at the poor cleric, the better to communicate. That's when the gun went off. Last seen, she was back behind the counter of the town dry cleaning establishment, executing business as usual and living with friends. It was just another of those marriages that couldn't be saved. Such things happen across America every day, even in the best of bowling-pin Christian families.

Chapter V. Gershwin's girlfriend, Casanova's cuties &c

Bachelors are a conspicuously, elusively, even mysteriously curious bunch, to be sure, and they surface (as folks say) from all walks and runs of life. A few of them are remembered mostly *as bachelors*; it's their identity: relentlessly self-invented fellows mostly of the right sort, independently-inclined chaps envied by married men (not a few of whom are overmastered by jealousy) and resented by certain kinds of prying women because they won't permit themselves to be trapped and tamed into the dungeons of domestic life.

We've had a tolerably close look at a few of them sociologically, demographically, physiologically, temperamentally and of course statistically. Now we'll have a still closer look at some of the better recognized, more outstanding instances of such fellows, ancient, modern and between, who have shared this enviable persuasion. They tend to resist our scrutiny because they're not all so otherwise temperamentally similar, because they predictably keep to themselves. If you rap on their doors, they may not respond. We can at least attempt, for the enlightenment of us all, to bring them together for a darned good roll call, if such is within the portals of possibility, to hear and otherwise extract their notions about life, love, destiny and all such searching avenues of mature bacheloristic existence and theory.

Our selection of a few of these more curious bachelors may not pivot upon such otherwise ordinary matters such as chronology, height, weight, nationality, zip code, blood type and count, golf handicap, credit rating, et cetera. Besides that, most of them are dead. Nor is it particularly to any avail to trace through the ages in search of some mystic, universally endorsed bacheloric message or some unifying thread. In the end we've decided not to do anything other than allow one historical figure to lead into the next, beginning with the historical Jesus and ending with yet another mythic figure, best left unidentified at this time. We earnestly recommend that the judicious reader refrain from repairing to the final pages of this contentious book.

One of the unfamiliar approaches to the historical Jesus has been to consider the man *as bachelor*. Today we would somehow never be inclined to think of him as pledged to some wife in holy or even unholy matrimony, although he is, of course identified with a number of women, primarily Mary, about whom he seems to have nothing good to say. Adam, as we've seen, reluctantly gave marriage a try and in no time it blew up in his face, an ominous portent if ever there was one. That's when our prototypical bachelor had been, so to speak, our first married man and in short order our first marital casualty. It's not a pretty Biblical picture. To further muddy the matrimonial waters, there has appeared a certain papyrus allegedly containing mention of Jesus' having had a wife, although we do not presume to say whether the document is genuine or ingenuous, although the apostles say nothing about this supposed marriage or this supposed wife. Had there been a wedding, they weren't even invited to the ritual reception. Some have said that if he were a bachelor, he would have been a conspicuously obvious one. If not, it begs the question of why not. There are several possible explanations. He apparently never became intimate with a woman because he entertained certain discreet reservations about doing so.

"The Famous Bachelors in History" is an outspoken essay published by New Zealand's *Ohinemuri Gazette* in November of 1918. Whoever composed the piece (it's unacknowledged) affirms that "the Divine Founder of Civilization" was, of course, "a bachelor" but hastens to add that many ostensibly outstanding men have acknowledged "their indebtedness to their wives for the great reputations they [who?] have made." Others attributed their greatness principally to their remaining in a single state, and have scorned to entertain the idea of matrimony.

One such person was the renowned but perpetually disgruntled Samuel Johnson (1707–1784) lexicographer, biographer, poet, and essayist who said that to marry a second time was *the triumph of hope over experience*. At 25, Johnson married a 45-year-old widow apparently for the purpose of using her money to open a boarding school. His extraordinary amanuensis and biographer James Boswell prudently remarked little about it in his huge Johnsonian biography, except that Johnson regarded it as "far from being natural for a man and woman to live in a state of marriage," adding too that "a savage man and a savage woman meet by chance; and when the man sees another woman who pleases him better, he will leave the first."

Long after Tatty Porter (that was her name) died in 1752, Johnson acknowledged that he had neglected her in their last dozen years.

Thomas Aquinas, bachelor that he appears to have been, pensively strolled the earth between 1225 and 1274 and attained sainthood—something that, at first glance, seems oddly out line with his conduct. It is patently impossible to call Aquinas a bachelor. Today we identify him and his work with *scholasticism*, which essentially means reconciling faith with reason, or to put it another way, reconciling Aristotle with the scriptures. This is and was no easy task, and a purely academic one that. Since he called it his *Summa Theologica* (1267–1273), one may assume it to be a scholastic summary of what is now known as *Thomism* and identified mostly with the Catholic Church as decreed by Pope Leo XIII in 1879.

Aquinas' interest in women, to put it another way, took a decidedly academic turn. For example, he was absorbed in clarifying whether woman was properly created in Eden before the Fall, or whether (being, as she was, a portrait of imperfection, easily led and influenced) she ought not to have been there in the first place. Said Aquinas, yes. Eve ought to have been in Eden because she was necessary for the procreation of the miserable human race. What said Aristotle about all this? That Eve is to be considered as an individual, and a misbegotten one, at that. Aquinas's exact words for her were deficient and misbegotten, expressed in his Latin *deficiens et occasionatus*, loosely meaning incomplete and accidental. Be she either misbegotten or defective, Aquinas viewed her charitably as perfect in her ability to reproduce. As one commentator remarks, "This hardly makes [Aquinas] a champion of the rights and dignity of women," since he views them as "inferior to men in both mind and body," albeit he "did not believe that women are the slaves of men"— encouraging, but, still and all, in his view, women are subject to the will of men simply because men are by and large the larger gender...where reason predominates. Next question?

Was it proper that woman was created from man's rib? Answer: Yes. Why? Because she was created out of his rib, not his head (symbolizing reason) and therefore is intellectually inferior. Aquinas' defenders have the devil's own time defending him against charges of blatant misogyny unless they assume that he viewed women as both superior and inferior to them. In the end, some argue, he is on the side of godliness and, after all, there are such things as women saints, something that has been passed off as *Christian Aristotelianism* or sometimes *Aristotelian misogyny*.

It doesn't end there, for instance in the question of whether woman was accidentally caused by the imperfections of the male reproductive system. These are, to be sure, touchy matters touching upon whether, to the contrary, women are justified by the necessity of further reproduction. Aquinas responds by saying that a woman is a *masoccionatus*, a *failed man*, and therefore something less than perfect. Still and all, she's not to be regarded as accidental.

Consider too that, as Aquinas says, the male seed takes its nourishment from the mother. We could go on, but won't. Had we to speculate, we'd have to say that Aquinas was not cut out to be some woman's husband, mostly because he was convinced of women's' innate inferiority. Nor would he have made much of a bachelor in the modem sense of that word, since he would not very well have fulfilled the role, even if he wished to.

The great Raphael Santi, *aka* Raphael (Sanzio (1483–1520), had enough sense not to marry, opting instead to become a lifelong bachelor and renowned painter, eventually chief architect of the Vatican. Clearly, Raphael's miraculous artistic calling precluded his interest in marriage, or so it appears.

He is believed to have been engaged for a time to Maria Bibbiena, a cardinal's niece, all the while maintaining a mistress (we don't have a problem with that) named Margherita Lute, a baker's daughter. There has been, to the contrary, a theory that he married the baker's daughter rather than the cardinal's niece, but we prefer to not to believe a word of it. For what it's worth, an accomplished woman's portrait called "Formarina" shows us a glimpse of a partially undressed figure sporting a ribbon with Raphael's name on it. Not only that, but the partially naked woman's left hand bears a wedding band that in later years appears to have been brushed over. Make of it what we will. There are those who claim that Raphael intended to marry the lovely Margherita, but put the wedding date off indefinitely, as bachelors have been known to do, then as now. One delay leads to another, and before anyone knew it, well, it never happened. As a kind of consolation prize the might-have-been-bride attracted what was certain immortally of her own, since her likeness appears as the face on the Sistine Madonna.

Consider too Michelangelo Bounarroti (1475–1564) who, also by way of his progress on the portrait of the Madonna, is probably most often remembered for his painting the ceiling of the Sistine Chapel between 1508 and 1512. Bachelor to the end, he yielded to someone's suggestion that he find a nice Italian girl, settle down and set his mind on reproducing himself. He replied dutifully that "I have too much of a wife in my art, and she has given me trouble enough. As to my children, if they are not worth much they will at least live for some time." There are signs that he had something going with the widow sonneteer Victorian Collona, although she lived in a convent and was rather limited in her *social mobility*, as some call it. Michelangelo drew representations of Cupid but never took him too seriously, and seems to have viewed his women as untouchable; none so much, ironically, as women who were presumed unchaste. His own heart and soul belonged not to a woman, but to his art as a painter, sculptor and poet.

And speaking of poets, confirmed bachelor Charles Lamb (1775–1834), sad to say, came from a family afflicted with what we'll call (understatedly) emotional instability in the days before it could be treated with a benignant-appearing pill, and he was committed (not to some woman but) to a mental asylum, as such places were then called. The Lambs, anything but meek, were rather demonstrable, if we may venture to say so. Charles' sister Mary stabbed their mother to death in a careless moment. Charlie (a tad unsteady himself) assumed responsibility for his sister's somewhat unpredictable behavior that caused her to glide into insanity every now and then, and between times be a fairly good, if eccentric, companion for the old fellow. He had to enter a home for lunatics where he received on occasion literary visitors laden with literary stories and anecdotes.

In the meantime, and with the best of intentions, Charlie told visitors that his excellent sister was far and away the "older and wiser" and also "better than me," a comment that we're inclined take with *a grain of salt*, as nitwits persist in saying. Charlie even authored a piece called "a bachelor's complaint" during which he had the nerve to proclaim that that "a bachelor is the equivalent of a hundred monkeys," which, when we consider it, doesn't make a whole lot of sense, poetical or otherwise. Nonetheless, we seize this opportunity (gratuitously) to nominate Charlie Lamb to our rigidly select Bachelorific Hall of Fame.

Let us continue by taking a somewhat closer look at music men such as Chopin, Liszt and Beethoven for what their strange lives reveal about the bacheloristic life in their day. Frederic François Chopin (1810–1849) we remember today as a romantically-inclined Pole who ventured to Paris where he took up with and kept the French woman novelist with the male name of George Sand who, after a good many conquests of her own, began to wear trousers. The two remained together between about 1838 and 1848, when he began to fail and when Sand began none too charitably refer to him as "my dear corpse." Chopin never married, partly because, like some fellows we discussed before him, he was consumed by his work and began a bachelorific life—a little less so when he lived with Sand, although he devoted some of his amorous hours to enviable beauties like Delphina Potoka, Konstancja Gladkowska and by all means Marie Wodzinska. He seemed to view Sand not too inappropriately as a female bachelor.

The reclusive Hungarian Franz Liszt (1811–1886), another romantically-inclined pianist and composer, was one who revolutionized the way pianos ought to be played, although he left no specific record of specifically how. He was also committed religiously, which has led to his being regarded as a Catholic composer; he early in life befriended Chopin. In 1833 he made the acquaintance of the Countess Marie d'Agoult but by 1847 he met the

Princess Carolyne zu Sayn-Wittgenstein and, according to historical records, the pair intended to marry in 1860, except that she had been married before. The Church interfered and the marriage, for better or worse, never happened, much to their regret. Chopin later took minor holy orders. By this time he had become constitutionally melancholic, but he may have been a better musician for it.

The boorish German Ludwig Van Beethoven (1770–1827), despite his ever-worsening deafness, became one of the outstanding composers of his time and ours. He was a notorious flirt with a tendency to concentrate his flirtatiousness and seductive skills upon unattainable women, but he seemed never to take women too darned seriously. According to Beethoven's biographer Stephen King (not the spook novelist), his bacheloristic personality was such that he had a predictably strong resistance to marriage, as did, for that matter, Brahms and Schubert. While this was going on, Haydn referred to his wife of 40-odd years as "the beast." Love wasn't exactly in bloom.

Saint-Saens' marriage to a 19-year-old lasted a whopping six years when he shifted gears in favor of a woman half his age, but he lived alone for the next 40. Through it all, Beethoven was deeply in love with himself but was, oddly enough, given to composing inspired love letters that were stashed away until after his death. His and other men's missives spilled over into flattering women with their sweet nothings designed to win their favors. Women rather annoyed Beethoven, however. To him, it was *all in the chase,* just another bachelorific gambit that, over a lifetime, won him all sorts of women to whom he sent messages signed *your faithful Ludwig.*

Niccolo Paganini (1782–1840), possibly the greatest violin virtuoso of his time, said that it was a darned good thing that he never married. This recommended him for inclusion on a list calling itself the "Famous Bachelors in History." His notably ugly Thoreauvian appearance caused some to liken to a devil, a ghost, even an ape—until they listened to his playing, after which he seemed more like an angel. Paganini was, as they say, *a bundle of contradictions.* The two seemed to neutralize each other. One woman nonetheless found him paradoxically attractive and had the urge to hold him nearly captive. Another kept him in her chateau for three years. Flexible person that he was, he suffered from a condition now called *Ellers-Daniel Syndrome,* meaning that his joints were astonishingly jointed, such that he could with apparent ease make love to the violin as others could not dream of doing. He did strike it up with Antonia Biondi, with whom he fathered a son, but outside wedlock. Gambler that he was, he forfeited huge sums at the gaming tables and, like Casanova, later owned part of a Parisian casino.

This brings us, with some trepidation, to Arthur Schopenhauer (1788–1860), a solitary German philosopher whose world outlook may best be described as terminal frustration, and who had pointedly nothing positive to say about women, possibly because he had proposed to one of them and been turned down. Nothing more. He thereafter felt so terminally rejected that he never got over it, and for this not very adequate reason he detested women and anything he happened to view as womanly. Schopenhauer is today what we all would feel secure in calling a negative bachelor: a fellow cut out for that sort of carefree life, and specifically cruising from pillar to post, bitching about women. Consider, for instance, his treatise *On Women*, which is not "onward with women," or maybe "upward with women," but more like "the lowdown on women," or even "the dirt on women," or "the awful truth about women." He says, for instance, things like "one need only look at a woman's shape to discover that she is not intended for too much mental or physical work." Anything else? Yes. "She pays the debt of life...by the pangs of child-bearing, child care and by subjection to man, to whom she should be a patient and cheerful companion." It gets worse. Women, he tells us, "are childish and short sighted," and are "big children all their lives." But take heart! Because women's reasoning powers are weaker [men must] take a [benevolent] interest in them." Schopenhauer's position has been appropriately called phallocentric, loosely translated as woman free. He lived out his bacheloric existence in solitude except for his dogs, although on one occasion a surprise visit by a woman turned into a nasty scene when he managed to incite her. She in turn sued him on some pretext or another, with the result that he was obliged to pay damages for the balance her life.

We should point out that while some bachelors are covertly or overtly misogynistic, they nonetheless on some level or another solicit women's company and their favors. Bachelors, most of them, have generally entertained a social dimension which prevents their falling headlong into morbid isolation. They are, after all, more or less likable, even engaging—social assets that prevent their slipping off the edge of the earth, headlong into oblivion.

Immanuel Kant (1724–1804), another Germanic metaphysician, is best known for this *Critique of Pure Reason* (1781) and also for fostering what's become known as *German Idealism*, something that did not always carry over to his view of women. His approach to the opposite sex had something to do with his being the son of a harness maker and a harness maker's daughter, who were sometimes believed to have embraced advanced and more refined tastes than one might first presume. Kant's view of women is not as coarse as Schopenhauer's, although he never married, preferring to keep company with his books, thereby fostering the impression, at least, of being a scholarly bachelor. He did venture to say that in marriage it is the husband's role to direct, and the wife's to obey, which has been taken to mean that husbands are superior in some respects, wives in others, expressive of his view of human equality wherein women need to be guarded and protected by men because women are emotional beings. "A woman," he once wrote, "is embarrassed little that she does not possesses certain high insights, that she is timid and not fit for serious employment." Still and all, "women have a superior feeling for the beautiful—so far as it pertains to herself."

By contrast, Blaise Pascal (1623–1662) distinguished himself in mathematics, physics and theology. His mother died when he was a small child, after which he formed a close attachment to his two older sisters. His intense religious convictions led him to become an ardent follower of Cornelius Janson's Catholic views, and he died while under the care of a surviving sister, having joined her at a Port Royal convent. After their father's death, Pascal set about accumulating women servants, developing an interest in the theatre, and gambling, bacheloristic excesses that seem to have been a stage in his younger life that eventually evolved into a metaphysical frame of mind, safely out of touch with ordinary womanhood. Pascal did author a treatise he called a "Discourse on the Passion of Love," the authenticity of which has been challenged because it sounds little or nothing like the Pascal we otherwise know, or think we do. He remained doggedly philosophical, as for example his remark on how "we are born with a disposition to love in our hearts," et cetera. He divided his attention between mathematics and religious philosophy.

Pascal brings to mind Sir Isaac Newton (1642–1727), another mathematician-physicist credited with discovering the law of universal gravitation, and optics. He grew up under the care of his mother from the age of three to 12, but she died in 1678, triggering what's been described as a Newtonian mental breakdown. Toward the end of his days Pascal lived with his niece and her husband. Pascal never married, and for that matter never much bothered about accumulating friends, making him a kind of uncompromising old (85 at his death) bachelor, inclined to depression and quarrelling. If he did bother with women, which is doubtful, we don't know who. We're told that in his early teen years he temporarily showed some interest in a girl (as young men tend to do), but after that he couldn't be bothered with them. "I can calculate the motion of heavenly bodies," Pascal said, "but not the madness of people."

Another of our excellent bacheloristic fellows was a chap named Françoise-Marie Arouet, known to us as *Voltaire* (1694–1778), recognized mostly for his *Candide or Optimism* (1959), a rapid-paced, cynical picaresque adventure tale, travel book, satire, romance, philosophical adventure, and allegory, written as a caustic, unsparing parody. Its targets are many, especially 18th century optimism, the travel book vogue, and the philosophical dialogue. When people asked Voltaire about the book, allegedly written by a certain *Dr. Ralph*, he became rather touchy. His father sent him to The Hague, where he met a lovely girl named Olympe Dunoyer whom he good-naturedly called *Pimpette*. Voltaire dabbled in a number of other, sometimes frivolous pursuits, among them real estate, military uniforms, objects d'art, commodities, and even loan sharking. He spent 1726 in England where he learned to read, write and speak the language and where he poured over Bacon, Locke and Newton. His brain was later preserved in a jar and his heart was presented to Napoleon III, who in turned donated it (and the brain) to the National Library. Voltaire was never buried, but he was every inch a bachelor. Ironist that he was, he entertained the subject of marriage in his *Philosophical Dictionary* (1764), claiming that he'd met a logician who assured him that "the more married men you have, the less crime there will be. Look at the frightful records of your criminal registers and you will find there a hundred bachelors hanged or broken on the wheel for one father of a family."

By contrast, we remember Adam Smith (1723–1770), the Scottish economist and moral philosopher for his *Inquiry into the Nature and Causes of the Wealth of Nations* (1776) that argued that *laissez-faire* economics would advance the best interests of society. Women did not evade his attention, although he sometimes viewed them through an economist's eyes. Example: "Scottish women frequently bear more than 20 children, while a fine lady is... generally exhausted by two or three," ergo, women with too much wealth at their disposal will decline faster. Similarly, "I think a woman's perspective is a little different [from] a man's...they see God a little differently than we do..." Smith was an odd sort of fellow, absent minded and eccentric appearing. He was quite fond of his mother, and needless to say declined to marry, being as he was a defenseless chap given to theorizing and speculating. The same was not so with Francisco Petrarch (1304–1374), the itinerant poet who first saw his feminine ideal and symbol of love where he had gone to pursue holy orders with a view toward becoming a *cleric*. The woman of his dreams was nonetheless somebody else's wife, whom Petrarch called *Laura* (assuming that she actually existed). Today Petrarch is celebrated among the *cognoscente* as the most influential of the Italian poets, whose work addresses effects of unrequited love. He became a major figure in the rise of Renaissance Humanism where his reputation invites comparison to Boccaccio and Dante. Not all of Boccaccio's love was unrequited, since he fathered at least two children out of wedlock, which tells us that he didn't spend all his days buried in monastic seclusion. This *father of humanism* gave us the so-called *Petrarchan woman* whose love is unattainable, like, for example, Shakespeare's

Juliet. It's all terribly romantic but one would at least have to ask, Was Petrarch a bachelor? We're uncertain whether anyone calling himself a cleric could be referred to as such, but even so his preoccupation with hard to acquire women at least bespeaks one bacheloric preoccupation. One could also argue that his Platonic relation with Laura was about as inconsistent with bachelordom as holy orders.

Petrarch leads us to consider the sad plight of Eloise and Abelard. Peter Abelard (1079–1142) was the controversial philosophical and theological scholar who fell into an affair of the heart with Eloise (or Heloise, 20 years his younger). As her tutor, he tutored her in a few inventive ways until she became pregnant, after which they were married. Nothing is quite so unromantic as matrimony, although her uncle prevailed upon her to become a nun, after which she was mutilated for having lost her innocence.

Henry David Thoreau, never married and possibly a-sexual, never paid much attention to women unless it was to engage them in esoteric exchanges. Even if he had wanted to marry, which he didn't, hardly any woman would have consented to it because of his aforementioned homeliness. Nathaniel Hawthorne wrote of him, "Mr. Thorou [*sic*]... is a singular character—a young man with much of wild original nature remaining in him. He is as ugly as sin, long-nosed, queer-mouthed, with an uncouth and somewhat rustic, courteous manners...but his ugliness is of an honest and agreeable fashion." Henry wrote a decorous piece called "Love" wherein in he spoke with a Thoreauvian flourish about women. In "The Maiden," he tells us, there exists "a fairer flower and sweeter fruit [referring to a woman] than my calyx in the field, and if she goes with averted face, confiding in her purity and high resolves, she will make the heavens retrospective and all nature humbly confess it its queen." That's all quite flattering, but all the same, when Thoreau built his famous 1845 Walden cabin (at a cost of $28.12), where he claimed to reside for two years, two months and two days, he also claimed to have lived by himself, although he carried on a pleasantly active social existence. Henry had a sister named Sophia, a self-effacing woman who attended him during his final illness, but that doesn't say much for his female associates. He, like Emerson, had a *rather frigid personality*. Nonetheless, Henry and his brother John were both believed to have fallen in love with the same woman—and at the same time, if that's to be believed. Her name was Ellen Sewell. John was engaged to her; knowing this, Henry proposed to her also, not in person but in a letter. We can presume why. When her father investigated Henry, he insisted that she fire off a letter of unequivocal refusal. She later married a Unitarian minister and remained married for nearly 50 years.

Truth be known, Henry was never too much into women, anyway. As a classic proponent of individualism and self-reliance, he spent one day stepping down a dirt road where he encountered what has been called a *skunk cabbage* that he booted out of his way, remarking, "There's what I think of marriage." He otherwise possessed certain familiar bacheloristic characteristics, especially his undaunted self-reliant, intensely private, eccentric attitudes, his self-contentedness, his pronounced sense of intellectual freedom, his books, his solitary happiness, his liberated mentality. He would not, for these and other reasons, have made some maid much of a husband because he could not be intimidated, lectured, to, ordered about, programmed, and deflated. Wrote he, "We need the tonic of wilderness—to wade sometimes in the marshes... and the meadow hen lurk and hear the booming of the snipe; to smell the whispering sedge where only some wilder and more solitary fowl builds her nest, and the mink crawls with its belly close to the ground. At the same time that we are earnest to explore and learn all things, we require that all things be mysterious and unemployable, that land and sea be infinitely wild, unsurveyed and unfathomed by us, because unfathomable. We can never have enough of Nature."

By the same token, red-haired Algernon Charles Swinburne (1837–1909) shared with Henry a predisposition for challenging social conventionalities, even to the point of attempting to scandalize. He considered himself an atheist in his younger years, following which it was anyone's guess what he'd defame—or embrace—next, although he had a marked tendency toward hero-worship. Women did not know quite how to take him, nor he them. Algy was more than a little excitable, and in different stages was attracted to the wonders of masochism and flagellation. He let it be known that he'd had a serious affair with a monkey and took a seriously misogynistic turn—with a leavening of sadomasochism, Obviously, Algy was not *cut out* (as idiots say) for the bachelorific life as we've described it. The best we can say is that the poor eccentric hadn't much of a future with women of any kind.

Neither, in another unusual way, did George Gershwin, dead at the age of 38 (1898–1937), the son of Russian Lithuanian Jewish immigrants who settled in Brooklyn. He made, with some persistence from his brother Ira, a name for himself with such noteworthy Broadway classics as his *Rhapsody in Blue* (1924), *Oh, Kay* (1926), *Funny Face* (1927), *Strike Up the Band* ((1927, 1930), *An American in Paris* (1928), *Show Girl* (1929), *Girl Crazy* (1930) and *Porgy and Bess* (1935). Gershwin was an endlessly committed worker who was a bit difficult to get along with, a bit difficult to know, and more than a little bit impatient. That he never married was the direct outcome of his work that began in New York as a song plugger for other people's music. Gershwin was influenced by other people's music, but in the end he composed in his own manner. He once expressed an interest in studying under, of all people, Maurice Ravel, who turned him down for a tutorial and famously inquired, "Why become a second rate Ravel when you're already a first rate Gershwin?"

George Gershwin's name is usually associated with one woman. She was Kay Swift, whom he saw off and on for a decade. Swift was a lyricist and composer in her own right and became a Gershwin's closest artistic associate.

In an obituary, Mark Steyn passed her off not as Gershwin's girlfriend but as the woman of whom Gershwin's mother Rose disapproved because she was not Jewish. She was, however, a well-connected New York socialite and a professional, conservatory-educated musician who became interested in his popular, nay, more than popular, songs. She met him at a party where he spent most of his time playing his own music on a piano, until he declared, "Well, I've got to go to Europe now." They remained in touch for the balance of his life. She was, in the meantime, divorced from her banker husband, after which it appeared that she might remarry. As Steyn put it, "The mercurial Gershwin doubted he would ever wed," and he didn't. She seated herself between George and Ira on the shaky opening night of *Porgy and Bess* in 1935. Steyn believed that Swift had a theory "that composers look like their music," as evidenced by George's "brash, reckless, assured" numbers. After all that, she traveled west and married a rodeo cowboy, asking, in Gershwin's parlance, "who could ask for anything more?" When she last saw him, he and Ira were boarding a plane for New York. After some urging and badgering from his confidants, he called her to say, "I'm coming back—for both of us," after which he died of a brain tumor, possibly the result of contemplating matrimony. Years later Katherine Weber, Swift's granddaughter, brought out a book called *The Memory of All That: Kate Swift and My Family's Legacy of Infidelities. It explores* Swift's marriage to James Paul Warburg, the internationally known investment banker and economist. It's all an intensely lachrymose story, but one wonders whether a determined bachelor like Gershwin could find happiness with the woman of whom his mother disapproved. Gershwin, as far as we know, never complained about the bacheloristic life and he apparently found it perfectly satisfactory—without irreparably ruining it. Kate lived to 95, two and a half times George's age.

Alfred de Musset (1810–1857), the Parisian literary lion (dramatist, poet, novelist), wrote *Les Nuits* (1833), an amorous account of if his adventures with the aforementioned George Sand, she being a convenient pretext for him to remain a bachelor, after his allegedly having (according to his account) fallen in love with this more than feckless woman. Here's what happened. The two of them set out toward Italy where Sand fell seriously ill with a fever (this makes absolutely no sense) because she could plainly see that Musset had become bored with her and carried his perpetually amorous desires to other women, only to be felled by what may have been the same fever, if not some sort of hex, for being not the best of male companions. In the meantime Sand made the acquaintance of a young Italian physician, a chap named Pietro Pagello, and between the two of them they restored Musset to his former eccentric self while she became Pietro's mistress, and Musset (bachelor to the end) hastened back to Paris to (as they say) lick his wounds (romanticist that he remained), but not without indulging in still another affair, this one with Louise Colet, best remembered as one of Flaubert's amours. It was at about this time that he developed a coronary problem to which he lent his own illustrious name: *the Musset Symptom*, a kind of vascular irregularity common among romantically possessed gentlemen and bachelors of finer than ordinary grain.

Mention of finer than ordinary sensibilities places us in mind of another bachelor, this one the American naturalist and conservationist John Burroughs (1837–1921), who was a remarkable man with a remarkable reputation, about whom the manic-depressive biographer Edward Renehan wrote with breathless enthusiasm, "John is so calm, so poised, so much at home with himself, so much a familiar spirit of the forests" that one cannot but receive him as "a child of the woods, fields, hills—native to them in a rare sense." Henry James, another chap with the rarest of senses, celebrated Burroughs as "more humorous, more amiable and more sociable Thoreau," and said that "the minuteness of Burrough's observation, the keenness of his perception [gave] him a real originality, and his sketches have a delightful oddity, vivacity and freshness." Indeed, Burroughs completed at least 28 books on "literature" and natural history, and was generously read in Wordsworth and Emerson. In 1857, however, he married a girl named Ursula North (1836–1917), whereupon Henry Ford gave him a touring car for some reason or another (besides touring). Renehan noted that "slender, attractive Ursula had been powerfully erotic," but after five years of marriage she "concluded that her husband's demands were immoral and intolerable" and they separated once for two months.

After Ursula died, he took an interest in Clara Barris (1864–1931), a physician employed at a psychiatric hospital. She was 33, he 64. Physician that she was, Barris, who had a more clinical attitude toward bodies and their functions, wrote Burroughs a flattering letter that encouraged him to send her an invitation to what he called his *hermit retreat* that he also knew as *Slabsides*, on the Hudson River. They never married, but like the man who came to dinner, she never left. In the meantime he designated her as his executrix and biographer, while her psychiatric interests made relations between the two a bit more accommodating. Barris had, in fact, taught psychiatric medicine, such as it then was, at New York's Women's College, and entitled her 1920 biography suggestively *John Burroughs: Boy and Man*. His marriage had been a complete washout, but it taught him never again to experiment with matrimony. He remained a bachelor for his final 59 years and that better suited his psychic requirements.

The French painter and sculptor Edgar Dégas (1834–1917) was, among other subjects, fond of depicting women in the form of ballerinas, women engaged in their toilette, women in cafés, women wherever he happened to find them. He is remembered too for his "Women with Chrysanthemums" (1865), "Foyer of the Dance" (1872) and even "Two Laundresses" (1882), "Greek Maidens," women bathing, ironing, doing this and doing that in a blatantly erotic manner that some collectors fancied for their collections. John Richardson, in an article called "Dégas and the Dancers" in the October 2, 2002, issue of *Vanity Fair*, alerted his readers to the misogynistic tendencies in the painter who so loved to depict women, saying, "Dégas created hundreds of paintings and sculptures which captured the harsh realities of 19th-century dancers' lives and hinged on his voyeuristic fascination with the pain ballet inflicted on female bodies," adding later that "he was not interested in capturing their onstage prettiness." He wanted instead to portray his "little monkey girls under stress, cracking their joints at the bar," as he said, "their youthful spirits cracked, their hamstrings in agony, their feet raw and bleeding." Noting too that Dégas—"a misogynist in a misogynistic society—equated dancers with animals," having later commented, "I have perhaps too often considered woman as an animal."

Robert L. Herbert, writing for *The New York Review of Books* (April 18, 1996), noted that Dégas also painted prostitutes, commenting that such women "might seem poor candidates for the admiration of art historians and critics who are women." "Many of the illustrations," he notes, "depict prostitutes sitting or reclining, often legs apart viewing the pubic triangle, and occasionally [with] their hands placed on their genitals," which they intend to share with their male clients, one of whom is entering a room with only the erotic edge of his clothing revealed.

Dégas lived the bachelorific life and, like certain others we have observed, was extremely close to the memory of his mother who died when he was 13. There are believed to be 83 self-portraits that reveal a variously sad and pouting young man looking a little more than suggestive. Having come from a socially conscious, upward bound family, in his later years he became interested in representing people for who and what they were, the manner they carried themselves, how they dressed. His misogyny led him to depict women as physically and emotionally tormented. He was of the opinion that his work superseded all else, and he consequently refrained from wasting his hours on other preoccupations. He also had a clear sense of place, that being Paris, more specifically Montmartre where he was born into a decidedly middle class household. He eventually became identified with dancers whose likenesses he froze forever on canvas. He is believed to have died in the solitary manner that he worked. From an undisclosed source comes a telling anecdote about a conversation between Dégas and an art dealer named Ambrose Vollard, to whom he is alleged to have said, "Vollard, you should get married. Don't you know what loneliness is when you grow old? Vollard then asks Dégas why, after all those years, he remained a bachelor. Dégas is alleged to have replied, "I was too much afraid of hearing my wife say, when I had finished a painting, "That's a pretty picture you've done."

As artists come and go, Van Gogh (pun intended) is possibly acknowledged in the popular mind as a recognized painter, although most of his work was accomplished in just over two years when he turned out 864 paintings and 1,000 sketches, among them sunflowers, in his otherwise not so shining life that terminated in suicide. His sallow faced self-portraits convey a brooding desperation. He was the son of a Dutch reformed pastor and a bookseller's daughter, and he was unusually emotional, partly because he'd suffered a great many traumas, including two awful encounters with women. Van Gogh was a passionate talker and a passionate painter who, with the aid of a razor, sliced part of his ear off and presented it to a sympathetic but incredulous prostitute. This was after he had passed some time in a mental asylum (as people called it) in Saint-Rémy for some psychiatric counsel, after which at age 37 he shot himself. Even today he is regarded by some as a "saintly man who painted those starry skies and sunflowers." There are others who regard him as selfish and manipulative. His women were often identified not by Dégas' feminine crotches but by the head, possibly symbolic of (if anything) intellect, rationality, will and so forth as we encounter it in "Head of an Old Peasant Woman With a White Cap" (1884), "Head of a Peasant Women" (1885), "Fisherman's Wife at the Beach" (1882), "Peasant Woman" (half-figure, 1884), "Head of a Woman With Her Hair Loose" (1885), "Peasant Woman With a Dark Cap" (1885), "Peasant Woman Taking Her Meal (1885). Van Gogh never discovered the wife for whom he longed. He assumed that other people viewed him as a mere eccentric and good for nothing, hence he became the solitary artist and unfulfilled bachelor, something that has endless implications. One of his women was Clasina Maria Hoornik, an alcoholic prostitute. A bachelor in spite of himself, he was left to manage with his instabilities and his insecurities on his own.

Consider too Edvard Munch (1863–1944), best identified by two easy pieces: "The Scream" (1893) and "The Kiss" (1895), who traded in such wonderful things as fear, death, hyper-anxiety and other forms of profound mental anguish, about which he knew a thing or two, since his father was afflicted with some varieties of mental illness. Munch willed his paintings not to relatives and friends but to the bureaucrats at the Oslo government, in return for which they built the Munch Museum of Art. Later in life he developed an alcoholic problem compounded by mental difficulties that led him to a Copenhagen mental hospital, after which he fell into a psychiatric condition. (Not surprisingly) he never married but referred to his paintings as his *children*. The folks at the Smithsonian chose to call "The Scream" nothing less than "a Mona Lisa for our time." They saw fit to view the painting as *a refreshing* exhibition "of our own age wracked with anxiety and uncertainty," apparently suggesting that ours is the only age tormented by those tensions, aptly represented by "a sexless twisted, fetal-faced creature, with mouth and eyes opened with in a shriek of horror" that Munch gruesomely described as "air turned to blood." These depictions were so intensely admired that they have been stolen from the Oslo Gallery and are apparently still missing.

In the meantime we are inspired by this "imposter whose personal tragedies, sickness and failures" are an inspiration for the rest of us. He wanted to be regarded as "a contemporary artist and not as an old master," explained the curator at the Munich Museum. "He embraced chance fearlessly," we are further told, along with the unparalleled disclosures that for some reason or non-reasons "he left his paintings out of doors in all kinds of weather," possibly to enhance their seeming weather-tormented effect. One of his more arresting works is "a depiction of his mother, confined with tuberculosis," wheezing wistfully from her chair which of course reminds us that the artist himself had tuberculosis and spat blood as a boy. His first sexual experienced arrived at about the age of 21 with a woman named Millie Thanow, a suitably distant relative, we are told, whom he had met at some sort of encounter in a woods. He reacted, we are also told, by being "maddened and trolled" while it lasted, and later "tormented and dissolute" when it dried up. Out of these encounters came the "Vampire (1893–1894) that illustrates "a red-haired woman...sinking her mouth into the neck of a desolate-looking lover." The poor fellow died at 81, still with what fools call *mental health issues* (which had been treated for a time by electrotherapy) that left him a defenseless bachelor. In May of 2012, "The Scream" sold at a Sotheby auction in excess of $119 million, supposedly well bloody worth it, confirming the painting's "reputation as one of the most famous and important works of art ever produced."

Henri Toulouse-Lautrec (1864–1901), whose growth was stunted, supposedly as a consequence of a childhood orthopedic mishap, was somehow thereafter ironically celebrated in Parisian cafes and music halls, not the least of which was the Moulin Rouge. There are some who claim that his dwarfishness was not the outcome of a childhood accident but, to the contrary, of inbreeding. It is possible that both were at cause. When he was 13, he fractured his left thigh; when he was 14, he fractured the right. Neither of the bones properly reset, complicated by what's come down to us (not literally, mind you) but come down to us as the *Toulouse-Lautrec Syndrome*, popularly known today as *osteopetrosis achondroplasia*, or still more popularly as *osteogenesis imperfecta* which means, in still plainer language, that one's legs refuse to develop in concert with most other children's. Lautrec was a bachelor whether or not he preferred it, which he apparently did, being as he was a little Chaplinesque chap characterized by a tall shirt and baggy pants, the roundest of eye glasses and a sporting cane. He loved women and women loved him. Some contemporary assessments of him allege that he spent his professional (and private) life *honoring all women*, meaning "not simply the few women he considered 'honorable'" but "the kindness and humanity of women of the 'underclass' who worked in *lowly professions*." Be that all it may, when his work was offered to the Louvre, it was turned down, possibly because he preferred to represent women as sirens and back alley tarts, as grotesque as himself. His was nearly a parody of the bachelorific life with its independent, self-sustaining, rather fun-loving preferences without the onerous burdens of matrimony, and his preferences for fallen women, at least of one of whom poisoned his life.

The German composer Johannes Brahms (1833–1897), who in 1853 made the acquaintance of Robert Schumann (1810–1856), became one of his allies and later suffered what was referred to as a nervous breakdown that led to a suicide attempt. Brahms placed himself at the Schumanns' service, although Schumann's wife was 14 years older than he when she offered her counsel (as is believed) and Brahms fell in love with her in an unrequited way, and remained so long after her husband died. Through it all, Brahms never married, although biographers believe that he was attracted in some way or another to women, even to the point that he declined to give one woman piano lessons for fear of becoming overly attracted to her. Clara, by this time, had lost four of her eight children and was, to put it gently, somewhat burnt out, having had her suicidal husband consigned to a mental asylum for two years. After decades of difficulty she turned to Brahms for support and friendship, something that provoked gossip. After having been offered the use of the Schumann household, he began to feel a bit guilty about ingratiating himself to his late friend's wife. She apparently appreciated his attention, having decorously written, "Often thank God for thy friend who has been sent to me in this time of bitterest trial, like a veritable angel of comfort." By 1858 he developed an infatuation with soprano Agathe von Siebold. A bit later the two exchanged engagement rings, only to have the arrangements dissolve, apparently having elicited his comment that "there I have freed myself from my last love," spoken like a true romantic after the two had (again) been driven apart by gossip over Brahms's perpetual bachelordom, though he apparently had an ongoing habit of chasing women until they became too close, after which he began again to consort with prostitutes. We have before noticed before the male tendency to pursue an objective until it became too reachable, then fade back. For what it's worth, he by this time organized a women's chorus in 1859, as if to accent women in wholesale numbers. Hence to some he appeared to be a rather inscrutable fellow, unwilling to marry, self-absorbed like certain other bachelors with their work and their reputations to guard and advance. Brahms' romances were one thing; his devotion to women quite another.

Who was Ludwig Josef Johann Wittgenstein? He was an Austrian philosopher whose years were 1889 and 1951 between which, we are informed, "all philosophical problems [arose] from the illusions created by the ambiguities of language," a presumptuous remark that made him, among those who know, dismissively "the greatest philosopher of the 20th century," but nonetheless a rather dismissively intense chap born into a wealthy iron and steel family. He tried teaching for a while and even enrolled in a teachers college. He had a nasty habit of physically attacking his students on philosophical grounds and bopped one of them over the head two or three times in the august name of enlightenment. He joined the military in World War I and as a POW had plenty of time to brush up his epistemology. Wittgenstein didn't have much encouraging to say about women, certainly nothing philosophic, and could at times be taken as downright misogynistic. Wittgenstein scholar Bela Szabados has concluded that this great head-bopping theorizer did not always think remarkable thoughts, and therefore may be less a great thinker that has traditionally been presumed. He opposed allowing women to vote, and ignored them socially, commenting under his breath one time, "Thank God, we have got rid of the women." We know that Schopenhauer was the first and most prominent influence on Wittgenstein, and we've seen examples of the former's outspoken antifeminism. Wittgenstein died from prostate cancer and lived out his last days at the home of his physician. His final ironic words were, "Tell them I've had a wonderful life."

Except for having a supposedly wonderful life, none of Wittgenstein's irrepressible attitudes and habits share much with Giacomo Casanova (1725–1798), born in Venice, died (appropriately) in Bohemia, a top shelf libertine and a profoundly professional bachelor if ever there was one. He did it all, or nearly so. Casanova (*new house*) began his extraordinary amorous career by being punted out of (of all places) a seminary, no place for a guy named Casanova, who perpetrated some uncommonly erotic stunts as if they were circus acts. Since he was theoretically in the service of the Roman Catholic Church, he inevitably puts us in mind of Chaucer's lecherous clerical scoundrels from the *Canterbury Tales*. He took up the violin, got himself locked up for some unspecified misdemeanor, escaped, assisted in organizing a Parisian lottery, adopted the jaunty name of *Chevalier de Seingalt*, crossed Europe, made the acquaintance of Voltaire in Switzerland, continued his travels through London, Berlin, Florence, St. Petersburg and into Spain, after which he returned to his native Venice and found employment as (of all things) a spy. Casanova could do more than seduce women; he could also engage the undivided attention of cardinals and popes along with the attention of Goethe, Mozart and Franklin. Known internationally (like Bryon) as a world class *seducer*, he found time to compose verses (possibly to that end), left us a new English rendering of Homer's *Iliad* and, more importantly, composed 12 volumes of his less than salty memoirs, christening himself *de. J. Casanova de Seingalt* (1826–1838). The manuscript is sometimes called his *histoire de ma vie* (*History of My Life*). A rather chatty but not altogether candid, less than complete anatomical disclosure of that prolonged parade of women and girls who submitted with apparent pleasure to his licentious purposes, the book finally appeared in 1821, pretty well bowdlerized, which neutralized some of its 3,700 pages of licentiousness. As recently as 2011, with its missing pages restored, the *Smithsonian* magazine found it "in turns hilarious, ribald, provocative, boastful, self-mocking, philosophical, tender and occasionally still shocking...the work of a man who has been dismissed as a frivolous sexual adventurer."

This womanizing rake's progress nearly went up in smoke during World War II, causing some serious concern for its continued survival, lest its descriptions of seductions of young girls (and at least one instance of incest) be regrettably lost to posterity. One commentator discovered more than 120 notorious love affairs with "countesses, milkmaids and nuns" peppered with "escapes, duels, swindles, stagecoach journeys, arrests and meetings with royals, gamblers and mountebanks." Through it all Casanova reacts differently from one female to the next and appears to be motivated to sex for sex's sake, with scarcely a thought about straying from what he seemed to view as conventional standards of morality. He tended to avoid prostitutes because they were by nature overly obliging, and because of the language barrier that inhibited his conversing with them with any appreciably seductive precision. Casanova, let's be clear, alas, never married, even though he could conceivably have made some woman a wretched husband. He wanted no part of entanglements, and he engaged readers with eroticism and by what he had to observe about elegant continental

18th century culture. Slippery chap that he was, he was condemned once for an undisclosed offense, languished for about 15 months in a lock-up, then (disguised as a monk) vanished. Such miraculous feats made him more of a drawing room hero than a fraud, an interloper, a common womanizer, a swindler, and a roving adventurer, who sought suitable company before whom to confess forthrightly as a *picaro*.

His elegant name inexorably lingers on. There are Casanova (or casa nova) restaurants around the globe, and a television series that describes itself as modeled "after a life spent seeking pleasure" that depicts Casanova's earnestly seeking *his own true love*. There is a Casanova agency somewhere out there trading in what we cannot presume to say. Such things tell us that, when all is done and said, the world covertly envies a seducer, an unmanageable bachelor, even a footloose womanizing roué. Even the term *Casanova* is part of our vocabulary, speaking of which, the English translation of the 1894 Casanova manuscript by Parisian Arthur Machen, entitled *Memoirs of Casanova Complete: The Unabridged London Edition of 1894*, with a heretofore unpublished chapter introduced by politician Arthur Symons, is now produced as a Product Gutenberg E Book. Said Casanova himself, "The chief business of my life has always been to indulge my senses; I felt myself born for the fair sex, I have ever loved it dearly, and have been loved by it as often and as much as I could. I have likewise always had a great weakness for good living, and ever felt passionately for every object which excites my curiosity," and later, "I have always been fond of richly-seasoned, rich dishes" such as macaroni prepared by a skillful Neapolitan cook, the *olla-podrida* of the Spaniards, the gluttonous codfish from Newfoundland, game with strong flavor, and cheese in the perfect state. As for women, I have always found the odor of my beloved ones exceedingly pleasant." The hundreds of pages that pass by are graced with a certain elegance, perilously short of the pornographic, a shared travel book where we find him repeating, "Dearest Christine, you are as lovely as one of God's angels. I have a great longing to give you a kiss." Today, the term *Casanova* refers to a sexual adventurer, a lady killer and unscrupulous seducer. Casanova himself was the son of professional actors and apparently inherited a verisimilitude and uncommon skill at role playing.

Bachelors, as we have repeatedly seen, come in all guises. Gottfried Wilhelm Leibniz, or Leibnitz (1646–1716), is variously recognized as philosopher, a mathematician, a metaphysician, a politician, and a prodigy who learned Latin at age seven and after that more than a few pages of Greek, following which his scholarly acumen transported him in a variety of learned directions that prompted him to form opinions in a variety of subjects scientific, social and practical. He endorsed the idea of a deterministic universe, for one thing, and differential equations for another, and what we sometimes known as symbolic logic. He never married and was believed to have been a bit on the *shady side*, sometimes believed to have been neutralized by his apparently redeeming good naturalness. He too grew up without a mother and was far too occupied to bother much with women. Today he is difficult to study because of his multifariousness, including his conversion to Catholicism, although those who read him tend toward his *Theodicy* (1710) and his *Monadology* (1714), although no single work captures the essence of his scholarly acumen. We find him conceding that "I have tried to uncover and unite the truth buried and scattered under the opinions of all the different philosophical sects, and I believe I have added something of my own which takes a few steps forward." Exactly why he never married, or never had much to do with women, remains a vexing mystery, except to say that Leibniz had a half-brother and a half-sister from his father's first marriage and believed, quite naturally, that matrimony was not, for a number of pressing reasons, a workable idea.

Søren Kierkegaard (1813–1855) is the Danish philosopher whose observations formed the development of existentialism, a guide to self-discovery and the meaning of self-existence. For what it's worth, he deigned to mention his mother, and was not much taken with his father's moodiness, melancholy and anxiety. We do know that Kierkegaard saw fit to break an engagement with a woman named Regine Olsen, and therefore did not see fit to make a leap of faith (an expression of his own invention) into matrimony. He wrote a treatise called *Fear and Trembling* (1843), another rhetorical *tour de force* (this one originating in *Philippians* 2:12) that we doubt had anything to do with his relations with Ms. Olsen or any other woman, but even so.

Neither had René Descartes (1596–1650), whose philosophic views are referred to as *Cartesian*. He is also fondly remembered for being a mathematician, philosopher and scientist, having published in psychology, physiology, mathematics, geometry optics and jurisprudence, not to mention his having speculated upon the existence of God. He lost his mother in the first year of his life, after which he was raised by his maternal grandmother and eventually taught in a Jesuit school and college, joined an army and apparently invented the philosophic standby that *I think; therefore I am*. He too never married, but did have a daughter, her mother being a comely maid servant. Descartes left France to live in the Netherlands for over 20 years, and he died in Stockholm. Almost the only marriage that interested him was the one between geometry and algebra. Like Leibniz, Descartes had a father who remarried and produced another son and daughter and, like Leibniz, did not apparently react well to the notion of marrying and remarrying. Both philosophers had better, more searching intellectual matters before them. Descartes lived by himself.

So did Nicholas Copernicus (1473–1543), the Polish (actually German) lawyer-turned astronomer who showed us that the sun, not the earth, is at the center of the solar system. His father died when Copernicus was ten. Did he ever marry? No. Was he a bachelor? Apparently so. Why did he not marry? We don't know. We are led to believe that like other theoreticians he was sufficiently absorbed in his work that it precluded much else. Such a life is by all means better suited to a bachelor, a man who has not volunteered to squander a goodly part of his time looking after a wife, children and property, which are marital preoccupations. His great grandfather had been a bricklayer, which was perhaps better suited to a man with a family, although he found time nonetheless to apprentice as a lawyer. Copernicus' parents evidently supported themselves by trading in copper. Nicholas was one of four children who, according to family records, prospered in familial enterprises, although he seemed to have had better bacheloric things to absorb his time and energies. Copernicus opened his attention to more ethereal pursuits, including religiosity, to the point where he endorsed monastic habits that are obviously at odds with ordinary bourgeois married life. He seemed to view himself as a religious poet, his purpose being to recommend Christianity and assert the necessity of faith. But what of marriage? "Marry, and you will regret it," he wrote. "Don't marry, you will also regret it; marry or don't marry. You will regret it either way. Believe a woman, you will regret it; believe her not. You will regret it both ways. Hang yourself; you will regret it; do not hang yourself. You'll regret it either way. Whether you hang yourself or do not hang yourself; you will regret it both." We're beginning to get the idea. "This," Copernicus assures us, "is the essence of all philosophy," not to mention the supremacy of indecision. For all his theology, his attitude toward ordinary events appears to be muddled and hopelessly confused. Aquinas, recall, assures us that the contemplative life rather shuts out the here and the now.

The French romantic impressionist painter Ferdinand Victor Eugene Delacroix (1798–1863) speaks to us mostly through his forms and colors, rather than as a pontificating philosopher tangled in the web of his own rhetoric. Delacroix had been impressed by the Catholic Church and its "appeal to man's deepest feelings," as expressed in his "Christ in the Garden," "The Lamentation" and "The Entombment." His journal posthumously published in three volumes between 1893 and 1895 offers some insights into the painter's personality and preoccupations, as does his correspondence (1936–1938) in five easy volumes. He lived what appears to have been a modest bachelorific life both in Paris and in nearby Champrosay, looked after by a housekeeper in these, the last years of the French Revolution. "Do all the work you can," he said once. "That is the whole philosophy of the good way of life." In other words, his mysticism superseded his appetite, which is not to suggest that he altogether ignored it, witness his "The Women of Algiers in Their Apartment," the outcome of Delacroix's cordial visitation to an Arabic harem, which was not as remarkable as it may sound, since harems at that time were heavily fortified, not only with women but with lethal-appearing guards. There is also his "Women With a Parrot," and even "A Naked Woman."

One woman was so overcome with whatever came over her while visiting the Louvre in 2013 that she accosted Delacroix's "Liberty Leading the People" (1830), depicting a woman of real flesh and blood, brandishing a flag with her bra most of the way off, while stepping over a heap of dead bodies. The deranged woman attempted to deface the painting with a permanent marker. Meanwhile, the allegorical message in the painting was apparently a depiction of the French people defeating a wicked monarch.

His "Head of an Elderly Woman," "Two Women at the Well" and "Head of a Peasant Women" are all of the same 19th-century genre which became particularly significant too for the depiction of French women, as further represented by Delacroix's "Medea About to Kill her Children" (1838), which has been interpreted as what happens when women have a modicum of liberation.

We have all heard of Boyle's Law, but chances are that we don't know, nor care to know, what the devil it means and why. Answer: "At constant temperature for a fixed mass, the absolute pressure and the volume of a gas are inversely proportional." That said, the person who first made that puzzling observation was, yes, a bachelor. Robert Boyle was his name (born 1627), the 15th child of Sir Richard Boyle and Lady Boyle, who was pretty well used up by this time. At 18, Boyle assisted in founding the Philosophical College, and at 25 he was busily studying anatomy, as one might expect of an intellectually inclined bachelor, although over time he became a devoted Christian an enthusiastic devourer of Bibles. He was still single or determined to be, and when in 1691 he died at the age of 64, he was (as far as we know) pure as the driven snow, as beanballs call it. He had authored a piece called *The Skeptical Chymist* in 1661, but he was every bit skeptical enough of women to evade them. Remembered as he is as the *father of modern chemistry*, he is not remembered for fathering anything (or anyone) else, although he did for a time live with one of his sisters.

In our relentless pursuit of bachelors, we would indeed be remiss (as dimwits say) if we did not have a closer look at Horace or, as some of more familiarly us know him, *Quintus Horatius Flaccus* who is believed to have been born in Apulia (southwestern Italy) in 65 B.C. and lived another 59 years. When we envision Horace, if we dwell upon him at all, we are put in mind of his short, stout, comparatively easy-going *Satires* in hexameters, the objectives of which were to recommend commonplace things like traditional morality, benevolently protecting the interests of small land-owners, warning against debt and usury and recommending self-reliance. James Romm of the *Wall Street Journal* reminds us (June 21, 2013) that whereas some poets suffer their way into truth, others get it by a less tortured path. "Horace...who knew neither the agony of passionate love, like his predecessor Catullus, nor the ecstasy of revelation like Socrates..." Horace, he continued, knew the "preludes of rustic live, recreational love affairs [Horace remained a lifelong bachelor] and above all, the joys of fine wine," but Horace never mentions his mother and is pretty well silent on the generic subject of women. Notwithstanding, in one of his odes, he writes, "Who is the lad now making love to you, Pyrrha? Poor naive, unsuspecting fellow, wait 'til he discovers your fickleness! I escaped from your clutches with difficulty, but somewhat battered, I am safe." We also find him warning, "Don't grieve overmuch, Albius, for heartless Glycera who has abandoned you for a younger lover. She is not worth it. Unrequited love is a common thing, moreover. Venus delights in bringing together persons not suited for each other. I, too, had a similar experience once."

But what had emotionally unstable Friedrich Nietzsche to say about women and matrimony? He was another German with a huge, regulation bushy mustache who drew attention to certain commonplace assumptions such as the foundations of Christianity (his grandfather having been a Lutheran minister) and what's usually referred to as conventionally-accepted notions of commonplace morality. Nietzsche was eight when his father died. At 23 he was still living with his mother and a year later he earned a doctorate. It wasn't until he was 37 that he was taken by a woman named Lou von Salome, 21, a philosophically inclined Russian, novelist, critic and general's daughter who, years later, became identified with Freud and still later wrote at some length about her involvement with Nietzsche. By 1809 he suffered what's been called a *mental breakdown*, possibly a stroke that left him an invalid for the balance of his life. As a child he had lived among women, lots of them, and was variously raised not only by his mother by also by a grandmother, two aunts and a sister. He once remarked that one should never know too precisely whom one has married, because to do so might demythologize that union. "When entering into marriage," he also wrote, "one ought to ask oneself, 'do you believe you are going to enjoy talking to this woman up into your old age? Most of the time you are together will be devoted to conversation.'" Nietzsche never married, but we can't imagine why, except that he was, shall we say, disinclined.

In the more popular mind, John Locke (1632–1704), born in England of Puritan parents, is identified with the idea that at birth one is endowed with a mental state called a *tabula rasa,* literally an *erased tablet, a blank blackboard, a blank mind* containing nothing until it is exposed to the world of ideas. It is a theory that extends back to Aristotle and Plato, and it assumes that one knows things by an *association of ideas* that build exponentially. It therefore refutes another idea, namely that one is born with certain inherent pieces of information (such as upon which horses to bet) derived from what's been called one's *racial memory,* accumulated over millions of years and inherited before birth. It's been called a *theory of knowledge,* one of the implications being that at birth all persons are (theoretically) equal, an Enlightenment idea canonized in the U.S. constitution. In his two treatises on government Locke articulated his (then) revolutionary notions about the rights of man and the so-called *social contract,* meaning essentially that certain freedoms must of necessity be relinquished for the protection of all, and that, accordingly, governments have clear responsibilities for their citizenry. In the meantime, Locke became romantically involved with the oddly named philosopher Damaris Cudworth Masham in 1682 and was also well acquainted with Leibniz. Her letter to Locke has generally been shown to support the view that Locke supported women's rights, arguing that women are not to be regarded as property but have the right to break the marriage contract should they wish to do so. Every inch a bachelor, he died unmarried and childless, in his country home, while Masham was left behind to compose her *Discourse Concerning the Love of God.*

Of course he was not the only person of that independent disposition. David Hume (1711–1776) is regarded as one who carried Locke's banner forward, by which we mean the notion that knowledge originates in experience. He was also skeptical enough to reject what might be called *rational theology.* When Hume reflected upon women, he seemed to think first of *modesty,* the avoidance of infidelity and the courage brazenly to enter a public washroom without infamy. He did, let it be noted, direct some of his attention to essays for "the female reader," whom he refrained from treating in a condescending tone. Interestingly enough, however, he defended polygamy, saying that "having a few wives" is "the only effectual remedy for the *disorder of love* and the only expedient for [which is] freeing men from that slavery to the females which the natural violence of our past has imposed upon us," which obliquely defends the bachelorific life. Did Hume marry? Hell, no. He was, however, full of advice for both sexes, as a sort of off-handed *pro bono* piece of his mind.

The same cannot be quite be said of Galileo (1564–1642), astronomer *par excellence*, who did not take his marching orders from Aristotle. Testing, for example, Aristotle's claim that heavy objects fall faster than lighter ones, Galileo eventually demonstrated that all objects fall at the same rate. So there. He didn't invent the telescope, but he did improve it to the point where he became the first human to view the moon's craters, and he may have been the first to see Neptune in person (had it been possible, he would have been first to shake his hand). Aquinas's Catholic Church taught everybody that all celestial bodies orbited the earth and ventured to say, moreover, that anyone who didn't accept this "fact" was a heretic. Galileo wasn't the first heretic, but he did endorse the unchurchly Copernican theory that the planets revolved around the sun, and for this bit of mischief he was summoned to Rome and told, in so many words, to keep his cockeyed theories to himself. He refused, and it cost him his final nine years under *house arrest*.

Having, as we say, a *mind of his own*, Galileo predictably remained a bachelor, something that fell a little short of getting him arrested. He had a remarkable mistress whose remarkable name was Maria Gamba, and with her he had at least one child. Galileo did not marry Gamba for three remarkably sound reasons: 1) she was too much younger than he, 2) she was not of his social rank and 3) he didn't care to get himself mired in matrimony. In his time and place, respectable women had two choices: marry, or enter a convent, and accordingly Galileo opted to send at least one daughter (he had three of them and one son) to the latter. Like Aquinas, he believed that men played by a separate code of conduct.

Thomas Hobbes (1588–1677), the English philosopher, carried a decidedly pessimistic attitude toward the human race and viewed life as "nasty, brutish and short." One can't get much more pessimistic than that. Hobbs is mainly recognized for his *Leviathan* (three volumes, 1651), arguing in support of the deterministic view of life, that one's destiny is controlled by heredity and environment, even to the extent that one has but little free will to make of himself what he wishes. Instead, he saw men in continuous struggle with one another and said that "the state of nature is a state of war." Hobbs nonetheless concerned himself with the *rights of women*, affirming that they are the equal of men, although he comes around to saying that it is fathers (not mothers) who have developed civilization, albeit a civilization that consists of a "general inclination of all mankind [to engage in] a perpetual and relentless desire of power after power that ceases only in death." Hobbs, oddly enough, never married, but in his spare time managed to father four sons. Rather than marrying, he devoted his last years to translating Homer and ignoring women, probably on grounds that the liberated person is by nature masculine, even to the point that it apparently excused women from being taken too seriously.

Literary people (poets, fiction writers, dramatists) are not to be mistaken for philosophers, which is not to suggest that they're not weighed down with opinions, positions, convictions, attitudes and inclinations, all of them subject to emendation and evolution as one might safely expect. Philosophers, of course, have gradually evolving views as well. Nevertheless, one does not look to literary figures, even the best of them, for philosophical guidance of the sort that we take too earnestly. Some of them might accurately be called *drugstore philosophers*. Shakespeare, for one good example, possessed rather commonplace drug store opinions on a range of matters, and though he is widely cited, he has little or nothing much noteworthy to say that we hadn't presumed before. Dante Alighieri's *Divine Comedy* is a systematically guided tour through the hills and dales of Hell, Purgatory and Heaven, in that order; it is itself guided by a range of philosophic positions theological and otherwise, while Dante is not himself to be read as a philosopher but more of a synthesizer of the ideas of preexisting ones.

Jonathan Swift (1667–1745) was the satirical priest who eventually fled the Catholic Church and who was in time ordained into the Anglican Church of Ireland. Today when we read Swift, it's ordinarily his *Gulliver's Travels* (1726), if not his *Tale of a Tub*, published in 1704 and written about eight years before. Beginning in about 1709, Swift launched a long series of missives to a woman named Esther Johnson (they were collected later as his *Journal to Stella*) and later another to one Rebecca Dingley. On a visit to London he became more than friendly with Hester Vanhomrigh, whose age has been estimated at about 20, possibly older, while Swift was 43. She became his fictional *Vanessa*, and when their mother died, she and her sister turned up in Ireland, where they became mostly an embarrassment to Swift, especially when the younger sister demanded to know precisely what was going on between Swift and his Stella. We cannot say with certainty what transpired between Swift and these variously contentious women, except that for him it became a huge headache. Vanessa died in 1723, apparently having written him out of her will. Stella died in 1728. Her will describes her as a mere *spinster*. After this, Swift's health went to hell with a brain tumor resulting in his deafness, blindness and madness. Why Swift did not marry, we don't definitively know. Rumor had it that he and Stella did indeed marry, but that is unconfirmed. He did admire women on one level or another and wished well of them. Privately he had his reservations (shall we say), and they weren't for a honeymoon. Instead of leaving his estate to a widow, he left it to a lunatic asylum.

Our subject is bachelorism, something about which everyone has some opinion, impression, attitude, position and so forth. There have been bachelors, a representative number, who became distinguished in one way or another. Not all of them are literary lions; some were literary pussycats toward whom a few gather near to hear what they think, thoughts that may not qualify as philosophic but that at least exert some influence and possibly some generally well-received point of view. Robert Burton (1577–1640) was one such figure who turned out his great compendium (as it's been called) titled *The Anatomy of Melancholy* (1621), calling himself *Democritus Junior*. The first Democritus (c. 460–c. 370 BC) became known as the *laughing philosopher*, i.e., something of a late night jokester. Burton developed a rhetorical style of his own that we will call *Burtonese*. He was, as George Sampson has ably written, "a permanent resident at Oxford, drawing upon the resources of his own Christ Church [college] library and the newly formed Bodleian [library] with a scholar's appetite which somebody observed in his case meant that he had far more an appetite for books than broads." The impulse to expand upon melancholic miseries originated, he said, from "the sin of our first parent," hardly an original idea. Burton obviously never married. It did him no apparent harm. Of all marital possibilities, Burton advised, "a noble man must marry a noble woman; a knight a knight's, a gentleman a gentleman's," ergo, if worst comes to worst, if marriage cannot be thwarted, one must at least marry within his rank and station. Burton's was another voice full of marital advice that he never followed. Said he, "'Tis no news for an old fellow to marry a young wench; but as he follows it, a woman's term is brief, and if 'tis not used in time, no one wants her for a wife." It has been written by someone whose identity is not known that he was "openly misogynistic and frequently denounced women in general and their unnatural insatiable lust in particular."

Edward Gibbon (1737–1714) was another Oxford man, but that said, he didn't learn a damned thing there, the same thing that Henry Adams said of Harvard. Gibbon's literary monument, as everyone knows, was *The Decline and Fall of the Roman Empire* (1776), a monster of a book to write and to read. Unlike Burton, Gibbon rather liked women, at least some of them. On a trip to Switzerland he reportedly fell in love with one whose name happened to be Suzanne Curchod, later *Madame Necker*, an allegorical name if ever we heard one, about whom one could say, as Samson did, that Gibbon's decline and fall was "an enduring monument of research, an imperishable literary possession and one of the highest encouragements to intellectual endeavor to be found in the history of letters," an unimaginably elevated compliment. While he was busily writing his monument, his Suzanne was busily making herself known to this fellow named Necker, whose political importance was such that he is believed to have ignited the wick that set the French Revolution into hellish motion, and who was King Louis XVI of France's financial minister. Scholars of romantic disposition are inclined to postulate that Gibbon had but one romantic interlude in his otherwise rather dishwater bland life. It ended when Gibbon's father, upon hearing about his son's engagement, refused to consent, assuming his consent to be necessary. Gibbon didn't contest it, and remarked later that he "sighed as a lover" and "obeyed as a son," meaning that he was an ostensibly reluctant bachelor, but a bachelor nonetheless.

Samuel Butler (1835–1902), more than Gibbon, was a man of varied talents, among them satirist, novelist, painter, musician, scholar and sheep herder. His father and grandfather were both ecclesial fellows who were ever urging him to pass his life disseminating the Word, but he responded by questioning things such as infant baptism and other such Christian staples. He published an article explaining that the author of Homer's *Odyssey* was, you guessed it, a woman, part of the purpose of which was to demonstrate that a woman can do anything a man can, almost. He is better known for a bunch of novels, among them *Erewhon* (an anagram for "nowhere," 1872) and *The Way of All Flesh* (spelled frontwards, posthumously, 1903). He is known to have had problems with his mother and satirized her as Christina Pontifex in the latter novel. Butler was a bit leery of women and observed that "brigands demand your money or your life; women require both." He was also not above saying that "in matrimony, to hesitate is sometimes to be saved," and that "wise men never say what they think of women."

When we consider the French novelist Marie Henri Beyle, known as *Stendhal* (1783–1842), we think first of *Le Rouge et le Noir* (*The Red and the Black*, 1831), published when he was 47. Red and black refer to Napoleonic ambition (red) versus the ecclesial (black), something that Stendhal detested. He was at times judged to be a comparatively unattractive fellow, vain, pretentious, vulgar and intellectually opportunistic. His pre-Freudian *l'Amour* (*About Love*, 1822) is both forthright and outstandingly sensuous; he became the first major realist and one of the early psychologists in the history of the French novel where his method was to accumulate innumerable minute details about his characters rather than weave a more conventionally engaging picture. One of these was his famous Julien Sorel, a figure that he invented after hearing about a young man who had murdered his mistress. Stendhal's mother died when he was seven and it has been suggested that he lived a life critical of authority and, as is not surprising, passed his life looking for the mother he'd lost. At one point he carried on a romance with the countess Clementine Curial, about whom Stendhal recorded, "No woman's departure ever caused me so much grief," and later Julie Gaulthier, with whom he had a rather unhappy arrangement, followed by a fraught liaison with Mathilde Dembrowski. Stendhal had a penchant for actresses and pursued women relentlessly, although at the same time he appears to have respected them on some level—but not enough to marry any of them.

The epileptic Gustave Flaubert (1821–1880), celebrated author of *Madame Bovary* (1857), lived with his mother after his father died, then with his niece, then alone, basking in near total isolation until he discovered Louise Colet, the previously-cited minor league poetess who in turn developed a serious interest in Alfred de Musset. She was a vain, impossible woman. Flaubert told her that as a child of six or seven he had, as a doctor's son, visited an asylum where he saw, "sitting in chairs, naked to the waist and all disheveled, a dozen women howling and clawing at their faces with their nails." Such were his impressions of women.

The name *Bovary* of course suggests *bovine*, referring to the sluggishness that one identifies with the cows and other barnyard beasts that graze through his novels, although Emma Bovary seems anything but bovine. To the contrary, she is a raven haired, blue-eyed beauty with full lips, but she destroys herself through romantic longing. The novel trots out a morbid succession of dead women, such as Roualt's wife, Charles Bovary's first wife (Heloise), Emma's mother and Emma herself. In the meantime, Colet stalked Flaubert for years until he told her that he tried to love her "in a way that isn't the way of lovers," whatever that may be taken to mean. William Grimes, writing for *The New York Times* (April 12, 2006), observed that Flaubert gave her his art. What he declined to give women was constancy, devotion and passion. Francine du Plessix Gray in *The New Yorker* (July 26, 1993) claimed that "Flaubert's views of women run the gamut from reverent awe to sexist disdain as virulent as can be found in the nineteenth century," adding that "on one hand he said that the female sex was a band of lascivious simpletons" who "mistake their hearts for their cunts and think the moon was invented to light their boudoirs." Flaubert told Colet that "our contemporary literature is drowning in women's menses," and complained about being feminized and softened by wear and tear, such that he himself had become bovine. He died with no wife, a few venereal infections, and a personal transformation into his own Emma Bovary. To amuse his friends he dressed as a woman and broke into a ridiculous dance. Like Emma, he was a doctor's child, and like her he was an unbridled sexual adventurer who never quite found a home.

Oliver Goldsmith, another rather cantankerous and voraciously authorial bachelor (1730?–1774), was an Irish poet, essayist and dramatist given to gambling who studied both law and medicine that he practiced without a license, and in lean times he held body and soul together by playing the flute. At other times he made his way with a pen, as when he authored his

History of England (1774) and a *History of Animated Nature*, a rather ambitious undertaking, although Goldsmith was fairly self-effacing. Through all of this he is remembered as a rather puerile, good-natured man who, in 1767, published *The Good Natur'd Man*. Dr. Johnson speaks of Goldy's intentional absurdity, something to be found in the pages of *The Vicar of Wakefield* (1766), a novel of enduring attraction and amusement, and an evergreen play entitled *She Stoops to Conquer* (1773). He may well have died of overwork and a kidney infection. He gave the impression, at least, of having no time and no money for women. His attitude toward them was captured in eight lines: "When lovely woman stoops to folly, / And finds too late that men betray, / what charm can sooth her, / What art can wash her guilt away? / The only art her guilt to cover, / To hide her shame from every eye/ To give repentance to her lover? / And wring his bosom—is to die." Goldsmith managed to avoid marriage because he was far too busy, and besides that, as he said, "All that a husband or wife really wants is to be pitied a little and appreciated a little." He had once resolved to emigrate to America, but he literally and figuratively missed the boat. He did, interestingly enough, pen a poem entitled "The Hermit" in 1765 depicting a loner who seems to approve of people who are decidedly hermetic, possibly but not necessarily an exercise in self-portraiture.

Unusual too was George Santayana, born in Spain (1863–1952) who came to America (but not Kafka's Amerika) in 1872 and studied at Harvard where he later taught philosophy before taking residence in France and England from 1914, publishing fiction and philosophy such as his *Platonism and the Spiritual Life* (1927) and more popularly *The Last Puritan* (1935). Richard Butler characterized Santayana as a "Catholic atheist," having become engaged in the matter of "belief and critical thought" that left him "a crusty bachelor of fifty, a talented student of law and art who had abandoned both pursuits for a more carefree existence." Santayana himself in a letter said that "such things are possible only to a thoroughly selfish old bachelor with money he doesn't have to look after, and no social engagements or dependents." Joseph Epstein's article entitled "Santayana's Chair," written after having read the first four volumes of Santayana's letters, surmised that "no one was more happily detached than Santayana. At 48 he had finally come into enough money to flee, with unalloyed delight, his day job in the philosophy department at Harvard. He lived out his days alone ('I find solitude the best company') in various temporary quarters in Europe ('to me it seems a dreadful indignity to have a soul controlled by geography'). A victim of what he called "the contemptible disease, he wished to observe the world as clearly as possible. "My philosophy, he wrote, "has always been that delusion is the only safe foundation for happiness." Similarly, William Holzberger has observed that "always a bachelor, Santayana lived by a strict routine, rising and retiring early, and devoting the full morning to writing." Newton P. Stallknecht has observed that Santayana "lived simply in retirement, but not in isolation ... [and], like the Pope, did not return visits."

The Austrian novelist Franz Kafka (1883–1924) was afflicted what's been called a regrettable inability to marry, even though he'd been engaged several times, more times, in fact, than he seemed to have acknowledged. What he left behind was *The Trial*, written between 1921 and 1922, *The Castle* (1926) and *Amerika* (1911–1914), among other works. If he seemed personally incomprehensible, so did his fiction; on one level it appears to be perfectly lucid while on another level it seems anything but. Kafka's world is every bit as confusing and nightmarish as bad dreams. To muddy the literary waters even more, Kafka burned nearly everything he had written with the exception of what he entrusted to his literary comrade Max Brod, supposedly insisting that Brod set fire to it all when he died. Fortunately, Brod did not honor the request.

After Kafka died from tuberculosis, Brod departed Prague, toting Kafkas's manuscripts, reportedly on the final train before the Nazis closed the borders, saving his life and saving the Kafka manuscripts. Brod survived until 1968, whereupon those papers fell into the hands of his secretary and (possibly) lover Esther Hoff who lived to the age of 101. Such were some of the legal and personal dilemmas that separated Kafka from his readers— readers that he never solicited in the first place. Kafka could now and again turn on the charm, however. Jacqueline Raoul-Duval's *Kafka in Love* (2012) shows us among other things that he collected women from a long distance, possibly so that he didn't actually have to confront them personally. When all was done and said, Kafka was a bit of a dandy after all, except that his disinclination to carry any of these romances forward (or shall we say *downward*) speaks to his determination never to marry. Being, as he was, a rather closeted subterranean literary man, he nevertheless did, so say some scholars, actively propose marriage to some of these prospects. Whereas his father had been a Jewish shopkeeper with a dominating personality, Kafka himself is said to have felt impotent and dependent, although he took a law degree from a German university and for a time found employment at an insurance company. Such was the essence of his isolation about which he wrote, "It seems so dreadful to stay a bachelor [and] to become an old man struggling to keep [his] dignity while begging for an invitation whenever [he] wants to spend an evening in company."

Jean-Paul Sartre (1905–1980) has been remembered as *the pope of existentialism* more than for his playwriting and literary criticism. He was captured by the Nazis between 1940 and 1941, after which he returned to his clandestine resistance of German occupation. For some time he embraced

Marxism, then drifted away from his own existentialism and composed three ambitious volumes on Flaubert. Sartre also assured us that loving relationships are doomed to fail, something that may come as less than a surprise to persons with a murky sense of romanticism. Sartre was a Parisian professor of philosophy who drank to excess, chain smoked, swallowed too many pills, weighed too much and inveighed too long about bourgeois values, although in his later years he charitably proclaimed that he was about to get cozy with the working class. When he died some fifty thousand of his admirers followed his cortège to the Montparnasse cemetery, to join Victor Hugo and Voltaire. Sartre had aggressively chased women, all the while maintaining a 50-year connection with Simone de Beauvoir, another existentialarian to whom he dutifully reported on whom he was currently pursuing. Sartre, who resembled a cross-eyed Peter Lorre, was anything but handsome, but in the eyes of many he was the foremost philosopher of the 20th century. He might just as well have been the philandering toast of Paris for his relentless adventuring with women whom he found attractive and more fun than men, whose company he found boring. Sartre told *Playboy* magazine that "Women play a rather large role in my life—but a small one in my books," and elsewhere said that "I have always tried to surround myself with women who are at least agreeable to look at. Feminine ugliness is offensive to me."

But what of Beauvoir? She and Jean-Paul met in Paris, 1929. He was 24, she 21. Once she got over his compromised appearance, she took a serious interest in him. A Louis Menard *New Yorker* article called "Stand by Your Man" (September 26, 2005) notes that "Sartre was about five feet tall, and he had lost almost all the sight in his right eye when he was three, he dressed in oversized clothes, with no sense of fashion, his skin and teeth suggested an indifference to hygiene. He had the kind of aggressive male ugliness that can be charismatic...he simply ignored his body. He was also smart, generous, agreeable, ambitious, ardent and very funny...he and Beauvoir decided that their love did not require marriage..."

They also agreed to tell each other everything, hence his keeping her posted about his erotic adventuring. He was collecting women like some footloose, more than ordinarily aggressive bachelor. She, in fact, struck up with some of them socially. She and Sartre became possibly the most celebrated—and talked about—couple in contemporary Paris. She developed a reputation as a leading women's writer with *The Second Sex* (1949–1950). Tourists plopped themselves down at cafes where the couple might turn up. Even *au courant* college courses in who knows what made a study of their coupledom. He made it entirely clear to her that he was a lifelong bachelor. He'd once been engaged to other women. Eventually they fell into their habit of bringing younger women into the tell-all home as part of a *ménage à trois*. Sartre, in the meantime, thought of himself as a "scholarly Don Juan," able to seduce women with his elegant rhetoric, since that may have been his only elegant feature. Meanwhile, his mother would not admit them to her home. Existentialism may have come to the service of seduction. A collection called *Witness to My Life: The Letters of Jean-Paul Sartre to Simone Beauvoir* (1926–1939) includes passages such as "tonight I love you on a spring evening. I love you with the window open. You are mine and things are mine, and my love alters the things around me, and the things around me alter my love." Spoken, as it were, by a calculating, philosophically-inclined seducer of the first water.

So-called Christian philosopher, physicist and manic depressive Blaise Pascal (1623–1662) is credited with having the first calculating machine, which was less than surprising since he had been recognized as a prodigy since childhood, and, as far as we know, never enrolled in a school of any kind, having been tutored by his father. He studied the classical languages by the age of 12 and quickly became an accomplished mathematician who carried his work well into then uncharted territories that in turn led him into medicine, such as it then was. We are assured that, unlike some of the figures we've seen, he never became anything close to a Jean-Paul Sartre libertine or a free thinker, but he still explored the theory of probabilities and eventually entered a convent after having reportedly constructed a perpetual motion machine, which we are inclined to doubt. One of Pascal's improbabilities was that he'd ever be led to the matrimonial altar, although he warned that "men of quality are not bothered by women of quality." Shortly after his death his sisters (one of whom was also a prodigy) entered a monastery and took the veil. Pascal's thoughts are advantageously entertained in his *Pensées de M. Pascal*, (posthumously 1670), although he wrote much and published little, leaving drafts behind for scholars to sort through and reach their own conclusions. "He who does not know his way to the sea," he said, "should take the river for his guide." Interestingly enough, Jacqueline Pascal (1625–1661) championed the rights of women and even defended their right to dissent from certain theological positions.

He brings to mind Benedict or Baruch Spinoza, the Sephardic Jewish lens-grinding Dutch philosopher (1632–1677) who was overflowing with speculative observations so intertwined that reading him is like hacking through thickets of thorny underbrush. His passion seemed to be that freedom consists of being one's self. He somehow or other offended sufficient numbers of his Jewish *community* that he became alienated for his alleged "monstrous deeds" and "abominable heresies." Suffice it to say that he was obliged to leave his Judaism behind and begin writing various speculative papers on God, nature and man, and had the extraordinary nerve to say that "a substance is prior in nature to its affections," something that we had long suspected but were too timid to repeat in public.

Spinoza had his reservations about women, for instance his bold assertion that "women are, like servants, subject to men," which we have no doubt won him the hearts and mind (as idiots say) of women everywhere, Christian, Jewish and beyond. He also proclaimed that women are not, by nature, the intellectual equals of men, something that may have been (we're not certain) one of his abominable heresies, another being that he refused to recognize women's political rights because of their "weak intellectual ability." He never the less willed his property to his sister.

Speaking of inequalities, we must not omit to say a few wonderful things about Jean-Jacques Rousseau (1712–1778), one of the more luminous luminaries of the so-called *French Enlightenment*. Besides being a political philosopher, he was a musical composer, an autobiographer, a servant, an engraver, a tutor and an ambassador who had at last considered entering the priesthood. It was a priest who introduced him to Françoise-Louise de Warens, estranged from her husband who, when he was 20, he took on as a lover while at the same time having an arrangement with one of the household stewards. Later in Paris he formed an attachment to a seamstress named Thérèse Lavasseur, a hotel chambermaid who bore him five children. They appear to have married, but the ceremony was somehow invalid. After that he formed a supposedly Platonic connection with Sophie d'Houdetot, a tax collector's daughter about whom Rousseau said that her features were scarred from smallpox. Along the way he produced the literary monuments for which he is now most admired, namely *Julie, or The New Heloise* (1761), *Emile, or Education* (1762), and of course his *Confessions* (1781).

What did Rousseau think about women? Not much. He proceeded on the theory that they were subservient to men and that their weakness was accountable to poor education and compromised social position. That said, he has been accused of saying things he didn't exactly mean, and he was not above contradicting himself. He said that women's education "should always be relative to men's," whatever that may mean. "To please, to be useful to us [men], to make us love and esteem them, to educate us when young, to take care of us when grown up, to advise, to console us, to render our lives easy and agreeable; these are the duties of women at all times, and they should be taught at infancy." He saw fit to pack those five children off to an orphanage (a foundling hospital), remarking that it was for their own good.

It should come as no surprise that the quintessential bachelor of bachelors is none other than Mr. Sherlock Holmes. By *quintessential* (let's be clear on this) we mean to say the *quintessence*, the *essence*, the *ideal embodiment*, the *most refined, essential, purest, most perfect form*. We're saying that Mr. 'olmes (as 'e's called in the old movies) more than anyone else, living or dead, mythical, imagined or real, cobbled together, invented, or captive, one who is arisen out of folklore's mist. We presume little to no distinction between real (living or not) people and those who are the products of a writer's pen or the painter's brush. Indeed, there was until 1970 a huge ceremonious Holmes statue opposite Conan Doyle's grave. Sherlock Holmes for generations has provoked differences of opinion about who and what he was, and about his somewhat obsequious companion Dr. John Watson, ever assuming, presuming, speculating to the place where droves of their literary followers were convinced that they were actual, living people: well-tailored, pipe-smoking chaps gifted with uncannily, metaphysically inquiring intellects. Their literary creator Sir Arthur Ignatius Conan Doyle (1859–1930) was surprisingly knighted in 1902 for his defense of the British in the Boer War. He was educated by the Jesuits in Edinburgh, although he eventually left the Catholic Church. After a year in Austria he took his medical degree at Edinburgh and practiced what we now know as *ophthalmology* which, of course, has caused many to suppose that his mysterious Sherlock Holmes relied upon extraordinary *perception* to solve certain of his otherwise clouded mysteries, more or less the same way other detectives have solved theirs.

It has been said that Doyle took to writing his first Holmes story while waiting at number 2 Upper Wimpole Street (designated today with an historic plaque) for the first medical patient to darken his door. He called that story "A Study in Scarlet" (1887). Curiously enough, in 1893 he (as it were) killed Holmes off only to have him, like Jesus, reappear after he was presumed no longer among the living. This, we are told, obliged Doyle to explain to his readers that, in the reality of fiction, along with his nemesis Professor Moriarty, Holmes had escaped being swallowed up by a mountainous crevasse. Later in a story called "The Return of Sherlock Holmes" (1905), Holmes miraculously reappeared with his friend and collaborator, the eccentric Watson, both of them bachelors. According to the A.C. Doyle Literary estate, Doyle's mother was both a bibliophile and an accomplished *raconteur*. His father was a professional alcoholic. Mary Doyle, as Arthur commentated, had a histrionic gift for "sinking her voice to a horror-stricken whisper."

In the meantime, Doyle was sent to a Jesuit English boarding school, the only pleasant aspect of which was writing his mother, something that he continued all his life, all the while inventing stories to amuse his classmates. In those days he was known as Arthur; he added the *Conan* later. When he at last ended his preparatory schooling, he and his mother signed papers that packed his father, then suffering from *dementia*, off to some institution for *lunatics*. Doyle's decision to pursue a medical education supposedly came through the influence a career-minded boarder his mother had taken in. At medical school he came under the influence of Dr. Joseph Bell, a practitioner with a keener than common sense of observation, deductive reasoning, logic and perceptive interpretation—characteristics later identified with Holmes and Watson. In his third year of medical school he accepted an appointment as a ship surgeon aboard the suggestively christened *Hope* that he later used in "Captain of the Pole Star." It was also at this time that he became quite the ladies' man, claiming, as bachelors sometimes do, that he was in love with five women at once. When he received his medical degree he called it *a license to kill*, after which he sailed on a steamer between Liverpool and Africa's west coast. He eventually opened his practice, dividing his time between ophthalmology and criminology.

He also married Mary Louise, aka Louisa Hawkins. By this time he was better known in America than in England. He resolved to enroll in more ophthalmologic studies, this time in Vienna, then opened the office on London's Wimpole Street. He had a literary agent by this time who marketed his fiction and struck an arrangement with the *Strand* magazine to publish Sherlock Holmes stories illustrated by Sidney Gaget, who in turn used his brother's image as the Sherlockian model. By 1891, at the age of 32, Doyle gave medicine up "with a wild rush of joy," and resolved that "I should at last be my own master," signing his name as *Dr. John Watson* and fathering a son named Kingsley (the first of five children between two eventual wives). While in Switzerland in 1893 he identified the exact place where Holmes and Moriarty ("the Napoleon of Crime") were to disappear in the Reichenbach Falls, after which fictive fatality an alleged 20,000 readers cancelled their subscription to *The Strand* in a gesture of literary protest. It was at that time that Louisa contracted tuberculosis, in spite of which he was able to extend her life to 1900. Her death and his father's death caused him to lapse into morbidity, such that he studied and expounded upon spiritualism and was for a time in touch with entertainer Harry Houdini. Doyle subsequently lectured on spiritualism around the world and exerted such influence that after his death nearly 6,000 spiritually enlightened people assembled at the Royal Albert Hall to hear him speak from beyond the grave.

Doyle sailed again to America in 1894, and scheduled lecture presentations in at least 30 cities. When the Boer War began in 1900 he expressed an interest in soldiering, but was rejected for being too old and too fat. He then entered the military as a medical doctor; he saw more people die from typhoid than from bullets. He wrote a 500-page chronicle described later as a "masterpiece of military scholarship" that earned him his knighthood, confirmed by King Edward VII who happened to be a devoted Sherlock Holmes reader. By this time Doyle had seen quite a bit of Jean Leckie, about whom the *London Daily Mail* as recently as August 13, 2014, published an article entitled "Adultery, My Dear Watson," subtitled "writer betrayed his dying wife with younger lover," claiming that Doyle "scandalously fell in love with...a younger woman who would become his second wife," all the while maintaining his correspondence with his mother, keeping her apprised with his adventuring, including various forms of living dangerously such as riding in hot air balloons and primitive airplanes, driving automobiles at impossible speeds, while at the same time dabbling unsuccessfully in politics (he ran for a seat in Parliament in 1900 and lost), body building—then lapsing into renewed depression after holding Louisa in his arms at the moment of her death. He was inclined at this time to impersonate Sherlock Holmes by offering advice to Scotland Yard and taking a more than ordinary interest in criminals, and in Jean Leckie, whom he married in 1907, after which he continued writing for the theater and fathering two more sons and a daughter. Doyle again attempted to enlist in the military (at age 55) in World War I, but instead authored a book he called *The British Campaign in France and Flanders.* He suffered the loss of his son Kingsley, his brother, two brothers-in-law and two nephews, after which he again explored the possibilities of the occult. He died from cardiac complications in 1930, having first informed his family that he was setting out on "the greatest and most glorious adventure of all."

Doyle was no bachelor; but he behaved like one. Identifying authors with their fictional characters, whether justified or not, went critically out of fashion decades ago. Nonetheless, there has been popular speculation over the years that Holmes represents Doyle's *alter ego*, his other self, his other identity, despite the fact that Doyle had been known whimsically to sign himself off as *Watson*. Holmes, in the meantime, appears to have no time for women except when they advance mysterious cases for him to untangle.

The woman to whom he seems closest is Mrs. Hudson, his matronly, unprepossessing housekeeper. Otherwise, he is dismissive of women, even to the point of veiled misogyny. We see this in "A Scandal in Bohemia" (1891) also titled as "Woman Wit," a tale that begins with Watson's observation that "to Sherlock Holmes she is always *the* woman," as if all women are stereotypical. "I have seldom heard him mention her [by] any other name. In his eyes she eclipses and predominates the whole of her sex...she was...the most perfect reasoning and observing machine that the world has seen; but as lover he would have placed himself in a false position. He never spoke of the softer passions, save with a gibe and a sneer."

Elsewhere in "The Sign of the Sneer," we encounter Holmes' remarking to Watson, "I am not a whole souled admirer of womankind, as you are aware." In "The Adventure of the Second Stain," (1904), we witness a woman's departure. Recalls Watson, "she looked back at us from the door, and I had a last impression of that beautiful haunted face, two startled eyes, and the drawn mouth. Then she was gone." Remarks Holmes with a smile, "Watson, the fair sex is your department," while the woman disappears, slamming the door behind her. "What was the fair lady's game?" Holmes inquires. "What did she really want?"

BIBLIOGRAPHY

Anderson, Sarah M. *Bringing Home the Bachelor*. New York: Harlequin, 2013.

Annis, Barbara and John Gray. *Work With Me: 8 blind spots between men and women in Business*. New York, Palgrave Macmillan, 2013.

Christenberry, Judy. *The Last Bachelor*. New York: Silhouette Books, 2002.

Chudacoff, Howard P. *The Age of the Bachelor: Creating An American Subculture*. Princeton, NJ: Princeton University Press, 1999.

Clemens Paul. *The Little Black Book: A Manual for Bachelors*. Garden City, NY: Doubleday, 1957.

Fine, Cordelia. *Delusions of Gender: How Our Minds, Society, And Neurosexism Create Difference*. New York: W.W. Norton, 2010.

Ford, Corey. *What Every Bachelor Knows*. Garden City, NY: Doubleday, 1961.

Foss, Kenelm. *Unwedded Bliss: Sixty Examples of Famous Folk Who, Eschewing the "Honorable State" and "Excellent Mystery" of Matrimony, Fulfilled Their Heart's Desire in Divers Ways*. Kingswood, Surry: World's Work, 1950.

Feather, Jane. *The Bachelor List*. New York: Bantam Books, 2004.

Gilder, George F. *Naked Nomads: Unmarried Men in America*. New York: Times Book Co, 1974.

Gray, John. *Men Are From Mars, Women Are From Venus: The Classic Guide to Understanding the Opposite Sex*. New York: Harper Collins Publishers, 2004.

Kahn, Fritz, et al. *Why Are You Single?* New York: Farrar, Straus, 1949.

Keen, Maurice. *Origins of the English Gentleman: Heraldry, Chivalry and Gentility in Medieval England*. Charleston, SC, 2002.

Maloff, Saul, ed. *All About Women*. New York: Harper & Row, 1963.

McCurdy, John Gilbert. *Citizen Bachelors: Manhood and the Creation of the United States*. Ithaca, NY, Cornell University Press, 2009.

McInerney, Jay. *The Last Bachelor*. New York: Bloomsbury, 2009.

Nathan, George Jean. *The Bachelor Life*. New York: Reynal & Hitchcock, 1941.

Neels, Betty. *The Bachelor's Wedding*. New York: Harlequin Books, 1996.

Nelson, Frederic. *Bachelors Are People Too*. Washington DC: Public Affairs Press, 1964.

Peacham, Henry. *The Complete Gentleman*. Oxford: The Clarenden Press, 1906.

Pitzulo, Carrie. *Bachelors and Bunnies: The Sexual Politics of Playboy*. Chicago; University of Chicago Press, 2011.

Ross, John A. *How to be Happily Divorced: A bachelor's guide for success and survival*. New York: Exposition Press, 1968.

Saunders, Kate. *Bachelor Boys*. New York: St. Martin's Press, 2005.

Seabright, Paul. *The War of the Sexes: How Conflict and Cooperation Have Shaped Men and Women from Prehistory to the Present*. Princeton, NJ. Princeton University Press, 2012

Snyder, Katherine V. *Bachelors, Manhood and the Novel, 1850-1925*. Cambridge, U.K and New York, Cambridge University Press, 1999.

Sommers, Christina Hoff. *The War Against Boys: How Misguided Feminism is Harming Our Young Men*. New York: Touchstone, 2001.

Spark, Muriel. *The Bachelors*. New York: New Directions, 2014.

Sparks, John. *Battle of the Sexes*. TV Books, 1999.

Springer, Kathryn. *The Bachelor Next Door*. New York: Harlequin Love Inspired, 2014.

Steel, Danielle. *Toxic Bachelors*. New York: Delacorte Press, 2005.

Trudeau, G.B. *Confirmed Bachelors are Just So Interesting*. New York: Ballantine, 1984.

Waehler, Charles A. *Bachelors: The Psychology of Men Who Haven't Married*. Westport Conn. Praeger, 1996.

Weisman, Carl. *So Why Have You Never Married*. New York: New Horizon, 2008

Wright, Alexander. *How to Live Without a Woman*. Indianapolis: Bobbs-Merrill, 1937.

Wodehouse, P.G. *Bachelors Anonymous*. New York: Overlook Press, 2012.

INDEX

Printed in the United States
By Bookmasters